STAR WARS

DAWN OF THE JEDI

BEFORE THE REPUBLIC (37,000–25,000 YEARS BEFORE THE EVENTS IN *STAR WARS:* EPISODE IV—*A NEW HOPE*)

This is an ancient time, lost in the annals of history. It is a time before a great Republic united the galaxy. A time before the first Jedi emerged to serve as the guardians of peace and justice. In this era, mysterious alien civilizations with unimaginable powers ruled their own dominions.

The events in this story begin approximately 36,453 years before the events in *Star Wars:* Episode IV—*A New Hope.*

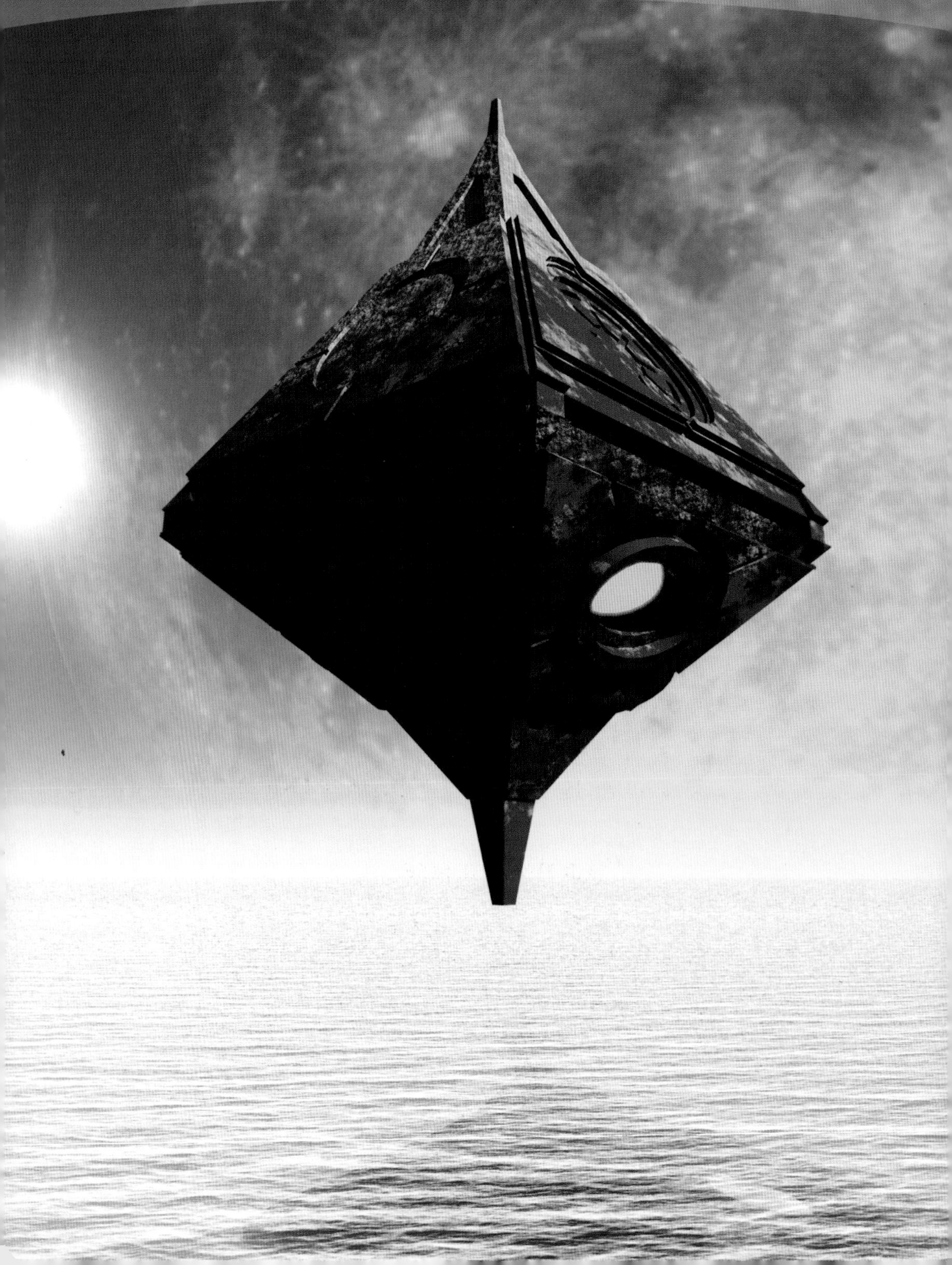

BOOK ONE

FORCE STORM

STAR WARS®

DAWN OF THE JEDI

STORY
JOHN OSTRANDER & JAN DUURSEMA

SCRIPT
JOHN OSTRANDER

PENCILS
JAN DUURSEMA

INKS
DAN PARSONS

COLORS
WES DZIOBA

LETTERS
MICHAEL HEISLER

COVER ART
GONZALO FLORES

BACK COVER ART
JAN DUURSEMA

DARK HORSE BOOKS
LUCAS BOOKS

president and publisher
MIKE RICHARDSON

editor
RANDY STRADLEY

assistant editor
FREDDYE LINS

collection designer
TINA ALESSI

Special thanks to **JENNIFER HEDDLE**, **LELAND CHEE**, **TROY ALDERS**, **CAROL ROEDER**, **JANN MOORHEAD**, and **DAVID ANDERMAN** at Lucas Licensing.

NEIL HANKERSON Executive Vice President TOM WEDDLE Chief Financial Officer RANDY STRADLEY Vice President of Publishing MICHAEL MARTENS Vice President of Book Trade Sales ANITA NELSON Vice President of Business Affairs DAVID SCROGGY Vice President of Product Development DALE LaFOUNTAIN Vice President of Information Technology DARLENE VOGEL Senior Director of Print, Design, and Production KEN LIZZI General Counsel MATT PARKINSON Senior Director of Marketing DAVEY ESTRADA Editorial Director SCOTT ALLIE Senior Managing Editor CHRIS WARNER Senior Books Editor DIANA SCHUTZ Executive Editor CARY GRAZZINI Director of Print and Development LIA RIBACCHI Art Director CARA NIECE Director of Scheduling

STAR WARS: DAWN OF THE JEDI Book One—Force Storm

This volume collects issues #1–#5 of the Dark Horse comic-book series *Star Wars: Dawn of the Jedi—Force Storm*.

Published by Dark Horse Books, a division of Dark Horse Comics, Inc.
10956 SE Main Street, Milwaukie, OR 97222
DarkHorse.com | StarWars.com

To find a comics shop in your area, call the Comic Shop Locator Service toll-free at 1-888-266-4226

LIBRARY OF CONGRESS CATALOGING-IN-PUBLICATION DATA

Ostrander, John.
Force storm / story, John Ostrander & Jan Duursema ; script, John Ostrander ; pencils, Jan Duursema ; inks, Dan Parsons ; colors, Wes Dzioba ; letters, Michael Heisler ; cover art, Gonzalo Flores ; back cover art, Jan Duursema.
    p. cm. -- (Star wars: dawn of the Jedi ; bk. 1)
Summary: "This is the beginning of the story of the true roots of the Jedi Order, the Star Wars of 25,000 years ago"-- Provided by publisher.
ISBN 978-1-59582-979-5
1. Graphic novels. I. Duursema, Jan. II. Flores, Gonzalo, ill. III. Title.
PZ7.7.O77For 2012
741.5'973--dc23
                        2012025527

First edition: December 2012
ISBN 978-1-59582-979-5
10 9 8 7 6 5 4 3 2 1
Printed at Midas Printing International, Ltd., Huizhou, China

IT IS AN ERA OF LEGEND, an era before the discovery of hyperspace travel, before the foundation of the Old Republic, and before the philosophies of the Jedi and the Sith were codified.

This is a tale of a great and mythic society, established and nurtured by powers unthinkably ancient and mysterious, on a collision course with an empire founded on darkness and death.

This is the beginning of the story of the true roots of the Jedi Order . . . the dawn of the Jedi.

Illustration by **JAN DUURSEMA**

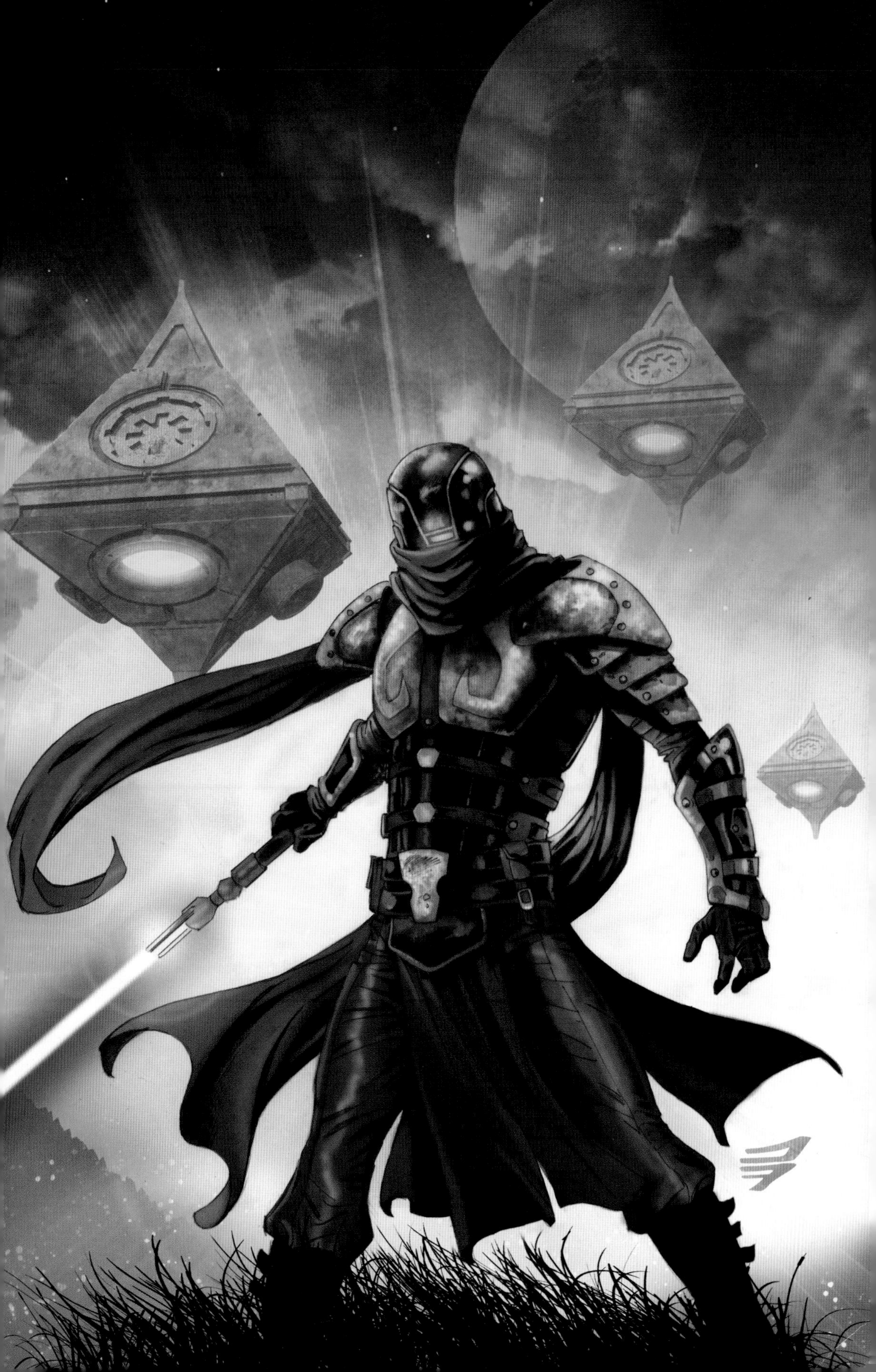

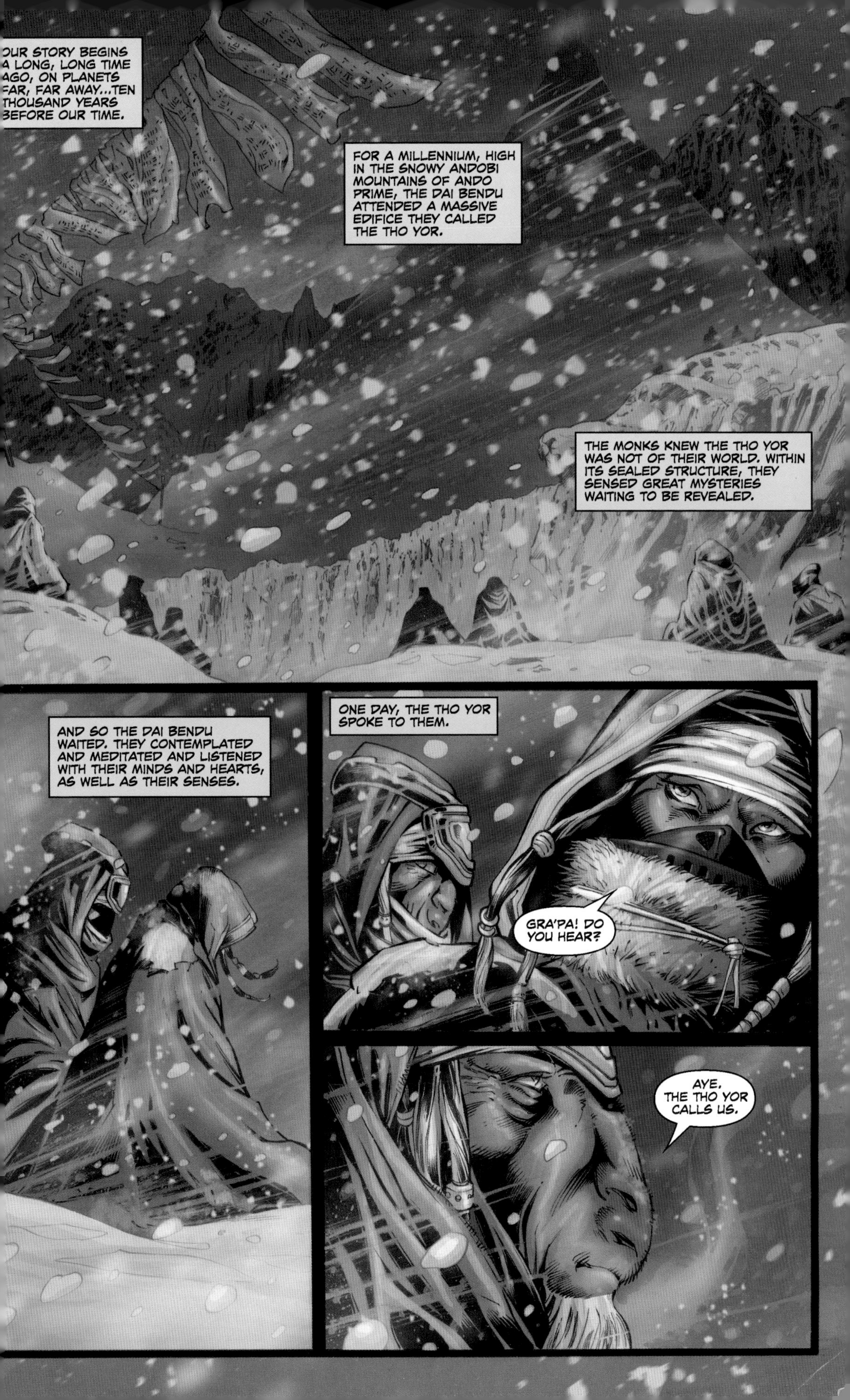
OUR STORY BEGINS A LONG, LONG TIME AGO, ON PLANETS FAR, FAR AWAY...TEN THOUSAND YEARS BEFORE OUR TIME.
FOR A MILLENNIUM, HIGH IN THE SNOWY ANDOBI MOUNTAINS OF ANDO PRIME, THE DAI BENDU ATTENDED A MASSIVE EDIFICE THEY CALLED THE THO YOR.
THE MONKS KNEW THE THO YOR WAS NOT OF THEIR WORLD. WITHIN ITS SEALED STRUCTURE, THEY SENSED GREAT MYSTERIES WAITING TO BE REVEALED.
AND SO THE DAI BENDU WAITED. THEY CONTEMPLATED AND MEDITATED AND LISTENED WITH THEIR MINDS AND HEARTS, AS WELL AS THEIR SENSES.
ONE DAY, THE THO YOR SPOKE TO THEM.
GRA'PA! DO YOU HEAR?
AYE. THE THO YOR CALLS US.

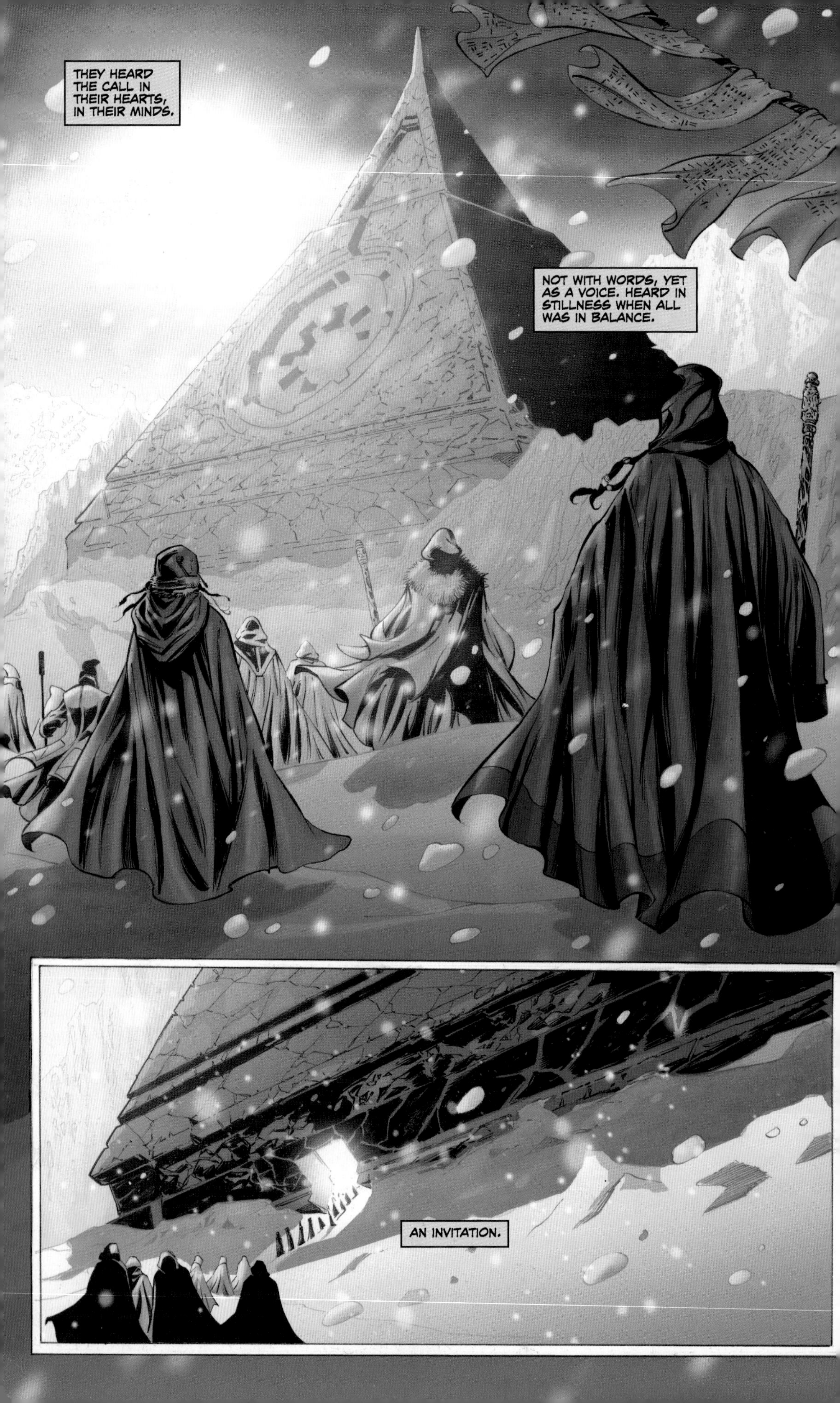
THEY HEARD THE CALL IN THEIR HEARTS, IN THEIR MINDS.
NOT WITH WORDS, YET AS A VOICE. HEARD IN STILLNESS WHEN ALL WAS IN BALANCE.
AN INVITATION.

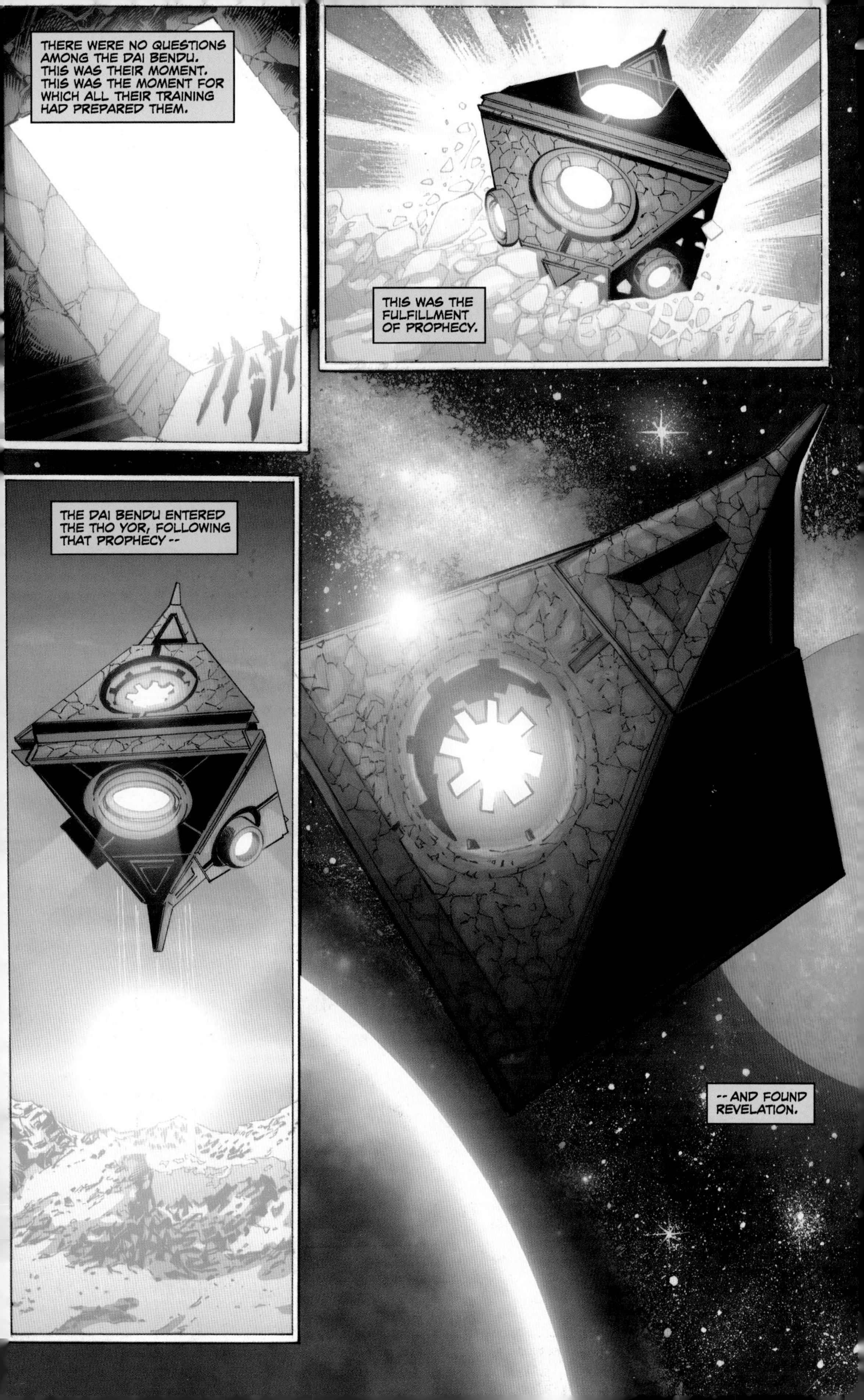
THERE WERE NO QUESTIONS AMONG THE DAI BENDU. THIS WAS THEIR MOMENT. THIS WAS THE MOMENT FOR WHICH ALL THEIR TRAINING HAD PREPARED THEM.
THIS WAS THE FULFILLMENT OF PROPHECY.
THE DAI BENDU ENTERED THE THO YOR, FOLLOWING THAT PROPHECY --
-- AND FOUND REVELATION.

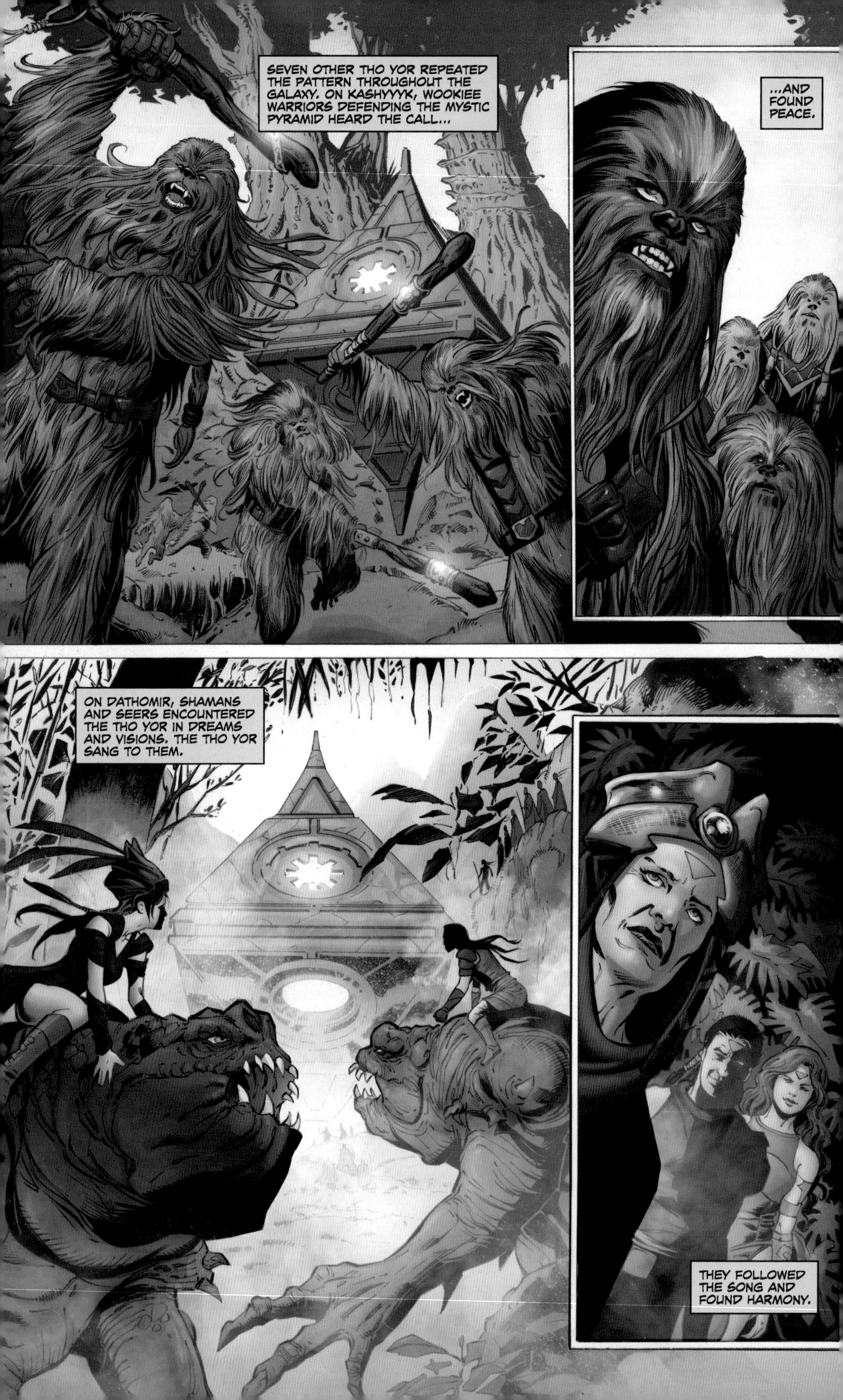
SEVEN OTHER THO YOR REPEATED THE PATTERN THROUGHOUT THE GALAXY. ON KASHYYYK, WOOKIEE WARRIORS DEFENDING THE MYSTIC PYRAMID HEARD THE CALL...
...AND FOUND PEACE.
ON DATHOMIR, SHAMANS AND SEERS ENCOUNTERED THE THO YOR IN DREAMS AND VISIONS. THE THO YOR SANG TO THEM.
THEY FOLLOWED THE SONG AND FOUND HARMONY.

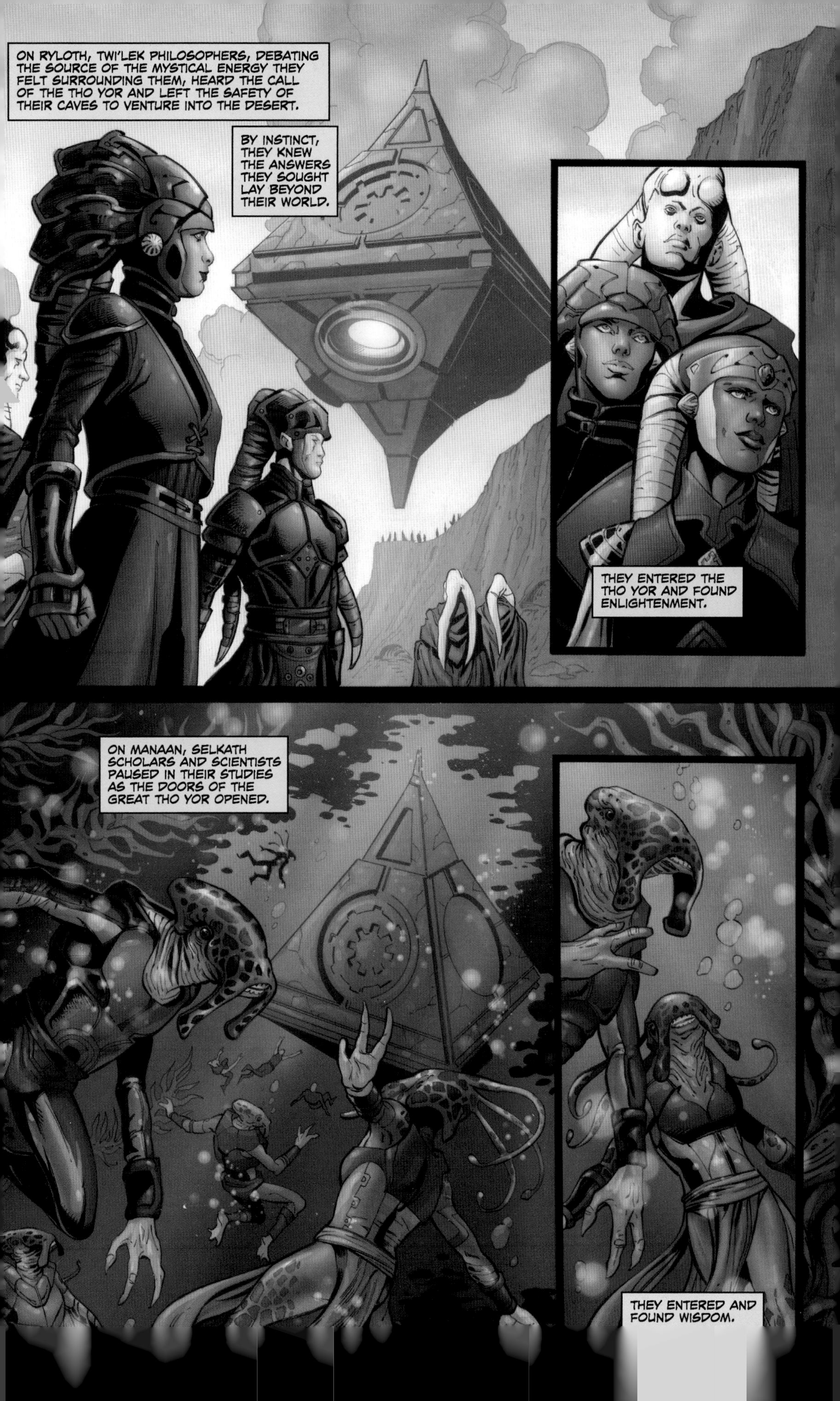
ON RYLOTH, TWI'LEK PHILOSOPHERS, DEBATING THE SOURCE OF THE MYSTICAL ENERGY THEY FELT SURROUNDING THEM, HEARD THE CALL OF THE THO YOR AND LEFT THE SAFETY OF THEIR CAVES TO VENTURE INTO THE DESERT.
BY INSTINCT, THEY KNEW THE ANSWERS THEY SOUGHT LAY BEYOND THEIR WORLD.
THEY ENTERED THE THO YOR AND FOUND ENLIGHTENMENT.
ON MANAAN, SELKATH SCHOLARS AND SCIENTISTS PAUSED IN THEIR STUDIES AS THE DOORS OF THE GREAT THO YOR OPENED.
THEY ENTERED AND FOUND WISDOM.

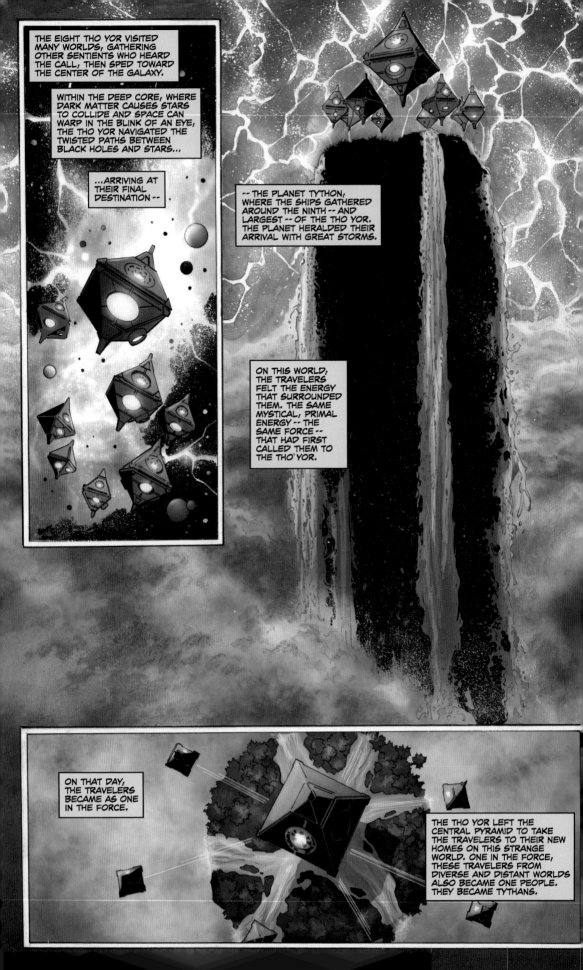

THE EIGHT THO YOR VISITED MANY WORLDS, GATHERING OTHER SENTIENTS WHO HEARD THE CALL, THEN SPED TOWARD THE CENTER OF THE GALAXY.

WITHIN THE DEEP CORE, WHERE DARK MATTER CAUSES STARS TO COLLIDE AND SPACE CAN WARP IN THE BLINK OF AN EYE, THE THO YOR NAVIGATED THE TWISTED PATHS BETWEEN BLACK HOLES AND STARS...

...ARRIVING AT THEIR FINAL DESTINATION --

-- THE PLANET TYTHON, WHERE THE SHIPS GATHERED AROUND THE NINTH -- AND LARGEST -- OF THE THO YOR. THE PLANET HERALDED THEIR ARRIVAL WITH GREAT STORMS.

ON THIS WORLD, THE TRAVELERS FELT THE ENERGY THAT SURROUNDED THEM. THE SAME MYSTICAL, PRIMAL ENERGY -- THE SAME FORCE -- THAT HAD FIRST CALLED THEM TO THE THO'YOR.

ON THAT DAY, THE TRAVELERS BECAME AS ONE IN THE FORCE.

THE THO YOR LEFT THE CENTRAL PYRAMID TO TAKE THE TRAVELERS TO THEIR NEW HOMES ON THIS STRANGE WORLD. ONE IN THE FORCE, THESE TRAVELERS FROM DIVERSE AND DISTANT WORLDS ALSO BECAME ONE PEOPLE. THEY BECAME TYTHANS.

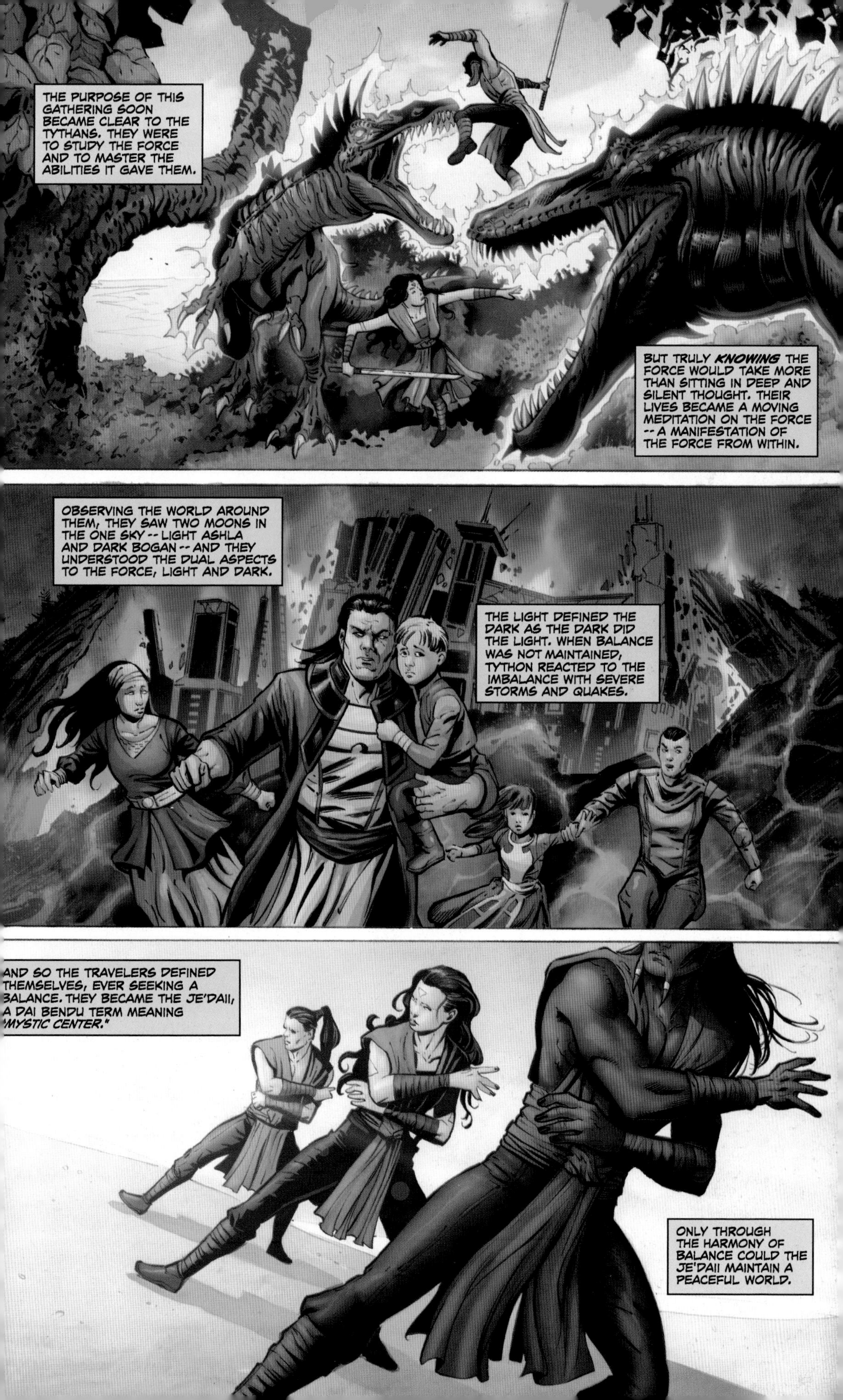
THE PURPOSE OF THIS GATHERING SOON BECAME CLEAR TO THE TYTHANS. THEY WERE TO STUDY THE FORCE AND TO MASTER THE ABILITIES IT GAVE THEM.
BUT TRULY *KNOWING* THE FORCE WOULD TAKE MORE THAN SITTING IN DEEP AND SILENT THOUGHT. THEIR LIVES BECAME A MOVING MEDITATION ON THE FORCE -- A MANIFESTATION OF THE FORCE FROM WITHIN.
OBSERVING THE WORLD AROUND THEM, THEY SAW TWO MOONS IN THE ONE SKY -- LIGHT ASHLA AND DARK BOGAN -- AND THEY UNDERSTOOD THE DUAL ASPECTS TO THE FORCE, LIGHT AND DARK.
THE LIGHT DEFINED THE DARK AS THE DARK DID THE LIGHT. WHEN BALANCE WAS NOT MAINTAINED, TYTHON REACTED TO THE IMBALANCE WITH SEVERE STORMS AND QUAKES.
AND SO THE TRAVELERS DEFINED THEMSELVES, EVER SEEKING A BALANCE. THEY BECAME THE JE'DAII, A DAI BENDU TERM MEANING *"MYSTIC CENTER."*
ONLY THROUGH THE HARMONY OF BALANCE COULD THE JE'DAII MAINTAIN A PEACEFUL WORLD.

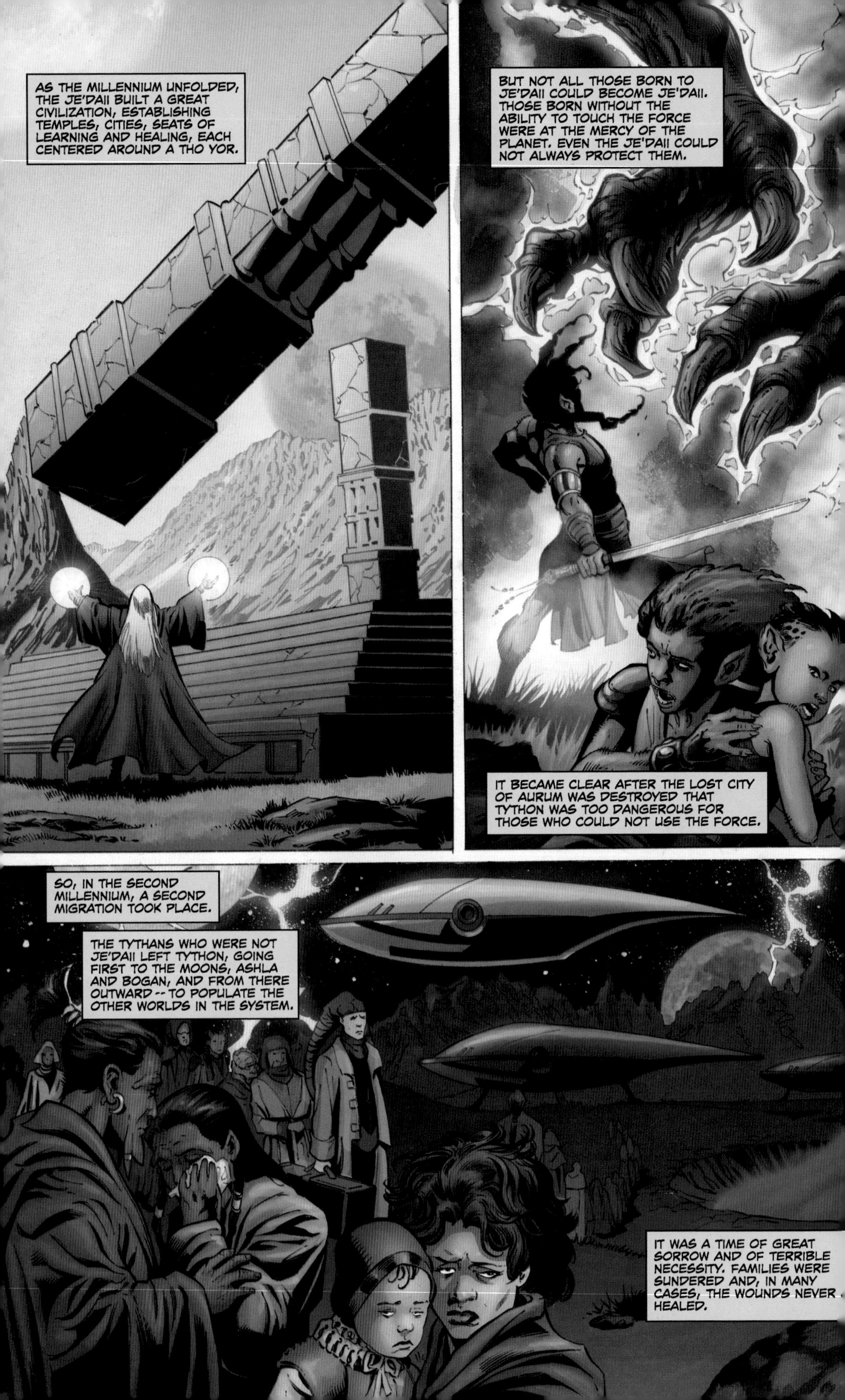
AS THE MILLENNIUM UNFOLDED, THE JE'DAII BUILT A GREAT CIVILIZATION, ESTABLISHING TEMPLES, CITIES, SEATS OF LEARNING AND HEALING, EACH CENTERED AROUND A THO YOR.
BUT NOT ALL THOSE BORN TO JE'DAII COULD BECOME JE'DAII. THOSE BORN WITHOUT THE ABILITY TO TOUCH THE FORCE WERE AT THE MERCY OF THE PLANET. EVEN THE JE'DAII COULD NOT ALWAYS PROTECT THEM.
IT BECAME CLEAR AFTER THE LOST CITY OF AURUM WAS DESTROYED THAT TYTHON WAS TOO DANGEROUS FOR THOSE WHO COULD NOT USE THE FORCE.
SO, IN THE SECOND MILLENNIUM, A SECOND MIGRATION TOOK PLACE.
THE TYTHANS WHO WERE NOT JE'DAII LEFT TYTHON, GOING FIRST TO THE MOONS, ASHLA AND BOGAN, AND FROM THERE OUTWARD -- TO POPULATE THE OTHER WORLDS IN THE SYSTEM.
IT WAS A TIME OF GREAT SORROW AND OF TERRIBLE NECESSITY. FAMILIES WERE SUNDERED AND, IN MANY CASES, THE WOUNDS NEVER HEALED.

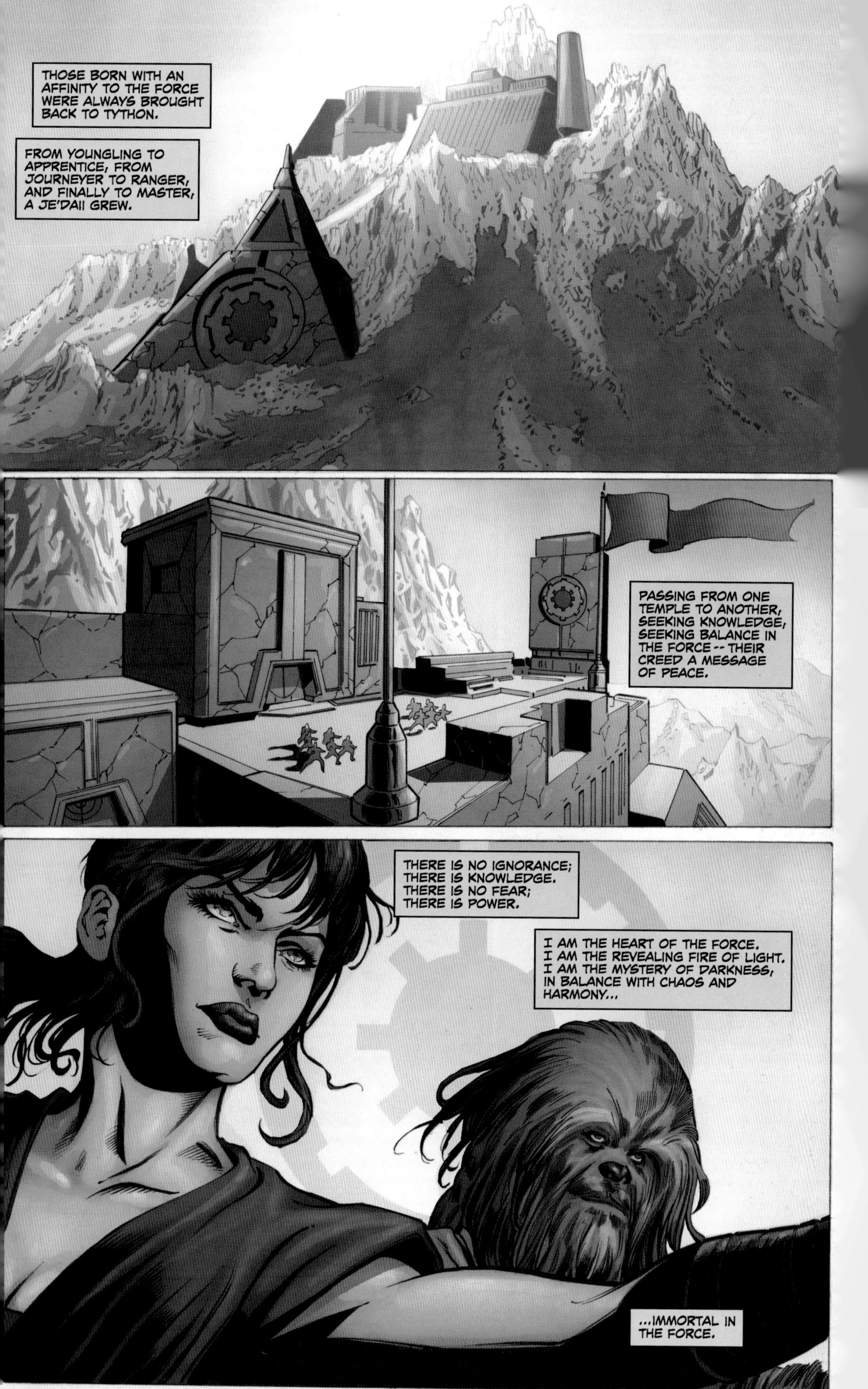
THOSE BORN WITH AN AFFINITY TO THE FORCE WERE ALWAYS BROUGHT BACK TO TYTHON.
FROM YOUNGLING TO APPRENTICE, FROM JOURNEYER TO RANGER, AND FINALLY TO MASTER, A JE'DAII GREW.
PASSING FROM ONE TEMPLE TO ANOTHER, SEEKING KNOWLEDGE, SEEKING BALANCE IN THE FORCE -- THEIR CREED A MESSAGE OF PEACE.
THERE IS NO IGNORANCE; THERE IS KNOWLEDGE. THERE IS NO FEAR; THERE IS POWER.
I AM THE HEART OF THE FORCE. I AM THE REVEALING FIRE OF LIGHT. I AM THE MYSTERY OF DARKNESS, IN BALANCE WITH CHAOS AND HARMONY...
...IMMORTAL IN THE FORCE.

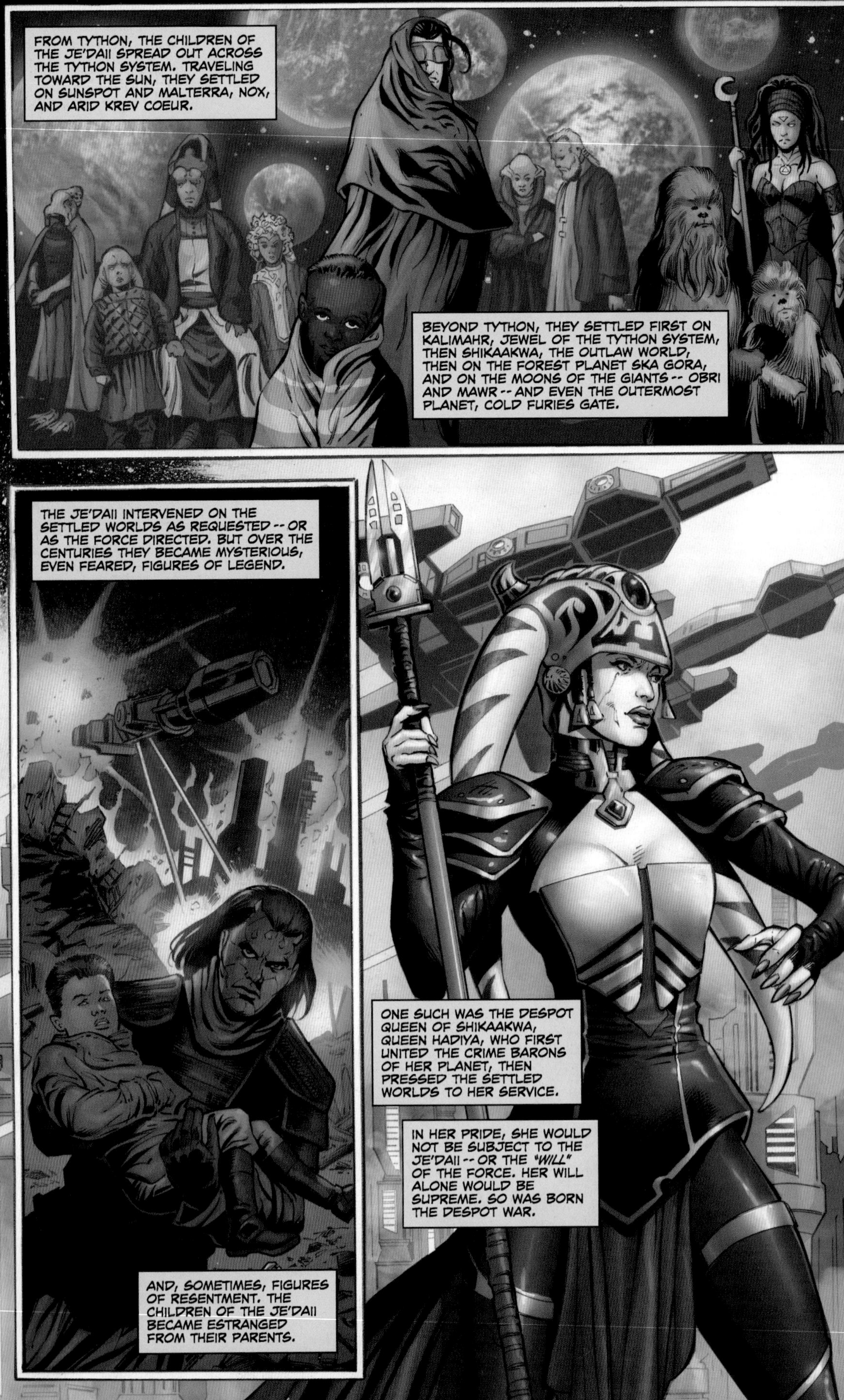
FROM TYTHON, THE CHILDREN OF THE JE'DAII SPREAD OUT ACROSS THE TYTHON SYSTEM. TRAVELING TOWARD THE SUN, THEY SETTLED ON SUNSPOT AND MALTERRA, NOX, AND ARID KREV COEUR.
BEYOND TYTHON, THEY SETTLED FIRST ON KALIMAHR, JEWEL OF THE TYTHON SYSTEM, THEN SHIKAAKWA, THE OUTLAW WORLD, THEN ON THE FOREST PLANET SKA GORA, AND ON THE MOONS OF THE GIANTS -- OBRI AND MAWR -- AND EVEN THE OUTERMOST PLANET, COLD FURIES GATE.
THE JE'DAII INTERVENED ON THE SETTLED WORLDS AS REQUESTED -- OR AS THE FORCE DIRECTED. BUT OVER THE CENTURIES THEY BECAME MYSTERIOUS, EVEN FEARED, FIGURES OF LEGEND.
AND, SOMETIMES, FIGURES OF RESENTMENT. THE CHILDREN OF THE JE'DAII BECAME ESTRANGED FROM THEIR PARENTS.
ONE SUCH WAS THE DESPOT QUEEN OF SHIKAAKWA, QUEEN HADIYA, WHO FIRST UNITED THE CRIME BARONS OF HER PLANET, THEN PRESSED THE SETTLED WORLDS TO HER SERVICE.
IN HER PRIDE, SHE WOULD NOT BE SUBJECT TO THE JE'DAII -- OR THE "WILL" OF THE FORCE. HER WILL ALONE WOULD BE SUPREME. SO WAS BORN THE DESPOT WAR.

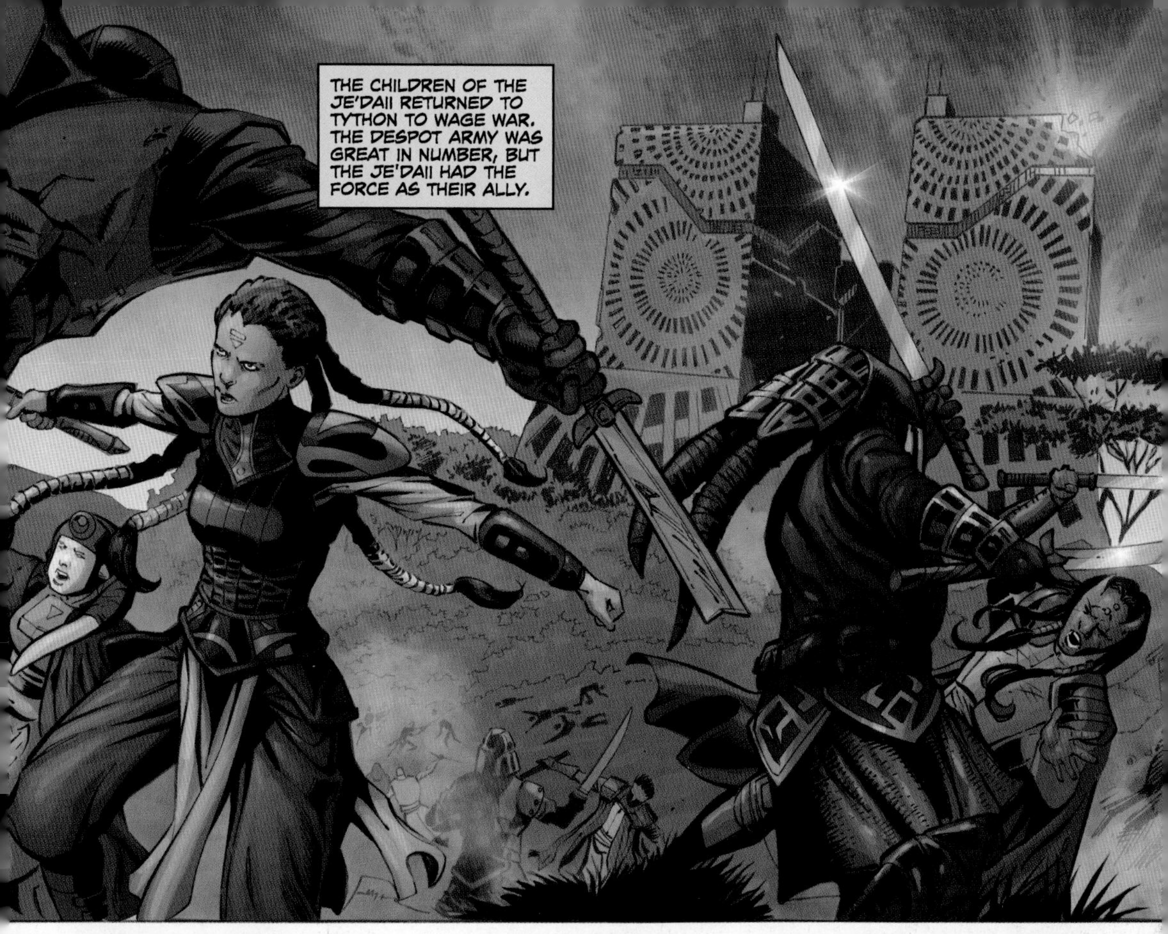
THE CHILDREN OF THE JE'DAII RETURNED TO TYTHON TO WAGE WAR. THE DESPOT ARMY WAS GREAT IN NUMBER, BUT THE JE'DAII HAD THE FORCE AS THEIR ALLY.

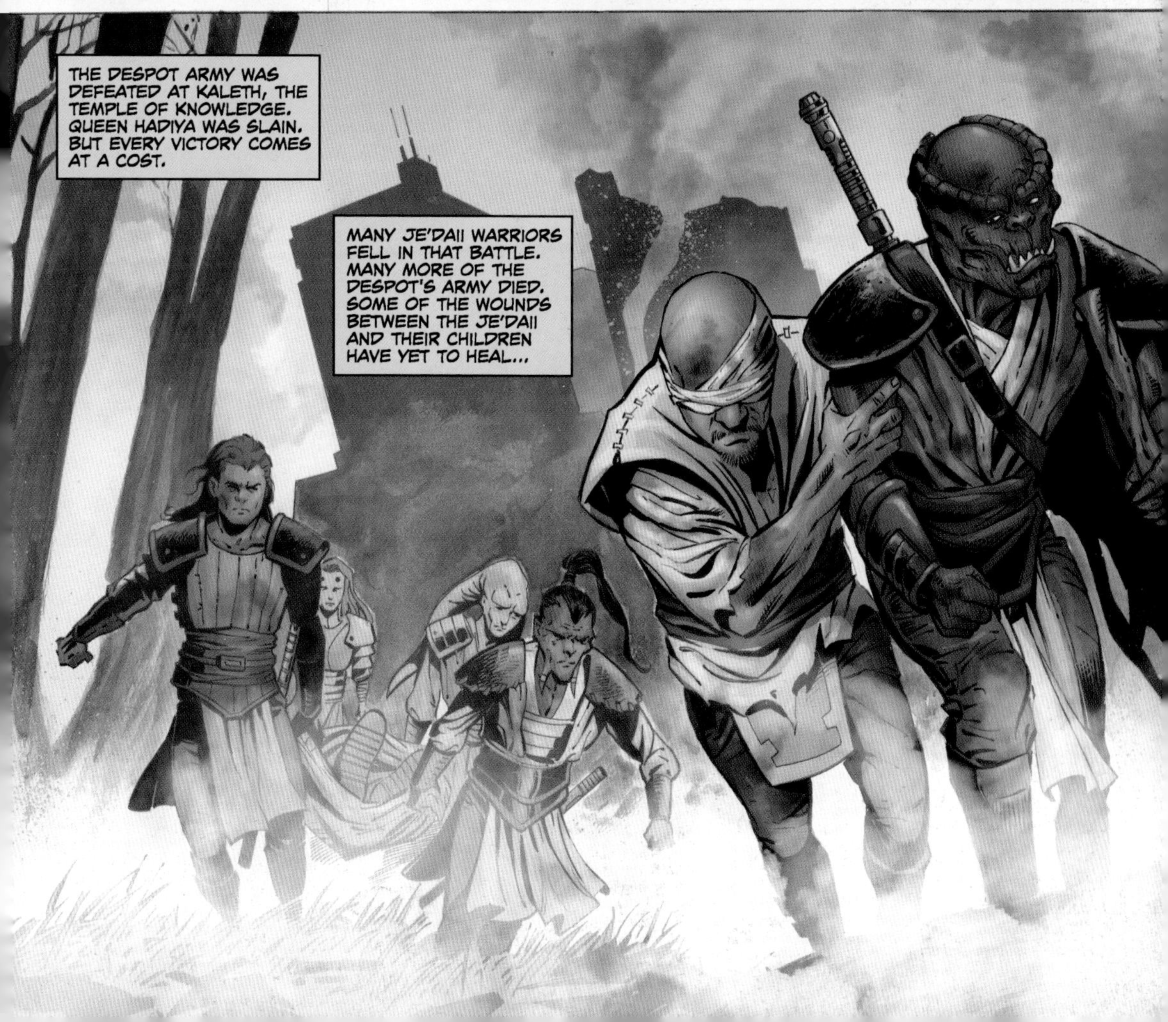
THE DESPOT ARMY WAS DEFEATED AT KALETH, THE TEMPLE OF KNOWLEDGE. QUEEN HADIYA WAS SLAIN. BUT EVERY VICTORY COMES AT A COST.
MANY JE'DAII WARRIORS FELL IN THAT BATTLE. MANY MORE OF THE DESPOT'S ARMY DIED. SOME OF THE WOUNDS BETWEEN THE JE'DAII AND THEIR CHILDREN HAVE YET TO HEAL...

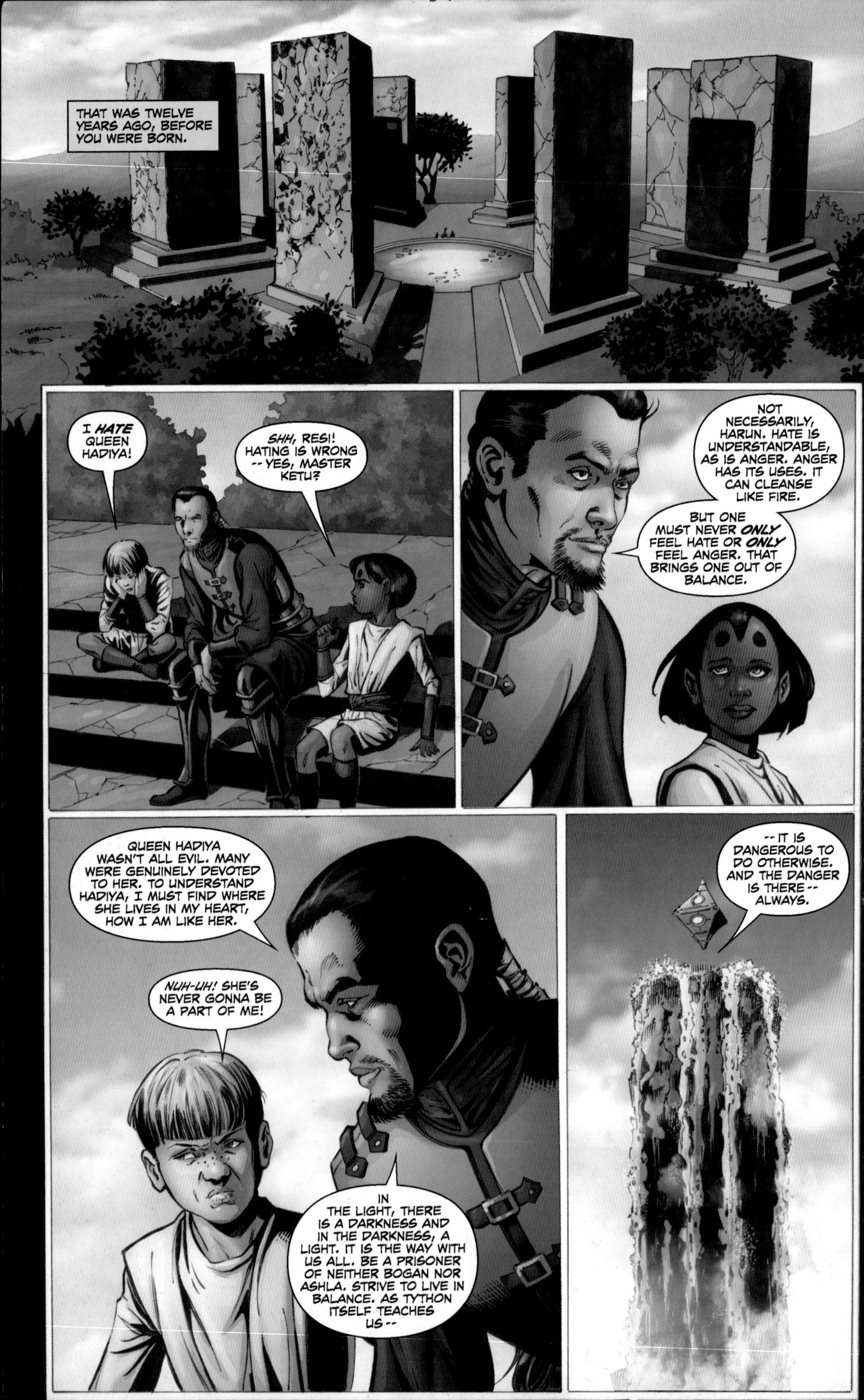
THAT WAS TWELVE YEARS AGO, BEFORE YOU WERE BORN.
I HATE QUEEN HADIYA!
SHH, RESI! HATING IS WRONG -- YES, MASTER KETU?
NOT NECESSARILY, HARUN. HATE IS UNDERSTANDABLE, AS IS ANGER. ANGER HAS ITS USES. IT CAN CLEANSE LIKE FIRE.
BUT ONE MUST NEVER ONLY FEEL HATE OR ONLY FEEL ANGER. THAT BRINGS ONE OUT OF BALANCE.
QUEEN HADIYA WASN'T ALL EVIL. MANY WERE GENUINELY DEVOTED TO HER. TO UNDERSTAND HADIYA, I MUST FIND WHERE SHE LIVES IN MY HEART, HOW I AM LIKE HER.
NUH-UH! SHE'S NEVER GONNA BE A PART OF ME!
IN THE LIGHT, THERE IS A DARKNESS AND IN THE DARKNESS, A LIGHT. IT IS THE WAY WITH US ALL. BE A PRISONER OF NEITHER BOGAN NOR ASHLA. STRIVE TO LIVE IN BALANCE. AS TYTHON ITSELF TEACHES US --
-- IT IS DANGEROUS TO DO OTHERWISE. AND THE DANGER IS THERE -- ALWAYS.

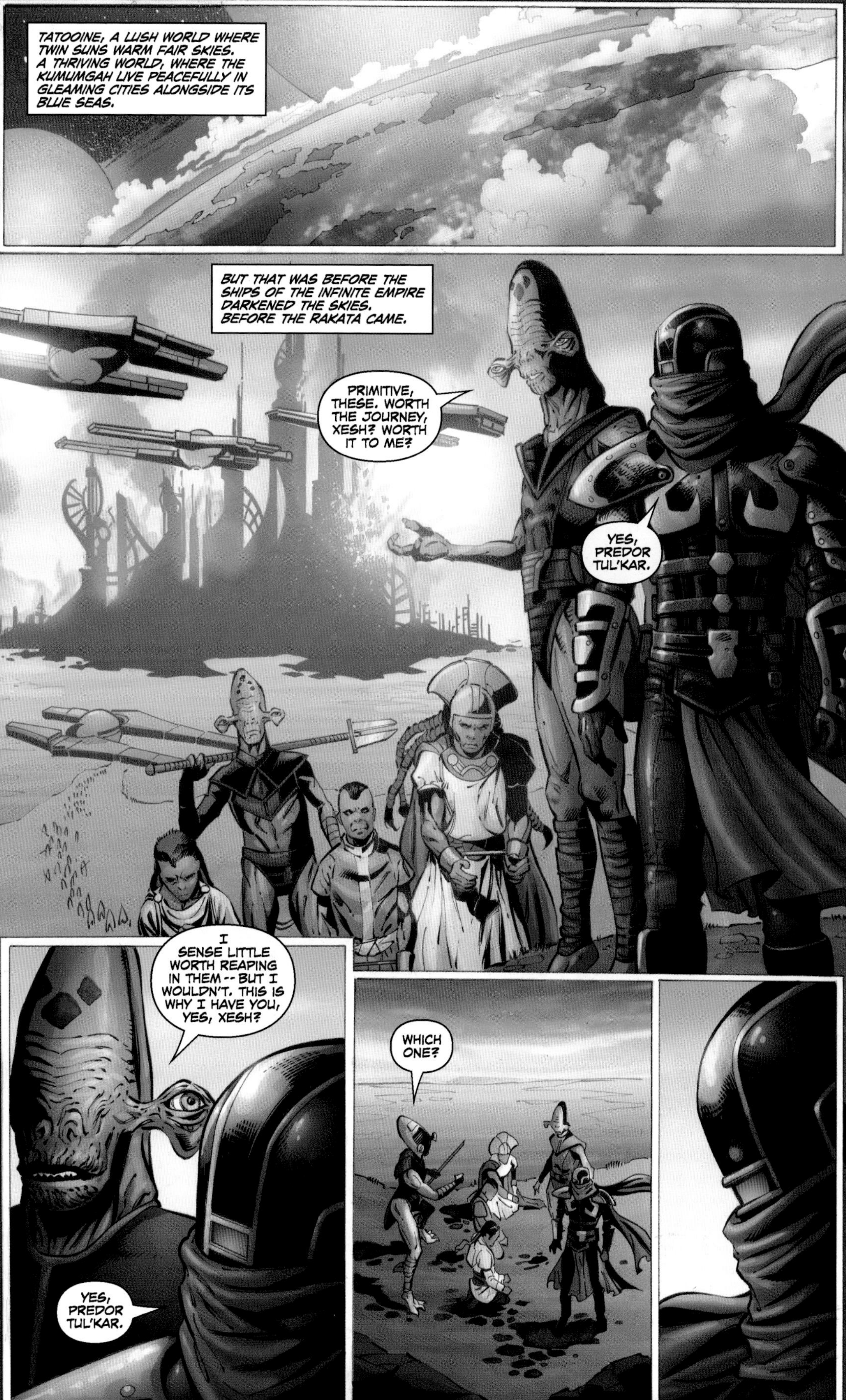
TATOOINE, A LUSH WORLD WHERE TWIN SUNS WARM FAIR SKIES. A THRIVING WORLD, WHERE THE KUMUMGAH LIVE PEACEFULLY IN GLEAMING CITIES ALONGSIDE ITS BLUE SEAS.
BUT THAT WAS BEFORE THE SHIPS OF THE INFINITE EMPIRE DARKENED THE SKIES. BEFORE THE RAKATA CAME.
PRIMITIVE, THESE. WORTH THE JOURNEY, XESH? WORTH IT TO ME?
YES, PREDOR TUL'KAR.
I SENSE LITTLE WORTH REAPING IN THEM -- BUT I WOULDN'T. THIS IS WHY I HAVE YOU, YES, XESH?
YES, PREDOR TUL'KAR.
WHICH ONE?

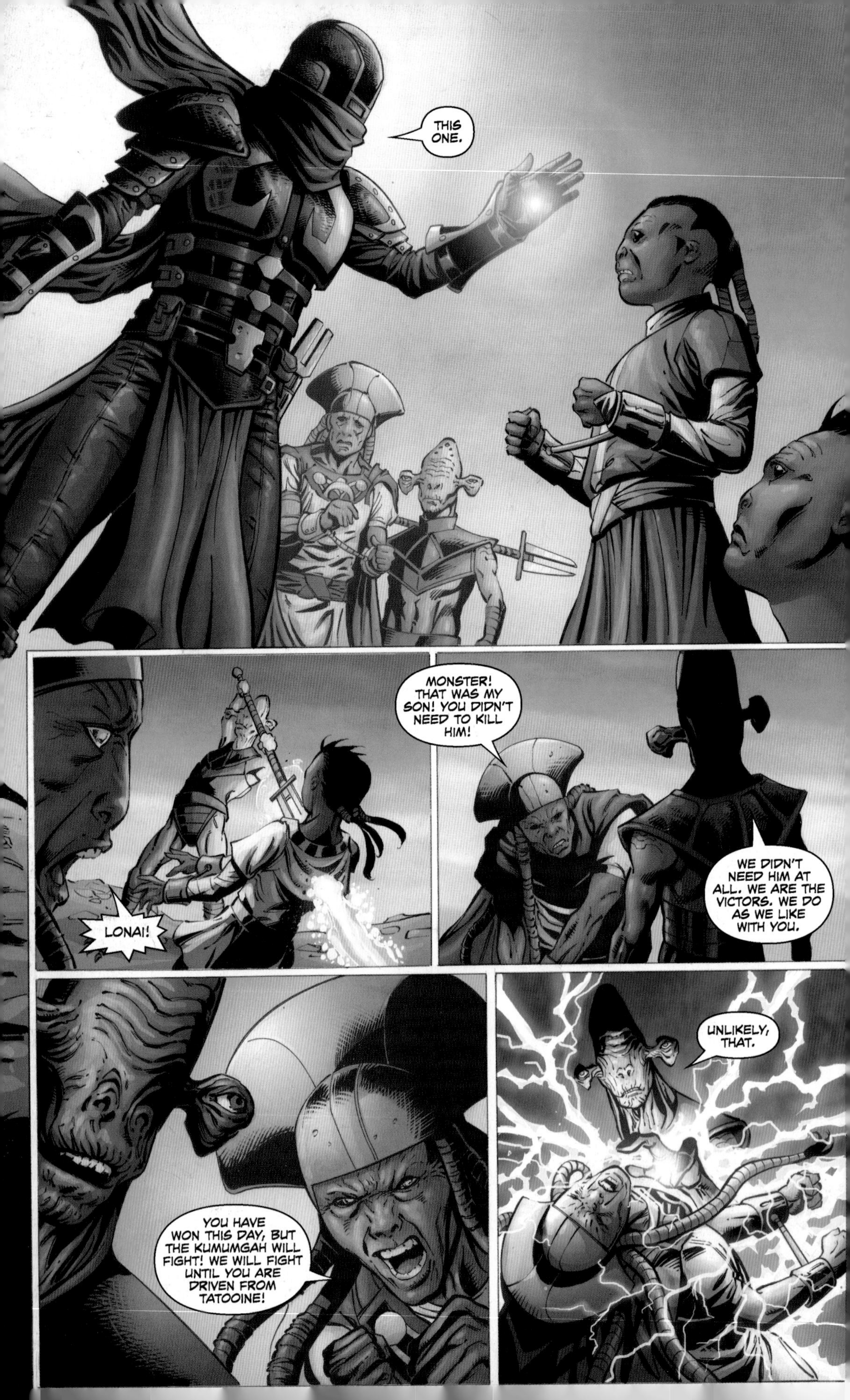
THIS ONE.
LONAI!
MONSTER! THAT WAS MY SON! YOU DIDN'T NEED TO KILL HIM!
WE DIDN'T NEED HIM AT ALL. WE ARE THE VICTORS. WE DO AS WE LIKE WITH YOU.
YOU HAVE WON THIS DAY, BUT THE KUMUMGAH WILL FIGHT! WE WILL FIGHT UNTIL YOU ARE DRIVEN FROM TATOOINE!
UNLIKELY, THAT.

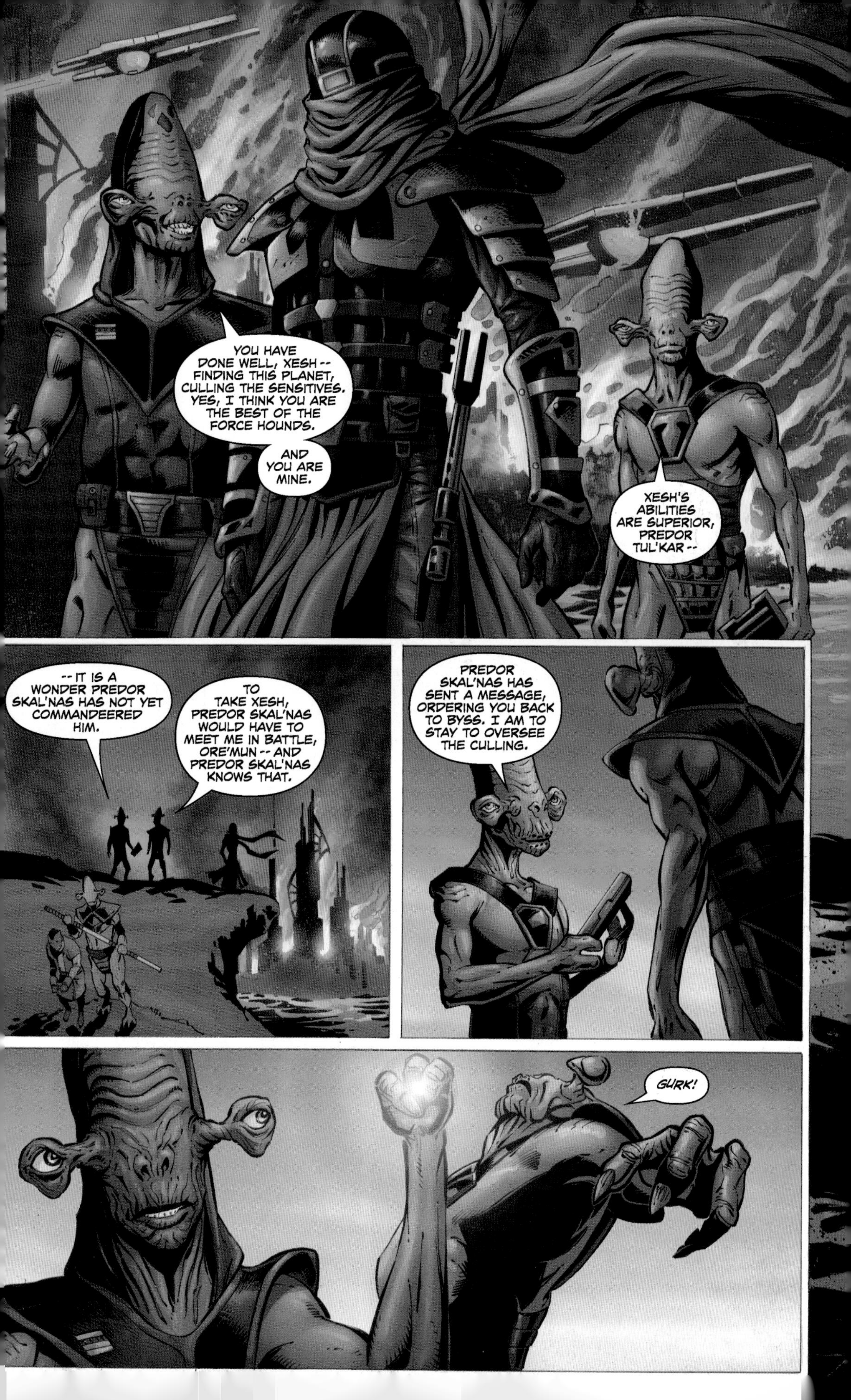
YOU HAVE DONE WELL, XESH -- FINDING THIS PLANET, CULLING THE SENSITIVES. YES, I THINK YOU ARE THE BEST OF THE FORCE HOUNDS.
AND YOU ARE MINE.
XESH'S ABILITIES ARE SUPERIOR, PREDOR TUL'KAR --
-- IT IS A WONDER PREDOR SKAL'NAS HAS NOT YET COMMANDEERED HIM.
TO TAKE XESH, PREDOR SKAL'NAS WOULD HAVE TO MEET ME IN BATTLE, ORE'MUN -- AND PREDOR SKAL'NAS KNOWS THAT.
PREDOR SKAL'NAS HAS SENT A MESSAGE, ORDERING YOU BACK TO BYSS. I AM TO STAY TO OVERSEE THE CULLING.
GURK!

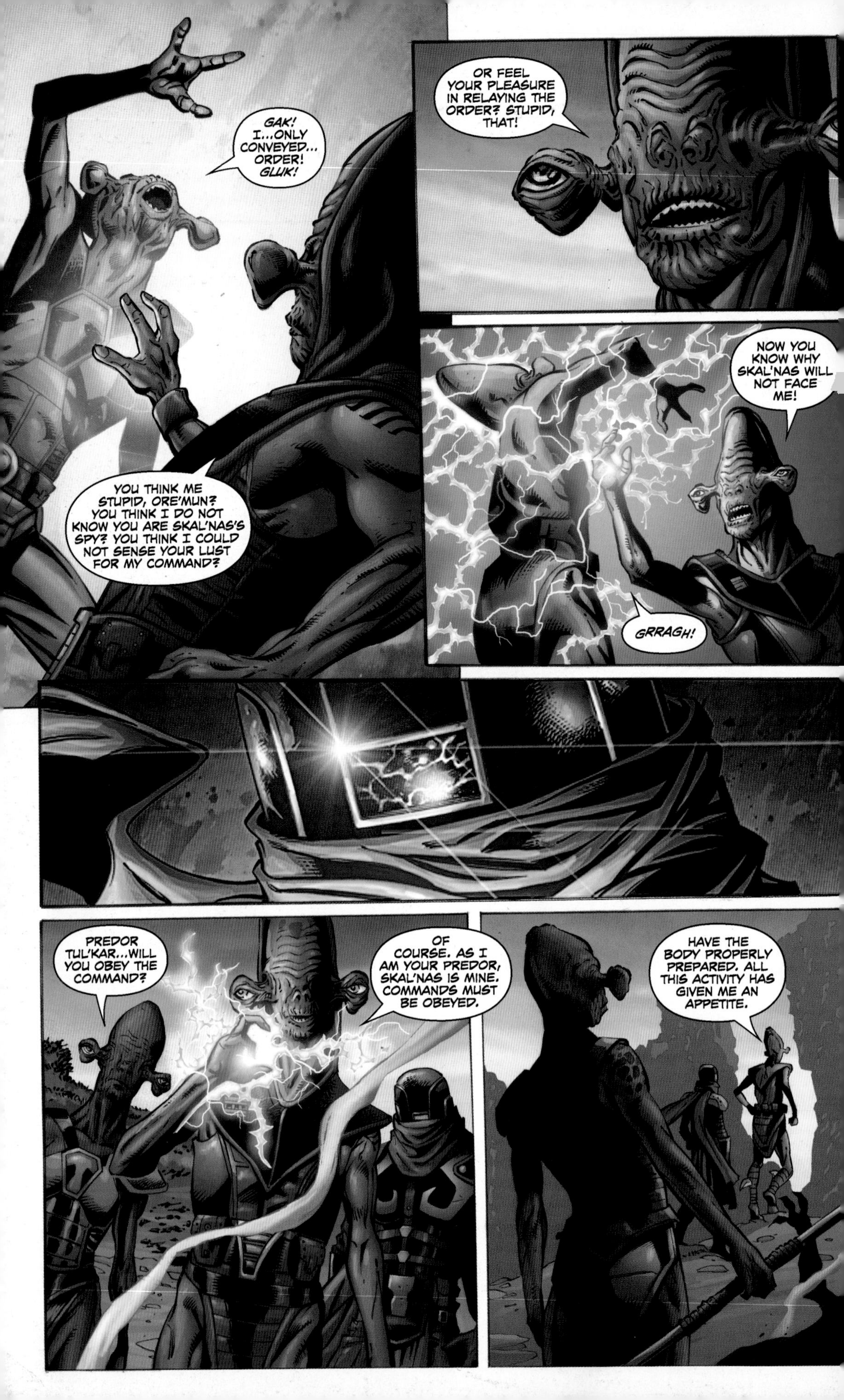
GAK! I...ONLY CONVEYED... ORDER! GLUK!
YOU THINK ME STUPID, ORE'MUN? YOU THINK I DO NOT KNOW YOU ARE SKAL'NAS'S SPY? YOU THINK I COULD NOT SENSE YOUR LUST FOR MY COMMAND?
OR FEEL YOUR PLEASURE IN RELAYING THE ORDER? STUPID, THAT!
NOW YOU KNOW WHY SKAL'NAS WILL NOT FACE ME!
GRRAGH!
PREDOR TUL'KAR...WILL YOU OBEY THE COMMAND?
OF COURSE. AS I AM YOUR PREDOR, SKAL'NAS IS MINE. COMMANDS MUST BE OBEYED.
HAVE THE BODY PROPERLY PREPARED. ALL THIS ACTIVITY HAS GIVEN ME AN APPETITE.

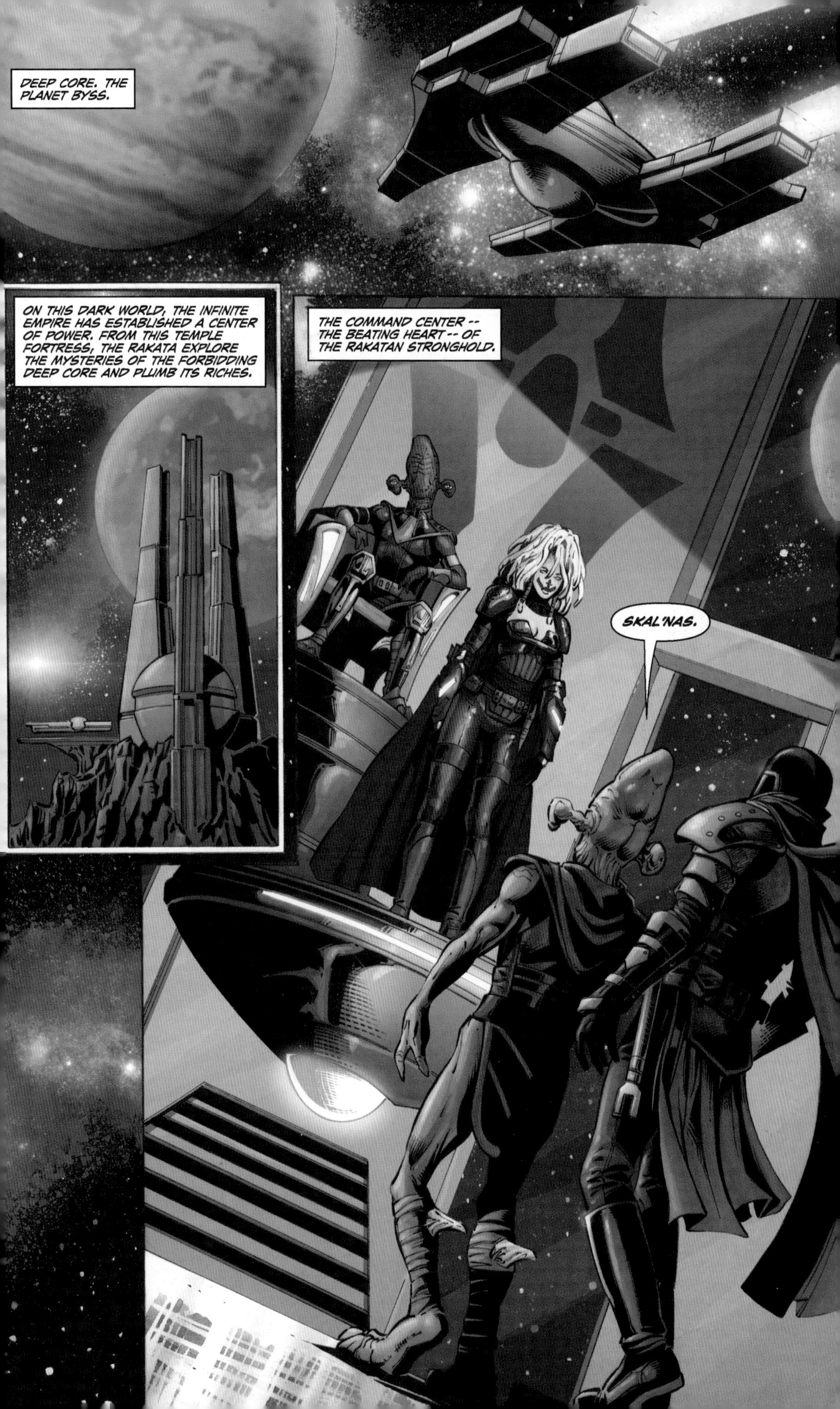
DEEP CORE. THE PLANET BYSS.
ON THIS DARK WORLD, THE INFINITE EMPIRE HAS ESTABLISHED A CENTER OF POWER. FROM THIS TEMPLE FORTRESS, THE RAKATA EXPLORE THE MYSTERIES OF THE FORBIDDING DEEP CORE AND PLUMB ITS RICHES.
THE COMMAND CENTER -- THE BEATING HEART -- OF THE RAKATAN STRONGHOLD.
SKAL'NAS.

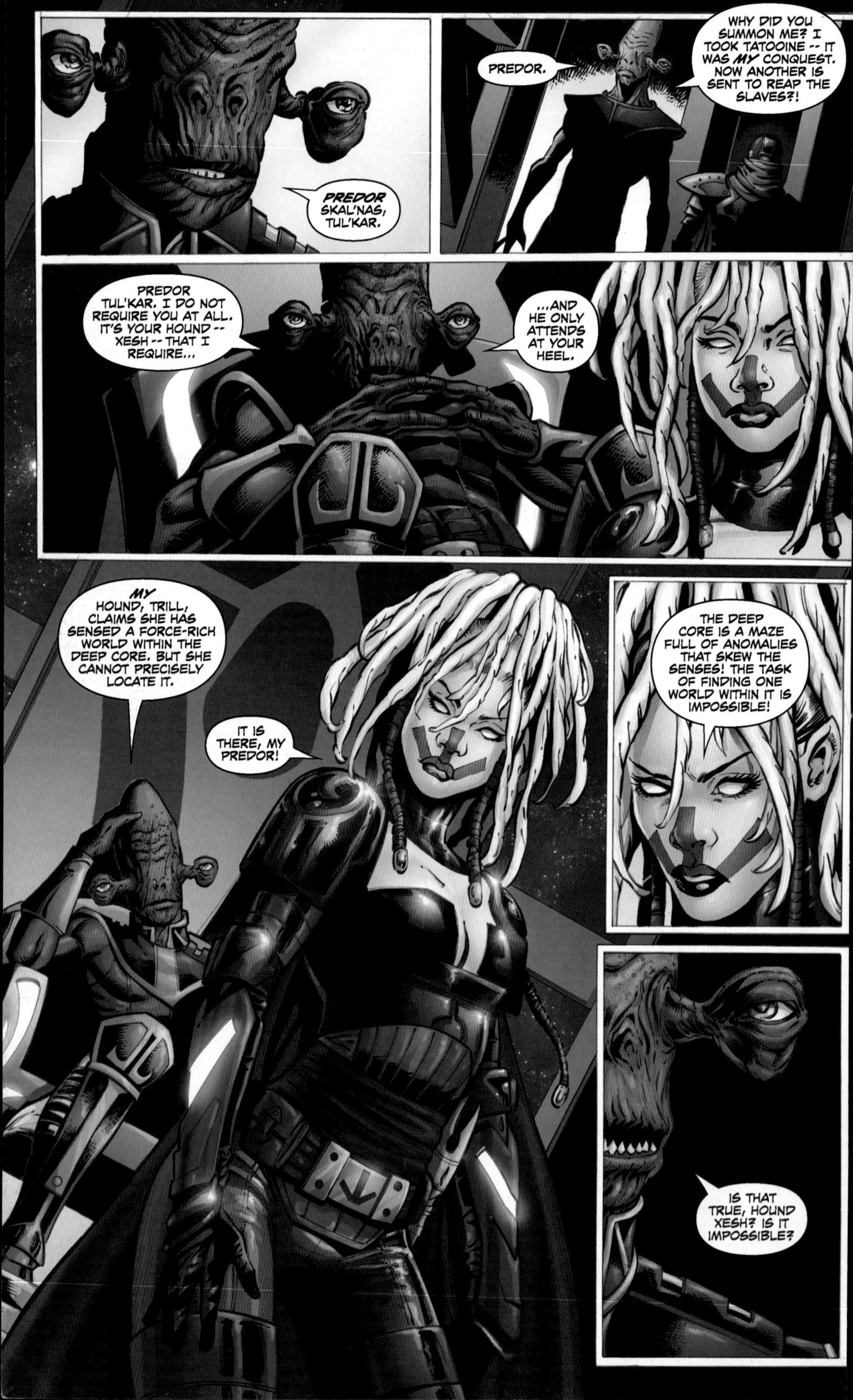
PREDOR SKAL'NAS, TUL'KAR.
PREDOR.
WHY DID YOU SUMMON ME? I TOOK TATOOINE -- IT WAS MY CONQUEST. NOW ANOTHER IS SENT TO REAP THE SLAVES?!
PREDOR TUL'KAR. I DO NOT REQUIRE YOU AT ALL. IT'S YOUR HOUND -- XESH -- THAT I REQUIRE...
...AND HE ONLY ATTENDS AT YOUR HEEL.
MY HOUND, TRILL, CLAIMS SHE HAS SENSED A FORCE-RICH WORLD WITHIN THE DEEP CORE. BUT SHE CANNOT PRECISELY LOCATE IT.
IT IS THERE, MY PREDOR!
THE DEEP CORE IS A MAZE FULL OF ANOMALIES THAT SKEW THE SENSES! THE TASK OF FINDING ONE WORLD WITHIN IT IS IMPOSSIBLE!
IS THAT TRUE, HOUND XESH? IS IT IMPOSSIBLE?

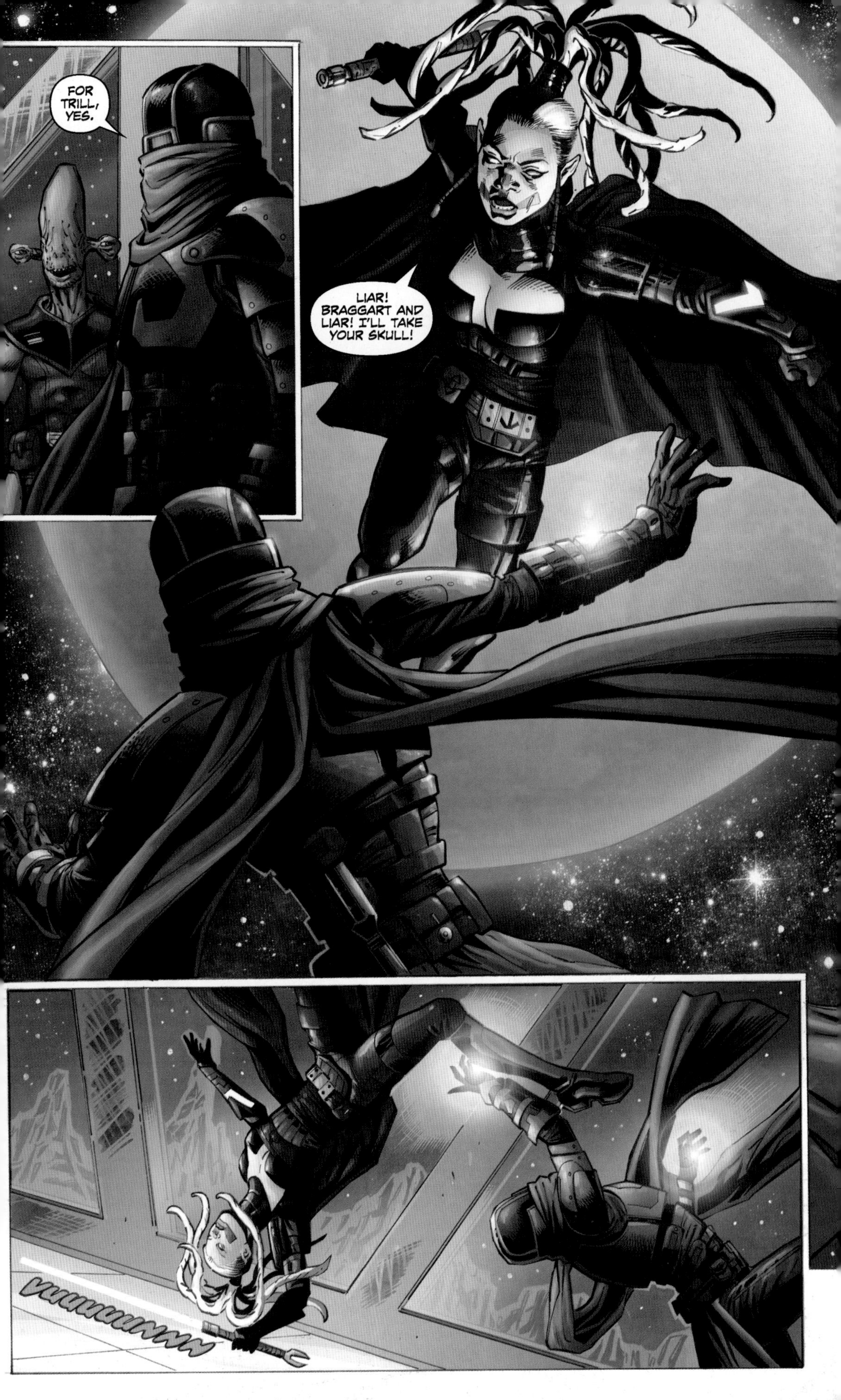
FOR TRILL, YES.
LIAR! BRAGGART AND LIAR! I'LL TAKE YOUR SKULL!
VVUUUUUUNNN

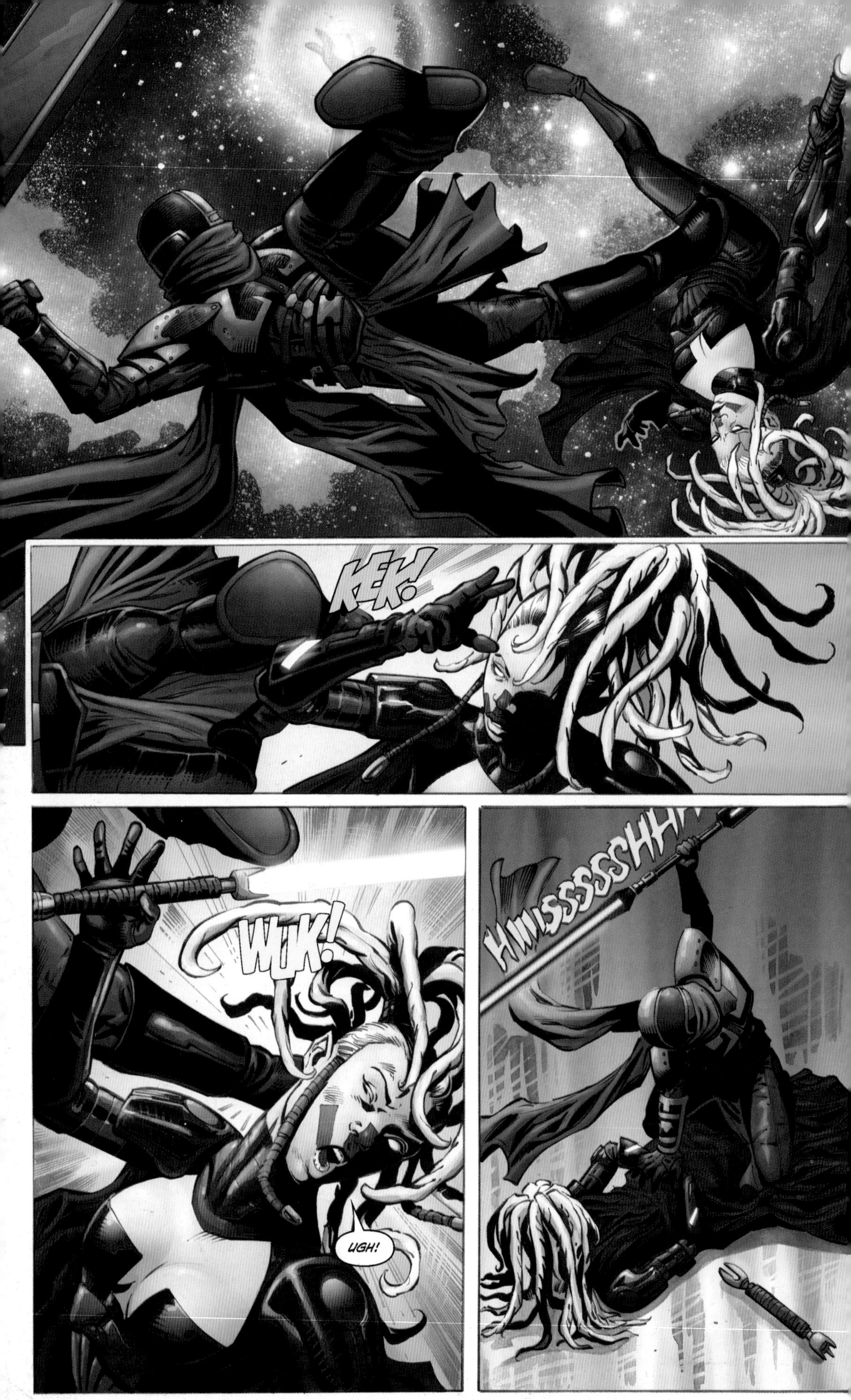
KEK!
WUK!
UGH!
HMISSSSSSHHH

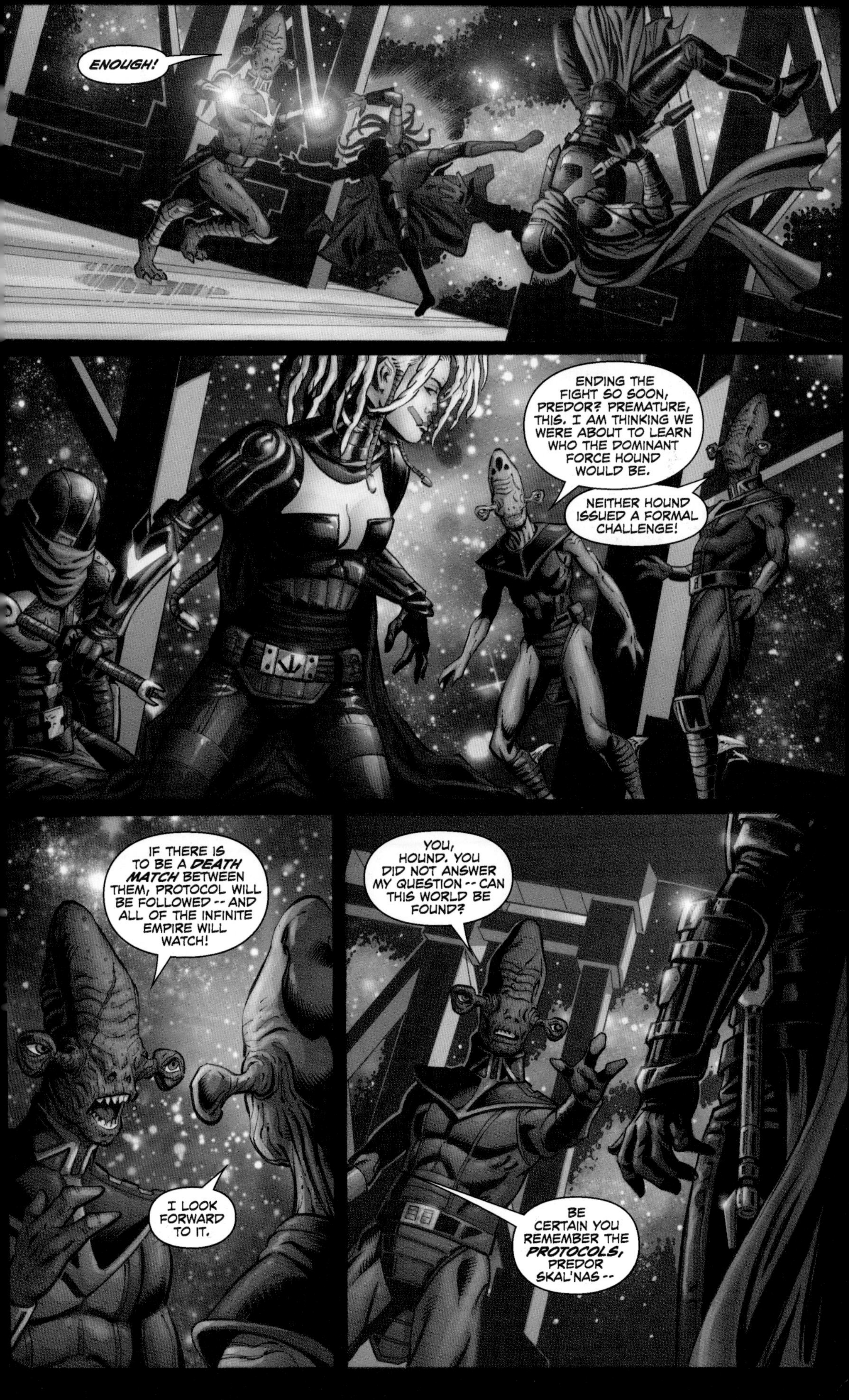
ENOUGH!
ENDING THE FIGHT SO SOON, PREDOR? PREMATURE, THIS. I AM THINKING WE WERE ABOUT TO LEARN WHO THE DOMINANT FORCE HOUND WOULD BE.
NEITHER HOUND ISSUED A FORMAL CHALLENGE!
IF THERE IS TO BE A *DEATH MATCH* BETWEEN THEM, PROTOCOL WILL BE FOLLOWED -- AND ALL OF THE INFINITE EMPIRE WILL WATCH!
I LOOK FORWARD TO IT.
YOU, HOUND. YOU DID NOT ANSWER MY QUESTION -- CAN THIS WORLD BE FOUND?
BE CERTAIN YOU REMEMBER THE *PROTOCOLS,* PREDOR SKAL'NAS --

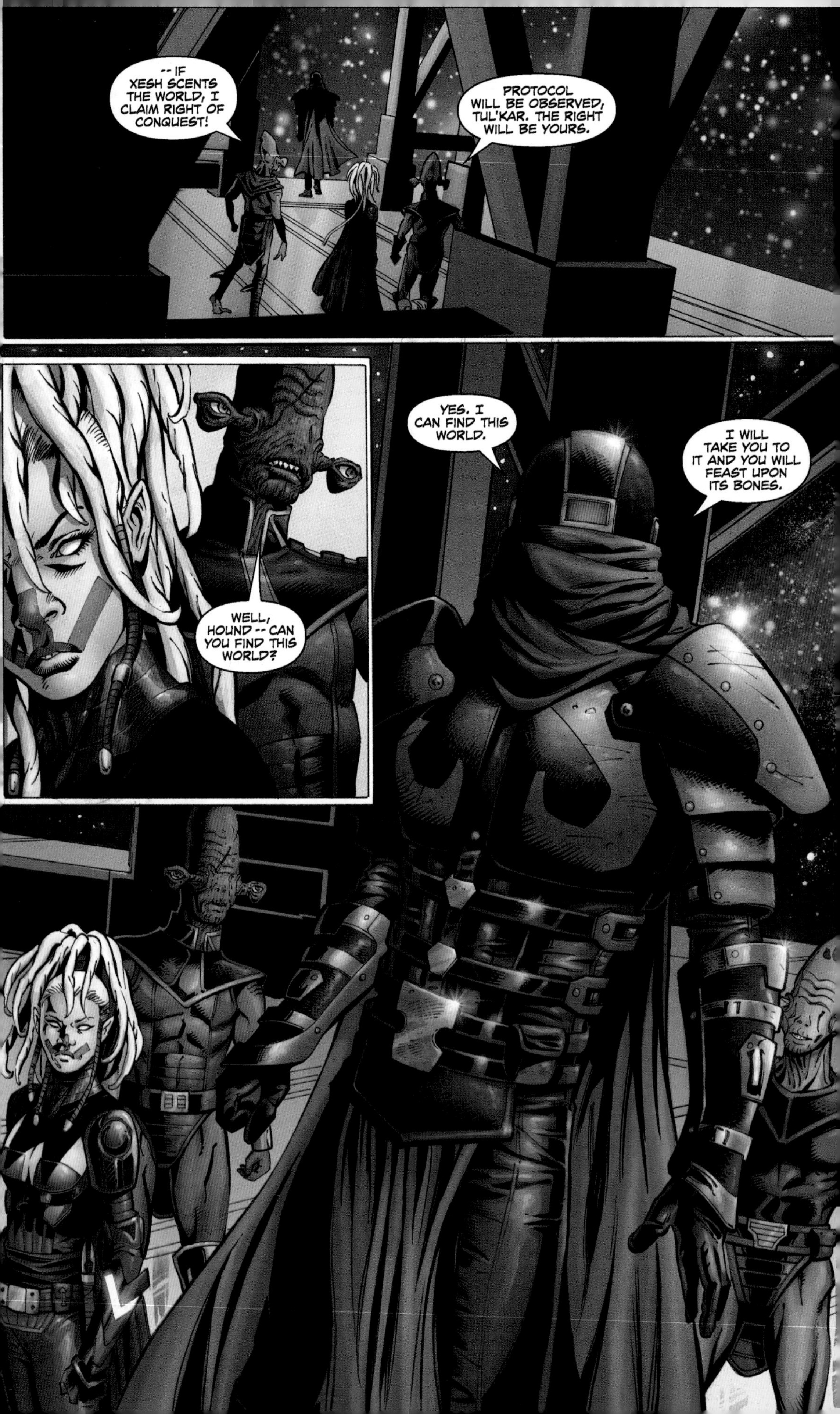
-- IF XESH SCENTS THE WORLD, I CLAIM RIGHT OF CONQUEST!
PROTOCOL WILL BE OBSERVED, TUL'KAR. THE RIGHT WILL BE YOURS.
WELL, HOUND -- CAN YOU FIND THIS WORLD?
YES. I CAN FIND THIS WORLD.
I WILL TAKE YOU TO IT AND YOU WILL FEAST UPON ITS BONES.

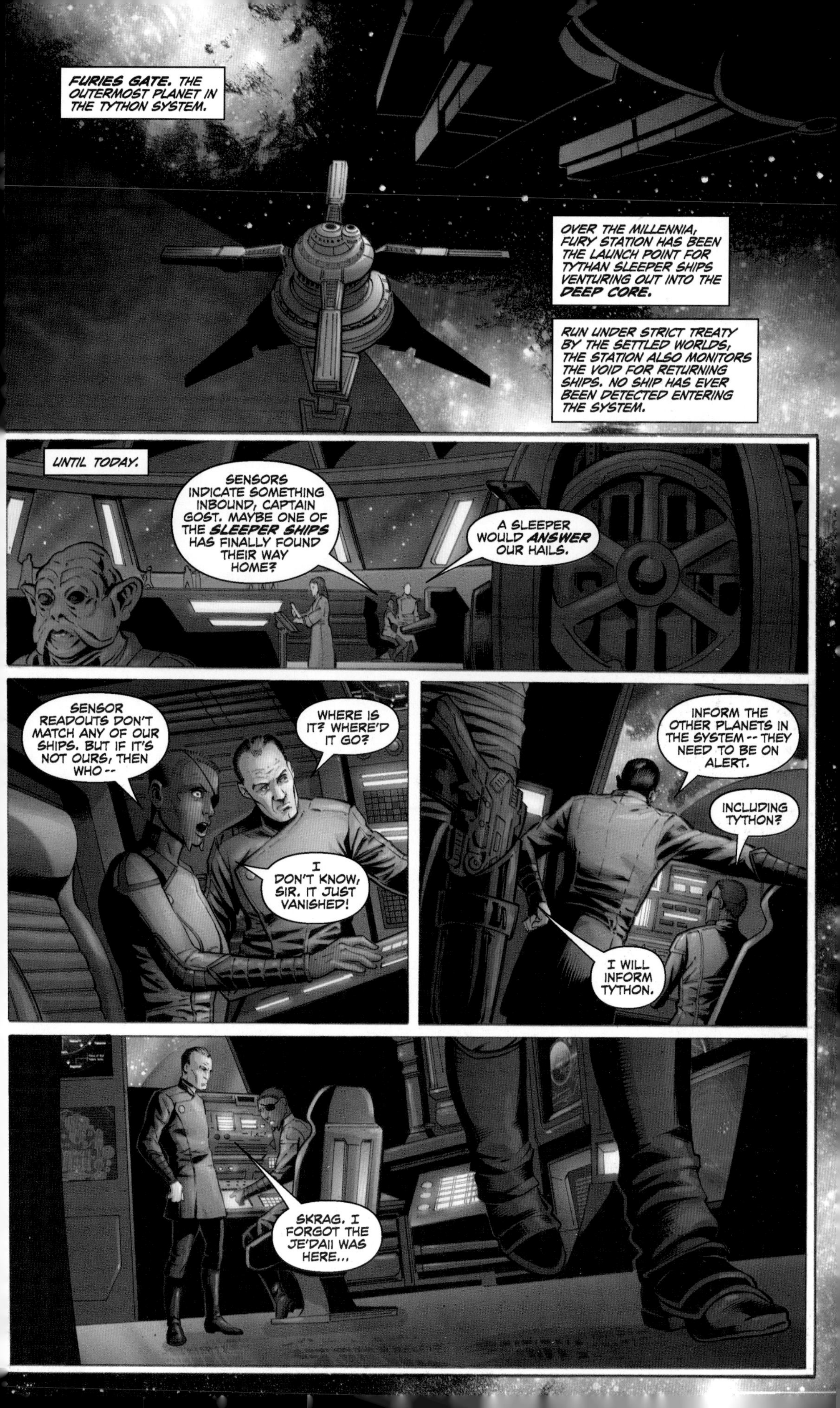
FURIES GATE. THE OUTERMOST PLANET IN THE TYTHON SYSTEM.
OVER THE MILLENNIA, FURY STATION HAS BEEN THE LAUNCH POINT FOR TYTHAN SLEEPER SHIPS VENTURING OUT INTO THE DEEP CORE.
RUN UNDER STRICT TREATY BY THE SETTLED WORLDS, THE STATION ALSO MONITORS THE VOID FOR RETURNING SHIPS. NO SHIP HAS EVER BEEN DETECTED ENTERING THE SYSTEM.
UNTIL TODAY.
SENSORS INDICATE SOMETHING INBOUND, CAPTAIN GOST. MAYBE ONE OF THE SLEEPER SHIPS HAS FINALLY FOUND THEIR WAY HOME?
A SLEEPER WOULD ANSWER OUR HAILS.
SENSOR READOUTS DON'T MATCH ANY OF OUR SHIPS. BUT IF IT'S NOT OURS, THEN WHO --
WHERE IS IT? WHERE'D IT GO?
I DON'T KNOW, SIR. IT JUST VANISHED!
INFORM THE OTHER PLANETS IN THE SYSTEM -- THEY NEED TO BE ON ALERT.
INCLUDING TYTHON?
I WILL INFORM TYTHON.
SKRAG. I FORGOT THE JE'DAII WAS HERE...

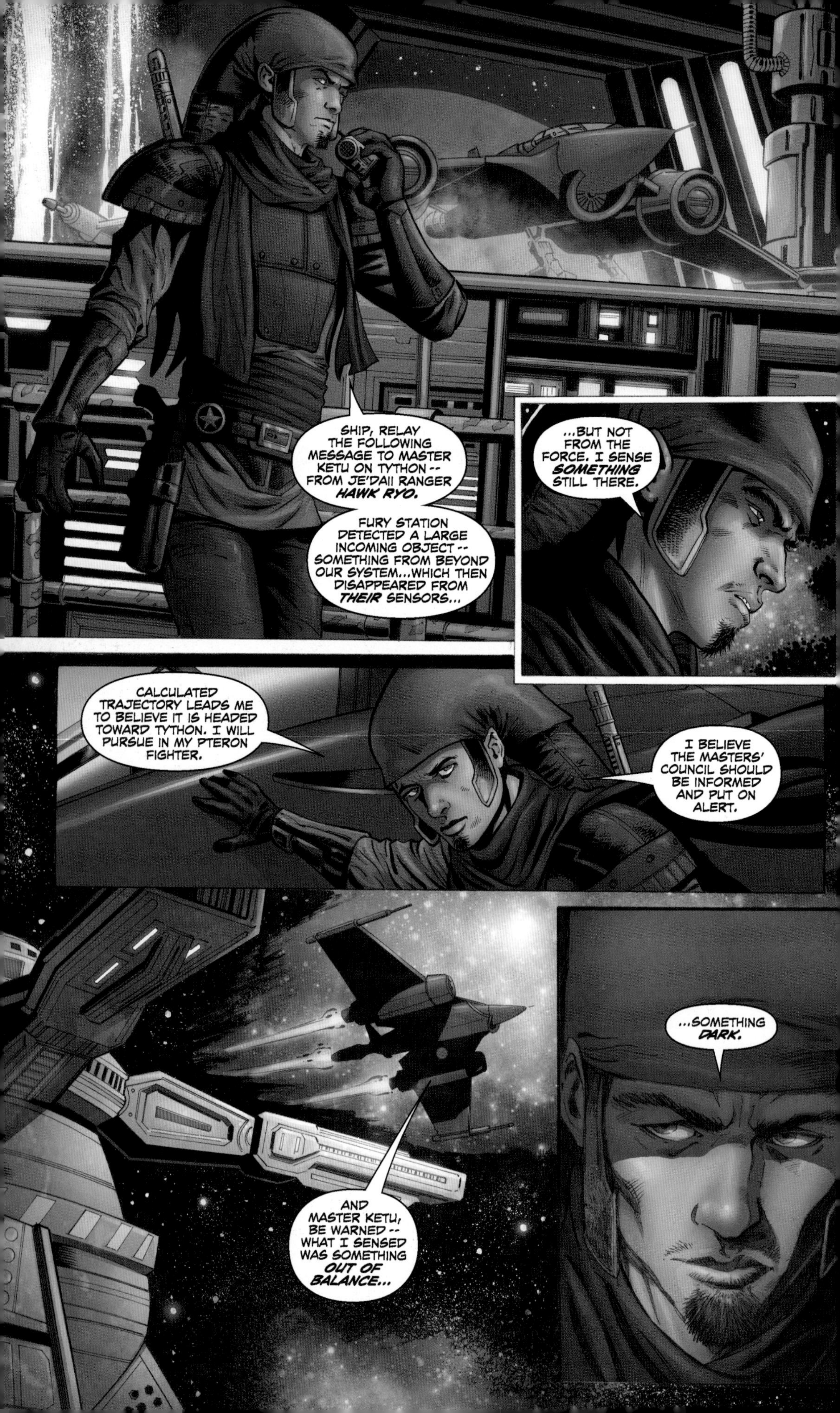
SHIP, RELAY THE FOLLOWING MESSAGE TO MASTER KETU ON TYTHON -- FROM JE'DAII RANGER HAWK RYO.
FURY STATION DETECTED A LARGE INCOMING OBJECT -- SOMETHING FROM BEYOND OUR SYSTEM...WHICH THEN DISAPPEARED FROM THEIR SENSORS...
...BUT NOT FROM THE FORCE. I SENSE SOMETHING STILL THERE.
CALCULATED TRAJECTORY LEADS ME TO BELIEVE IT IS HEADED TOWARD TYTHON. I WILL PURSUE IN MY PTERON FIGHTER.
I BELIEVE THE MASTERS' COUNCIL SHOULD BE INFORMED AND PUT ON ALERT.
AND MASTER KETU, BE WARNED -- WHAT I SENSED WAS SOMETHING OUT OF BALANCE...
...SOMETHING DARK.

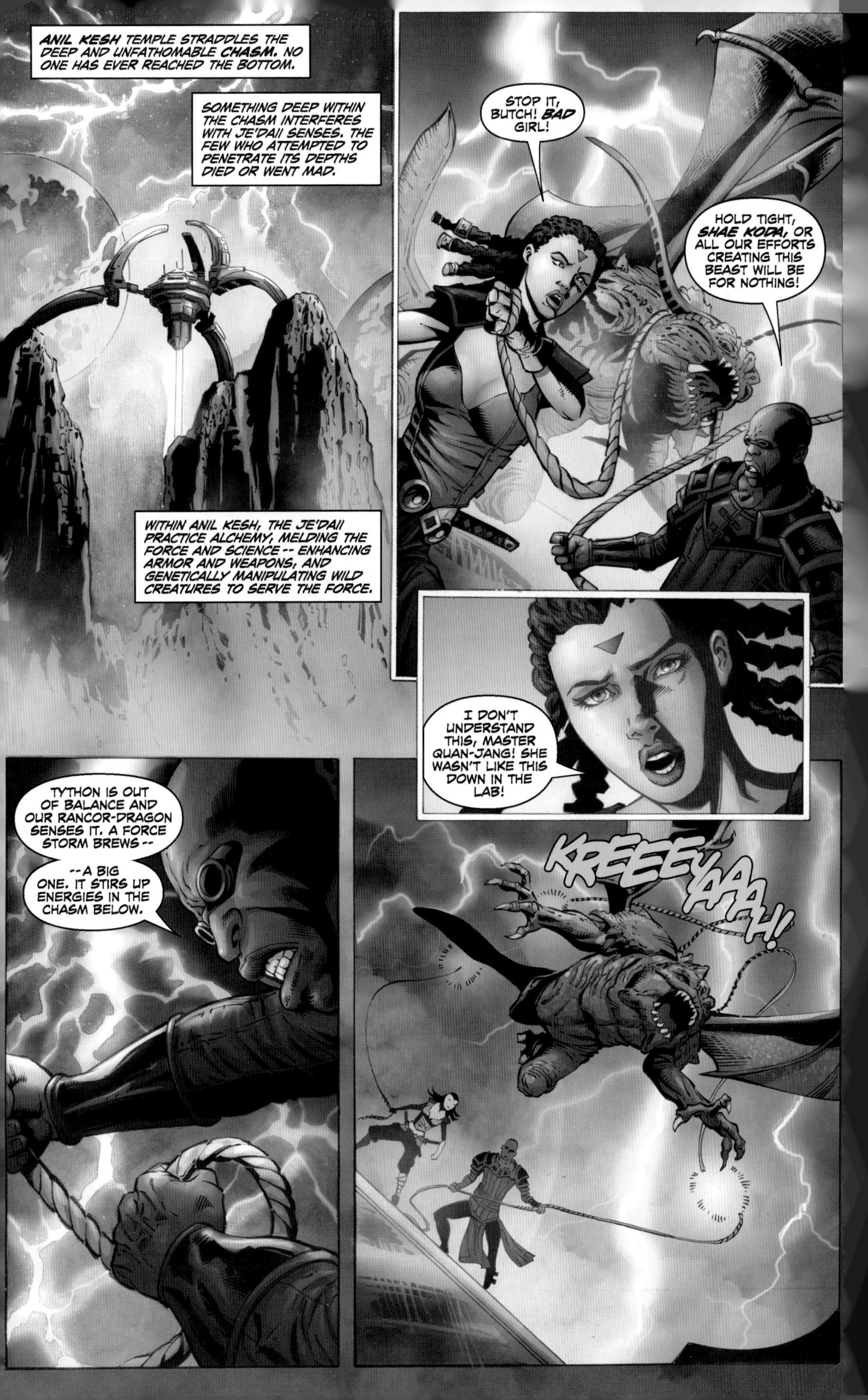
ANIL KESH TEMPLE STRADDLES THE DEEP AND UNFATHOMABLE CHASM. NO ONE HAS EVER REACHED THE BOTTOM.
SOMETHING DEEP WITHIN THE CHASM INTERFERES WITH JE'DAII SENSES. THE FEW WHO ATTEMPTED TO PENETRATE ITS DEPTHS DIED OR WENT MAD.
WITHIN ANIL KESH, THE JE'DAII PRACTICE ALCHEMY, MELDING THE FORCE AND SCIENCE -- ENHANCING ARMOR AND WEAPONS, AND GENETICALLY MANIPULATING WILD CREATURES TO SERVE THE FORCE.
STOP IT, BUTCH! BAD GIRL!
HOLD TIGHT, SHAE KODA, OR ALL OUR EFFORTS CREATING THIS BEAST WILL BE FOR NOTHING!
I DON'T UNDERSTAND THIS, MASTER QUAN-JANG! SHE WASN'T LIKE THIS DOWN IN THE LAB!
TYTHON IS OUT OF BALANCE AND OUR RANCOR-DRAGON SENSES IT. A FORCE STORM BREWS --
--A BIG ONE. IT STIRS UP ENERGIES IN THE CHASM BELOW.
KREEEYAAAH!

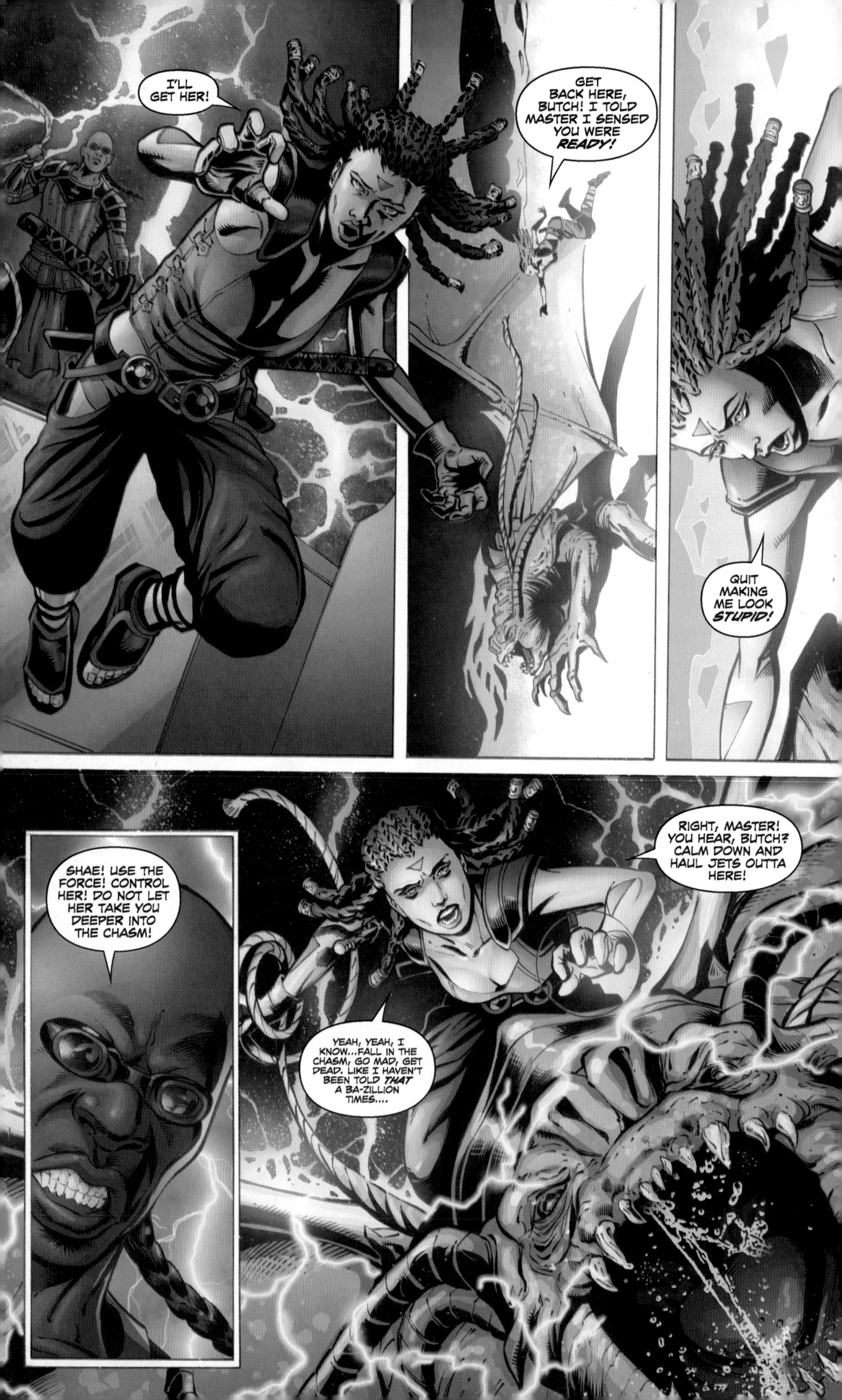
I'LL GET HER!
GET BACK HERE, BUTCH! I TOLD MASTER I SENSED YOU WERE READY!
QUIT MAKING ME LOOK STUPID!
SHAE! USE THE FORCE! CONTROL HER! DO NOT LET HER TAKE YOU DEEPER INTO THE CHASM!
RIGHT, MASTER! YOU HEAR, BUTCH? CALM DOWN AND HAUL JETS OUTTA HERE!
YEAH, YEAH, I KNOW...FALL IN THE CHASM, GO MAD, GET DEAD. LIKE I HAVEN'T BEEN TOLD THAT A BA-ZILLION TIMES....

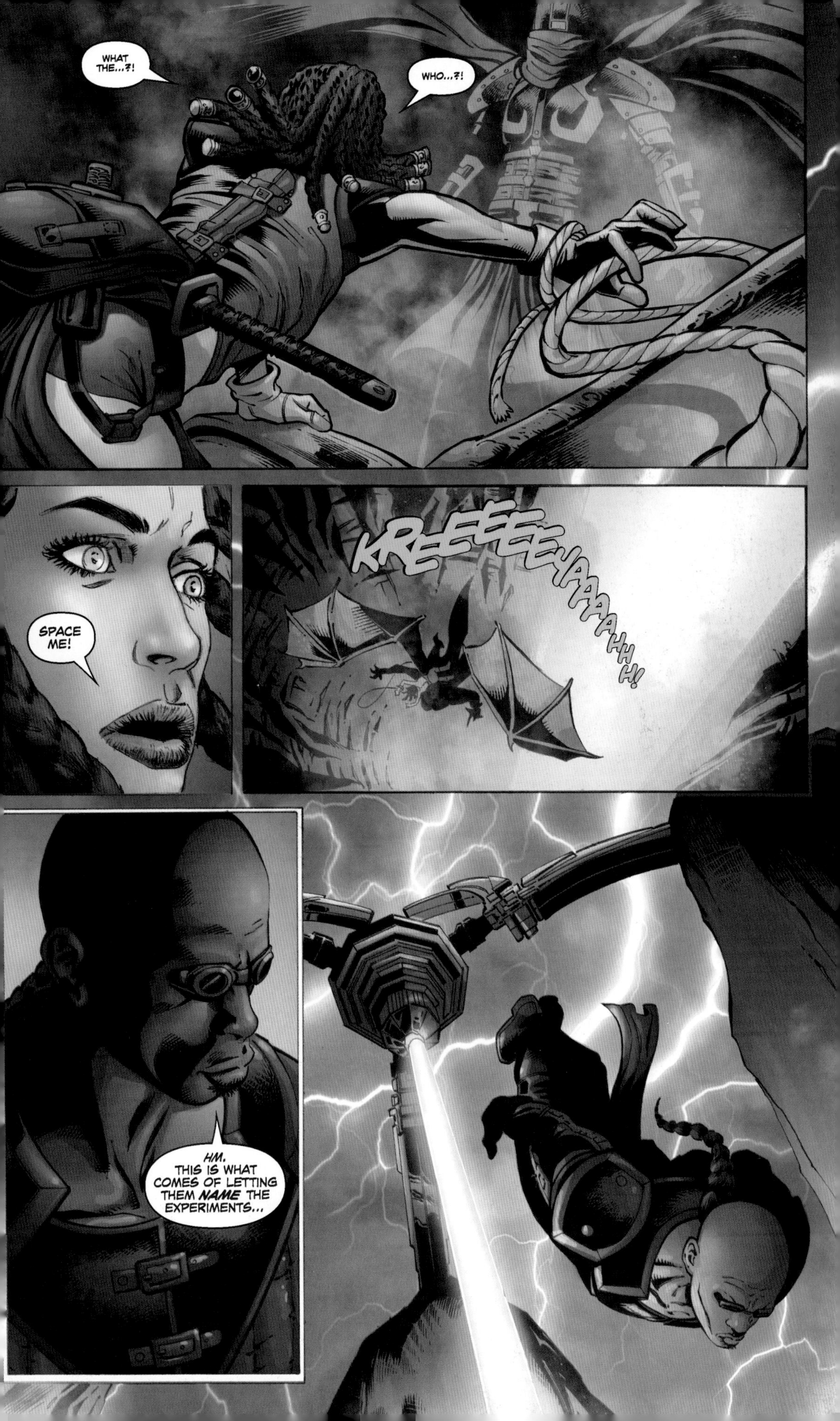
WHAT THE...?!
WHO...?!
SPACE ME!
KREEEEEEYAAAAHHH!
HM. THIS IS WHAT COMES OF LETTING THEM NAME THE EXPERIMENTS...

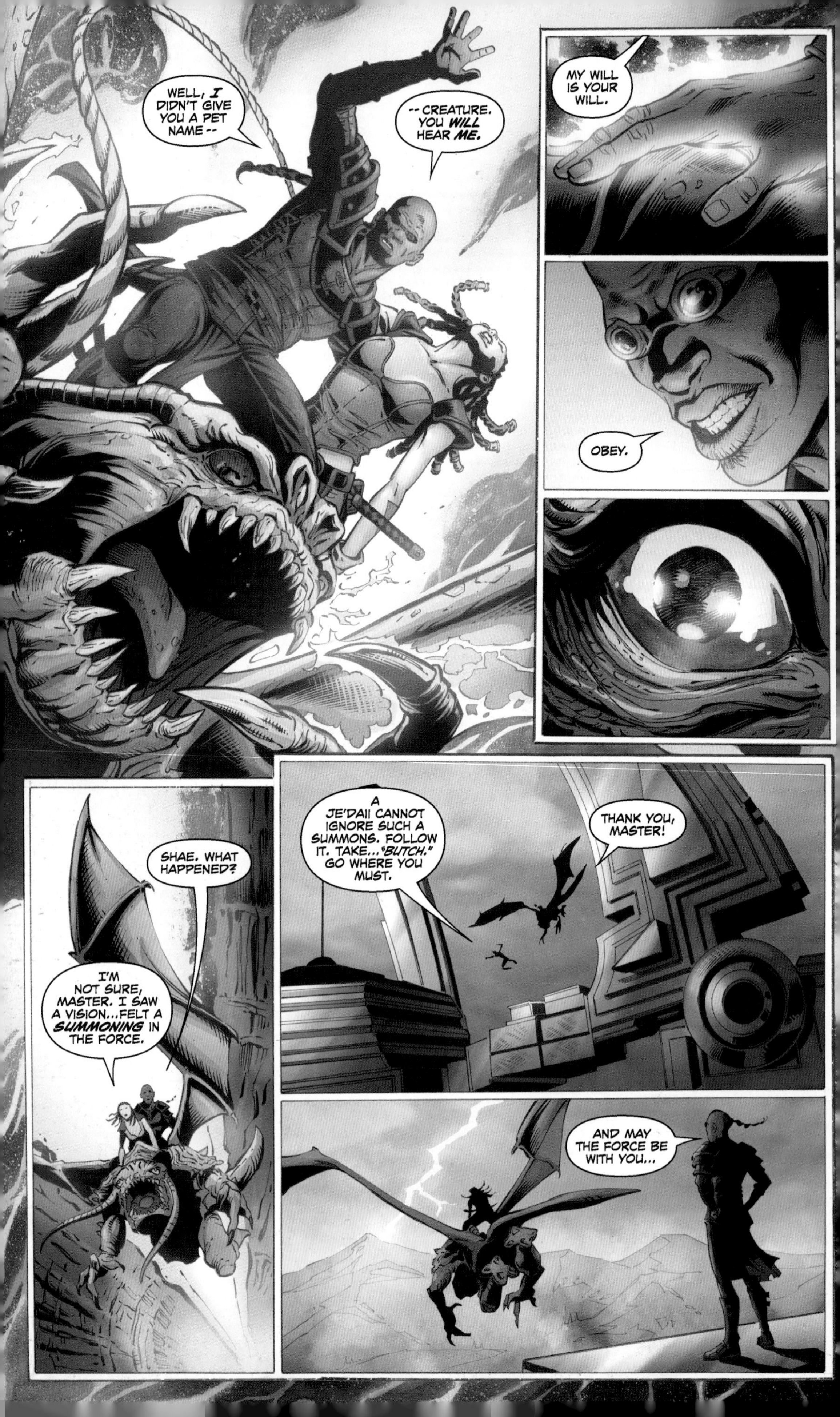
WELL, *I* DIDN'T GIVE YOU A PET NAME --
-- CREATURE. YOU *WILL* HEAR *ME.*
MY WILL IS YOUR WILL.
OBEY.
SHAE. WHAT HAPPENED?
I'M NOT SURE, MASTER. I SAW A VISION... FELT A *SUMMONING* IN THE FORCE.
A JE'DAII CANNOT IGNORE SUCH A SUMMONS. FOLLOW IT. TAKE... "*BUTCH.*" GO WHERE YOU MUST.
THANK YOU, MASTER!
AND MAY THE FORCE BE WITH YOU...

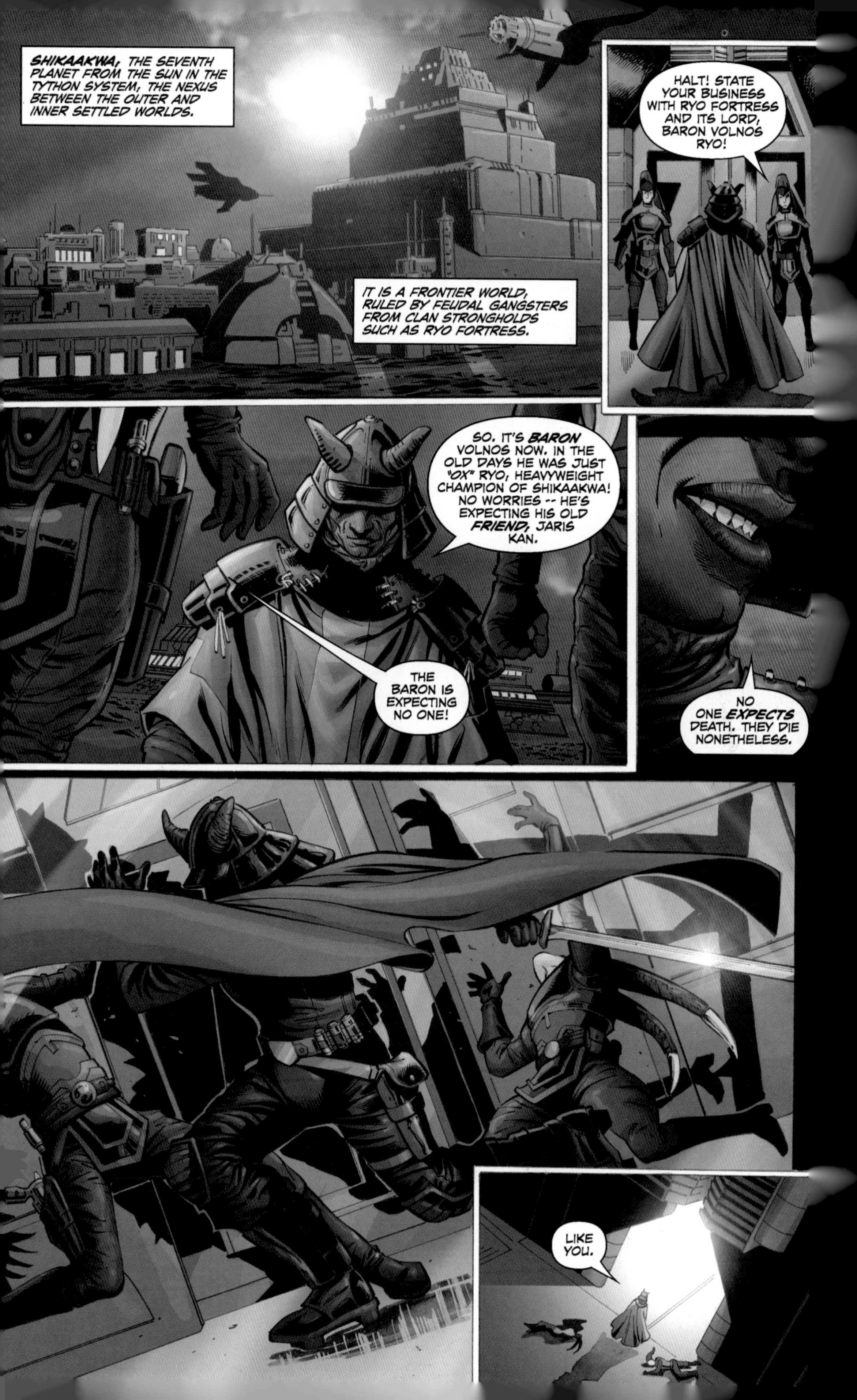

SHIKAAKWA, THE SEVENTH PLANET FROM THE SUN IN THE TYTHON SYSTEM, THE NEXUS BETWEEN THE OUTER AND INNER SETTLED WORLDS.
IT IS A FRONTIER WORLD, RULED BY FEUDAL GANGSTERS FROM CLAN STRONGHOLDS SUCH AS RYO FORTRESS.
HALT! STATE YOUR BUSINESS WITH RYO FORTRESS AND ITS LORD, BARON VOLNOS RYO!
SO. IT'S BARON VOLNOS NOW. IN THE OLD DAYS HE WAS JUST "OX" RYO, HEAVYWEIGHT CHAMPION OF SHIKAAKWA! NO WORRIES -- HE'S EXPECTING HIS OLD FRIEND, JARIS KAN.
THE BARON IS EXPECTING NO ONE!
NO ONE EXPECTS DEATH. THEY DIE NONETHELESS.
LIKE YOU.

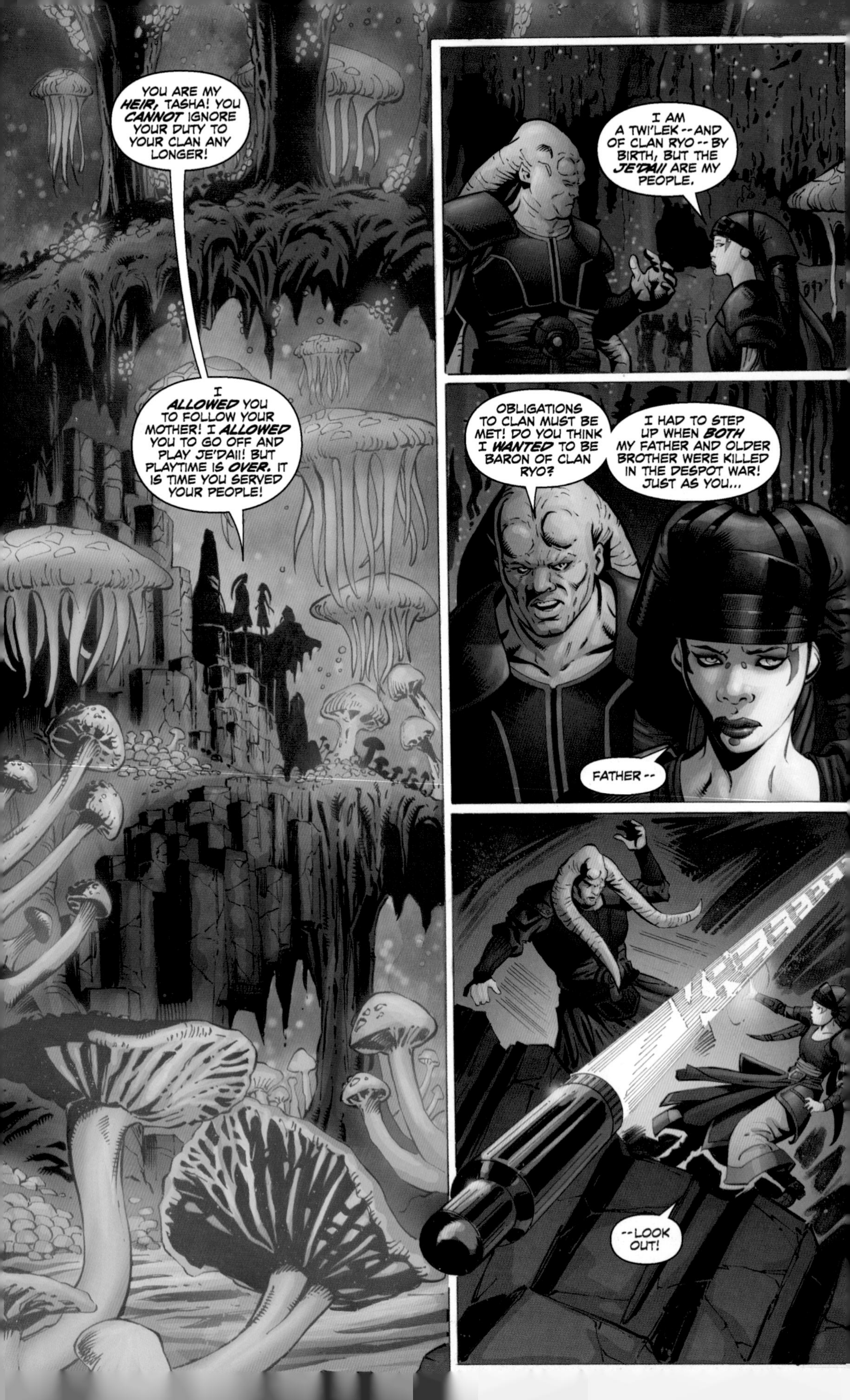
YOU ARE MY HEIR, TASHA! YOU CANNOT IGNORE YOUR DUTY TO YOUR CLAN ANY LONGER!
I ALLOWED YOU TO FOLLOW YOUR MOTHER! I ALLOWED YOU TO GO OFF AND PLAY JE'DAII! BUT PLAYTIME IS OVER. IT IS TIME YOU SERVED YOUR PEOPLE!
I AM A TWI'LEK--AND OF CLAN RYO--BY BIRTH, BUT THE JE'DAII ARE MY PEOPLE.
OBLIGATIONS TO CLAN MUST BE MET! DO YOU THINK I WANTED TO BE BARON OF CLAN RYO?
I HAD TO STEP UP WHEN BOTH MY FATHER AND OLDER BROTHER WERE KILLED IN THE DESPOT WAR! JUST AS YOU...
FATHER--
--LOOK OUT!

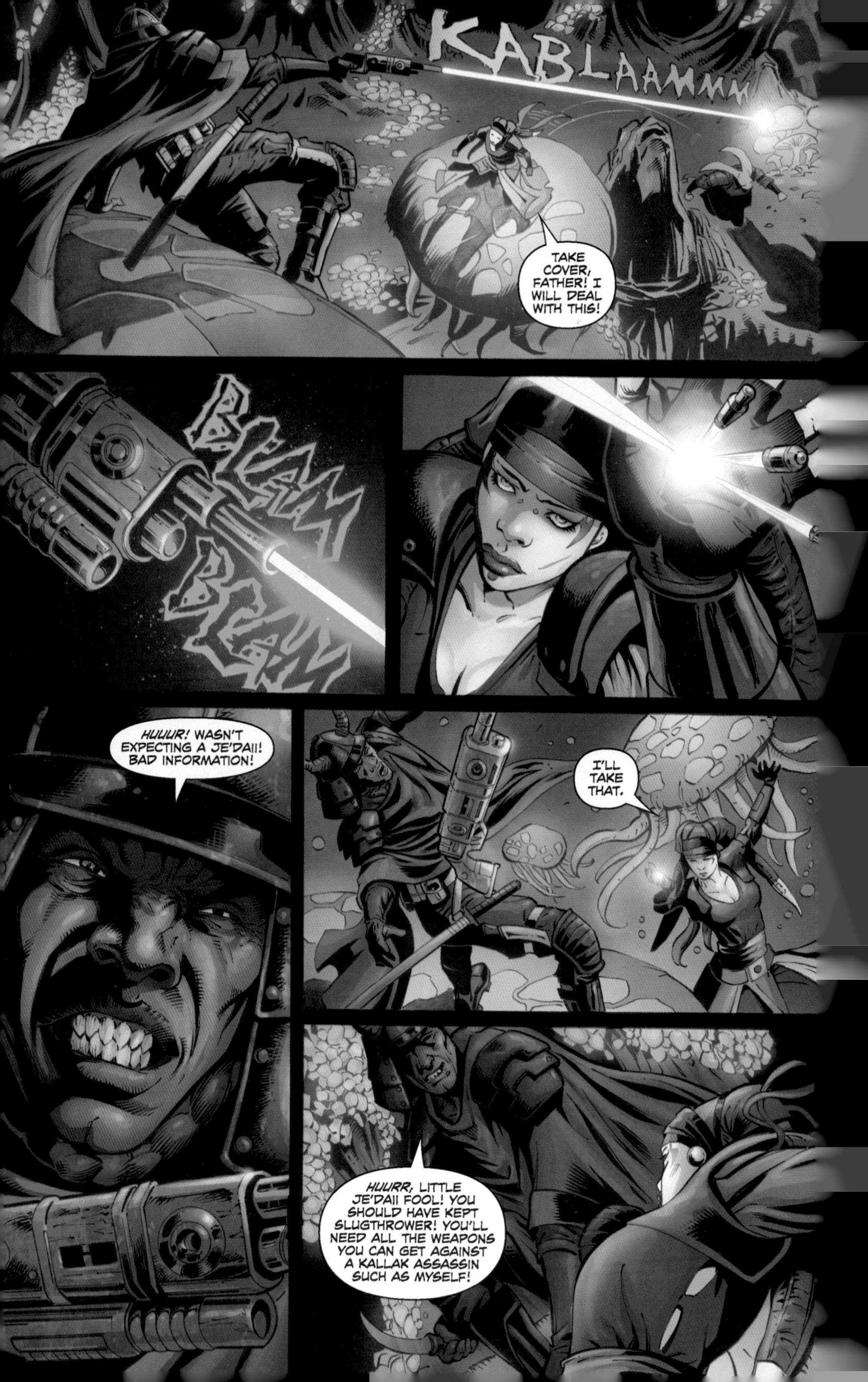
KABLAAMMM
TAKE COVER, FATHER! I WILL DEAL WITH THIS!
HUUUR! WASN'T EXPECTING A JE'DAII! BAD INFORMATION!
I'LL TAKE THAT.
HUURR, LITTLE JE'DAII FOOL! YOU SHOULD HAVE KEPT SLUGTHROWER! YOU'LL NEED ALL THE WEAPONS YOU CAN GET AGAINST A KALLAK ASSASSIN SUCH AS MYSELF!

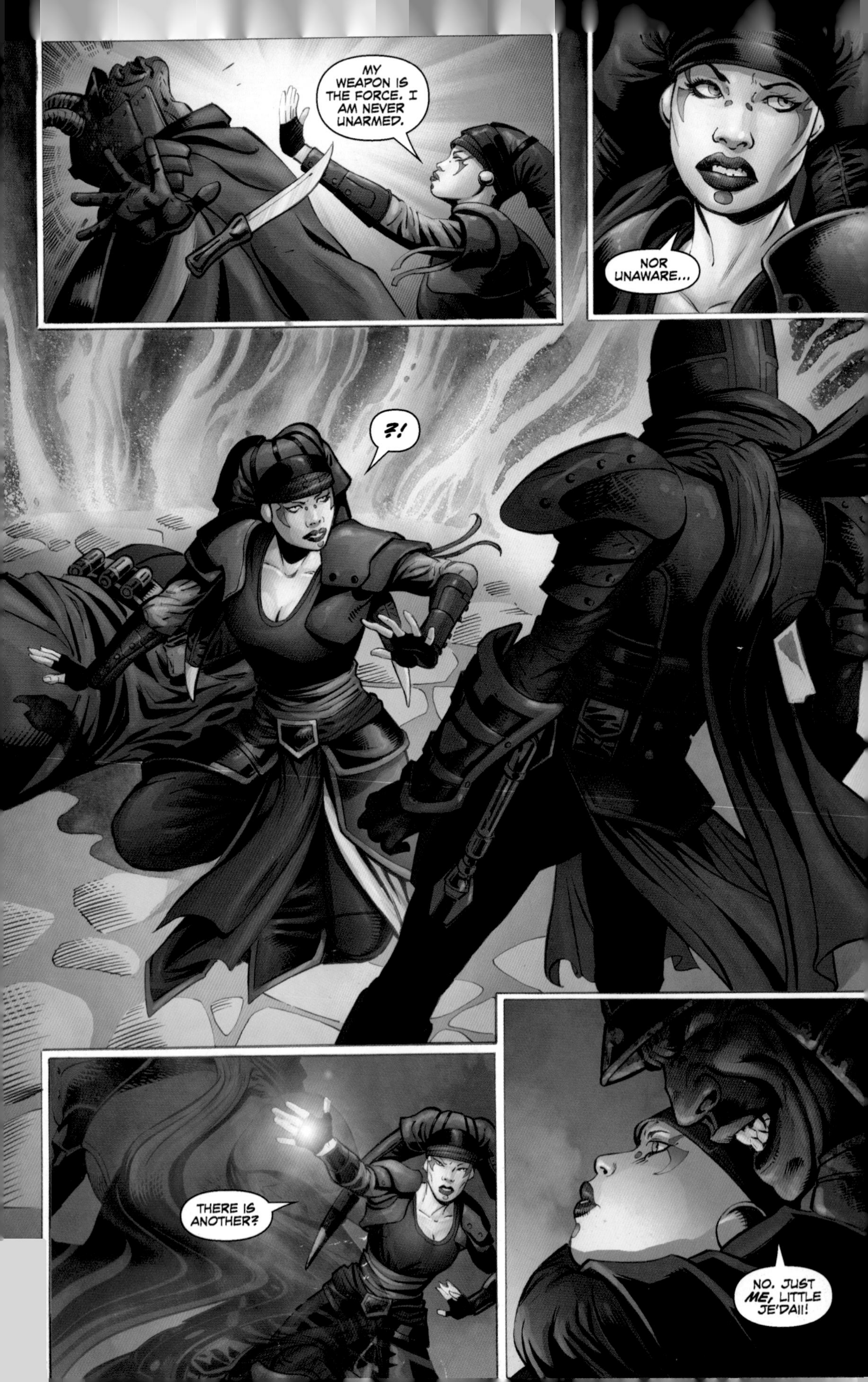
MY WEAPON IS THE FORCE. I AM NEVER UNARMED.
NOR UNAWARE...
?!
THERE IS ANOTHER?
NO. JUST *ME*, LITTLE JE'DAII!

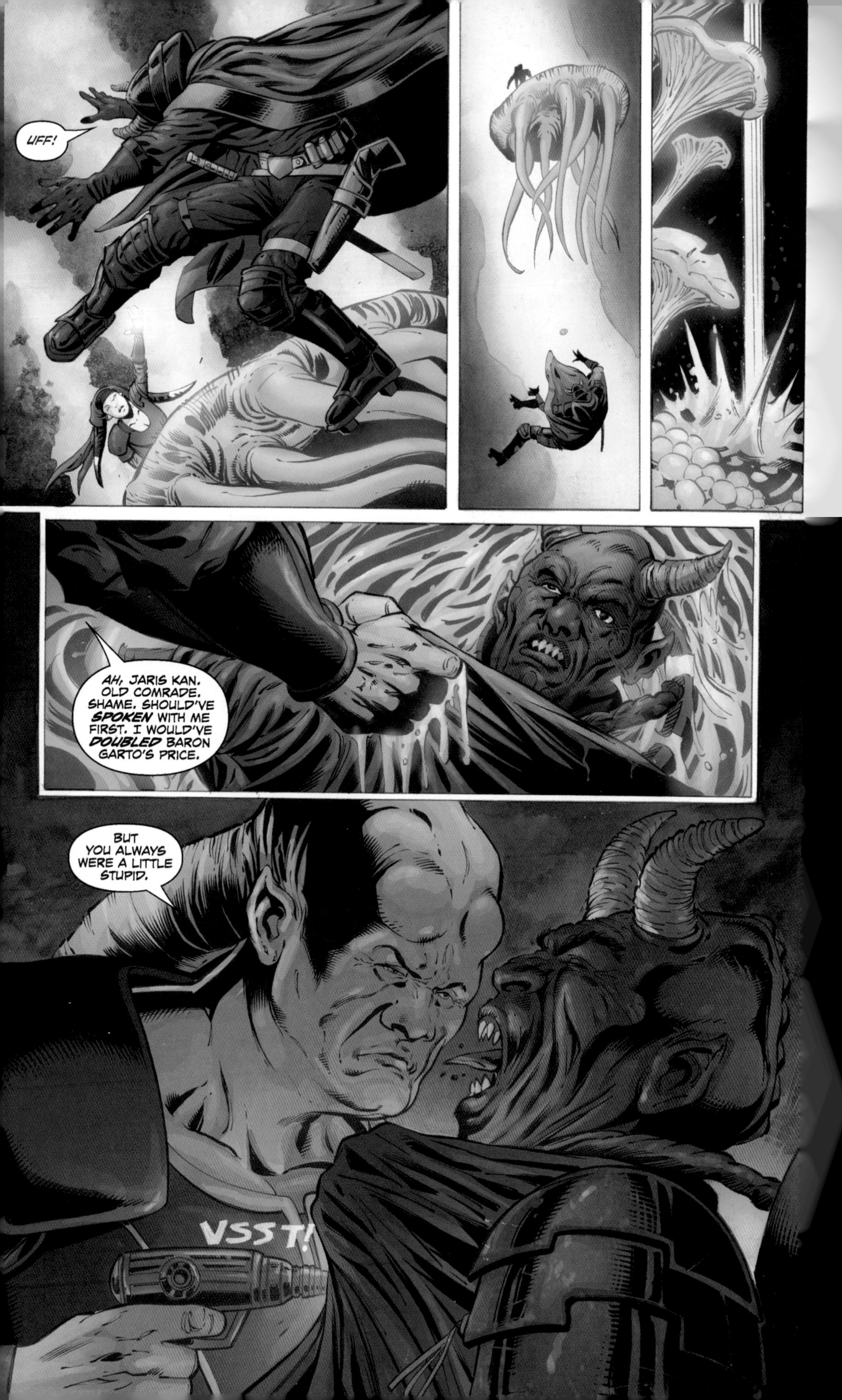
UFF!
AH, JARIS KAN. OLD COMRADE. SHAME. SHOULD'VE SPOKEN WITH ME FIRST. I WOULD'VE DOUBLED BARON GARTO'S PRICE.
BUT YOU ALWAYS WERE A LITTLE STUPID.
VSST!

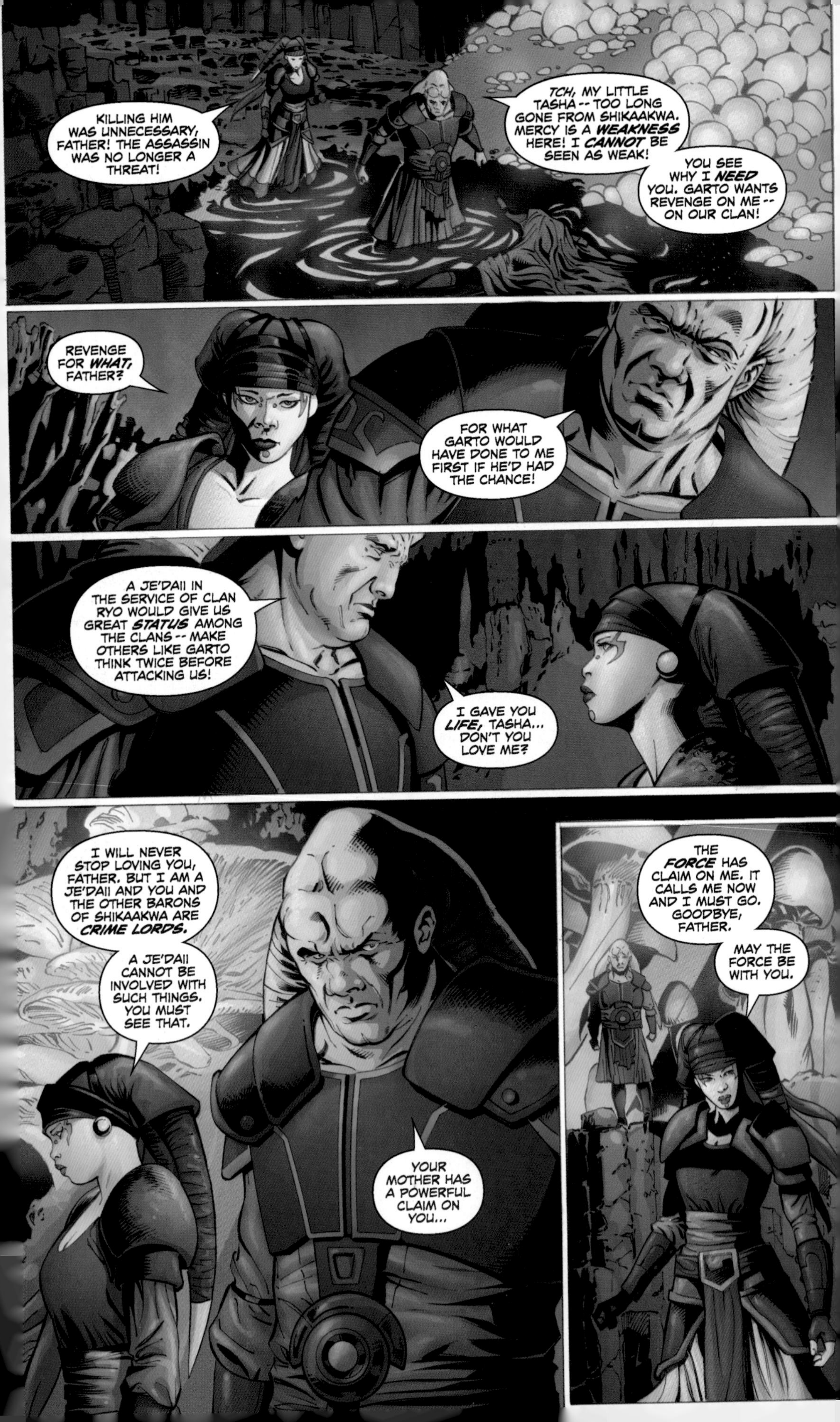
KILLING HIM WAS UNNECESSARY, FATHER! THE ASSASSIN WAS NO LONGER A THREAT!
TCH, MY LITTLE TASHA -- TOO LONG GONE FROM SHIKAAKWA. MERCY IS A WEAKNESS HERE! I CANNOT BE SEEN AS WEAK!
YOU SEE WHY I NEED YOU. GARTO WANTS REVENGE ON ME -- ON OUR CLAN!
REVENGE FOR WHAT, FATHER?
FOR WHAT GARTO WOULD HAVE DONE TO ME FIRST IF HE'D HAD THE CHANCE!
A JE'DAII IN THE SERVICE OF CLAN RYO WOULD GIVE US GREAT STATUS AMONG THE CLANS -- MAKE OTHERS LIKE GARTO THINK TWICE BEFORE ATTACKING US!
I GAVE YOU LIFE, TASHA... DON'T YOU LOVE ME?
I WILL NEVER STOP LOVING YOU, FATHER. BUT I AM A JE'DAII AND YOU AND THE OTHER BARONS OF SHIKAAKWA ARE CRIME LORDS.
A JE'DAII CANNOT BE INVOLVED WITH SUCH THINGS. YOU MUST SEE THAT.
YOUR MOTHER HAS A POWERFUL CLAIM ON YOU...
THE FORCE HAS CLAIM ON ME. IT CALLS ME NOW AND I MUST GO. GOODBYE, FATHER.
MAY THE FORCE BE WITH YOU.

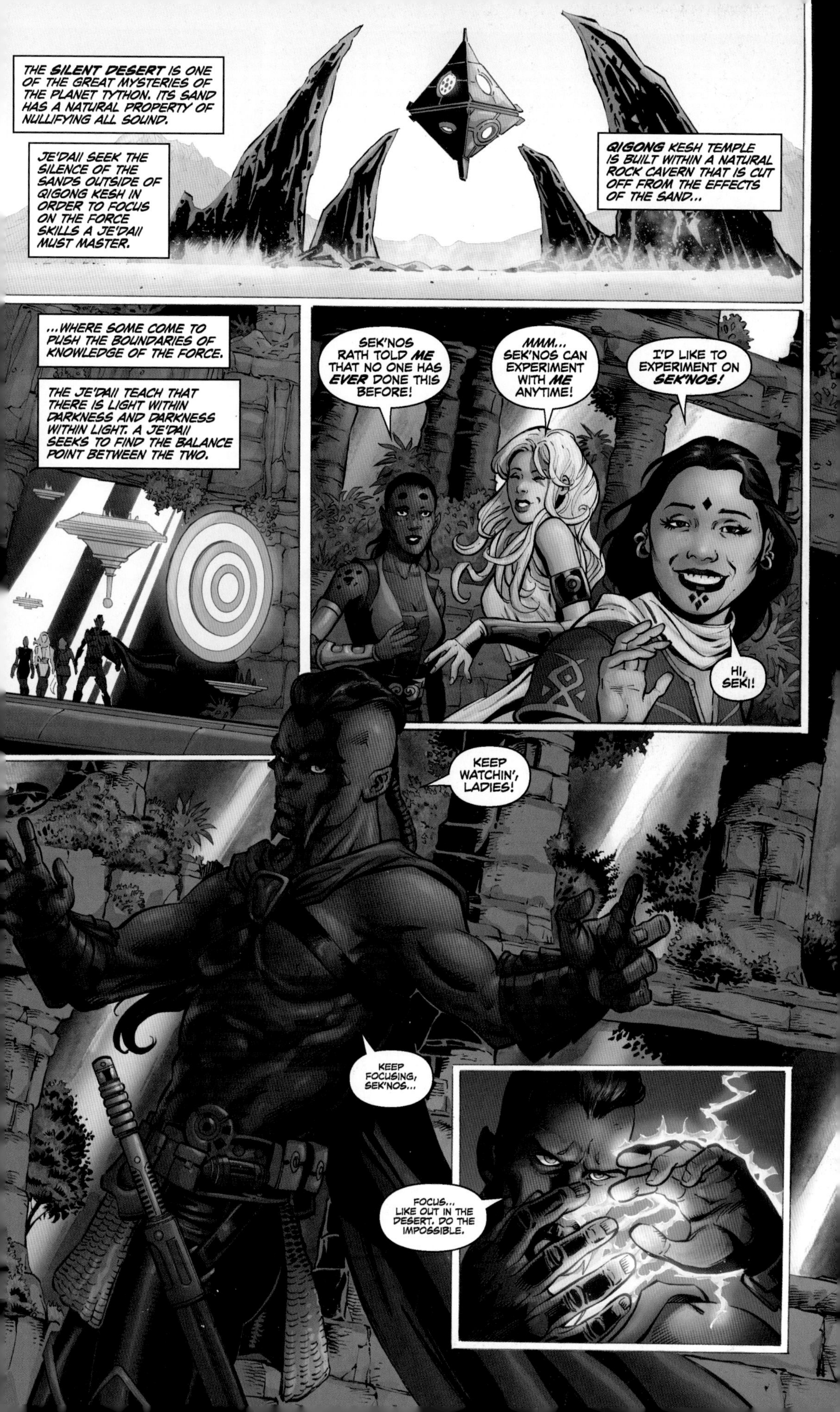
THE SILENT DESERT IS ONE OF THE GREAT MYSTERIES OF THE PLANET TYTHON. ITS SAND HAS A NATURAL PROPERTY OF NULLIFYING ALL SOUND.
JE'DAII SEEK THE SILENCE OF THE SANDS OUTSIDE OF QIGONG KESH IN ORDER TO FOCUS ON THE FORCE SKILLS A JE'DAII MUST MASTER.
QIGONG KESH TEMPLE IS BUILT WITHIN A NATURAL ROCK CAVERN THAT IS CUT OFF FROM THE EFFECTS OF THE SAND...
...WHERE SOME COME TO PUSH THE BOUNDARIES OF KNOWLEDGE OF THE FORCE.
THE JE'DAII TEACH THAT THERE IS LIGHT WITHIN DARKNESS AND DARKNESS WITHIN LIGHT. A JE'DAII SEEKS TO FIND THE BALANCE POINT BETWEEN THE TWO.
SEK'NOS RATH TOLD ME THAT NO ONE HAS EVER DONE THIS BEFORE!
MMM... SEK'NOS CAN EXPERIMENT WITH ME ANYTIME!
I'D LIKE TO EXPERIMENT ON SEK'NOS!
HI, SEKI!
KEEP WATCHIN', LADIES!
KEEP FOCUSING, SEK'NOS...
FOCUS... LIKE OUT IN THE DESERT. DO THE IMPOSSIBLE.

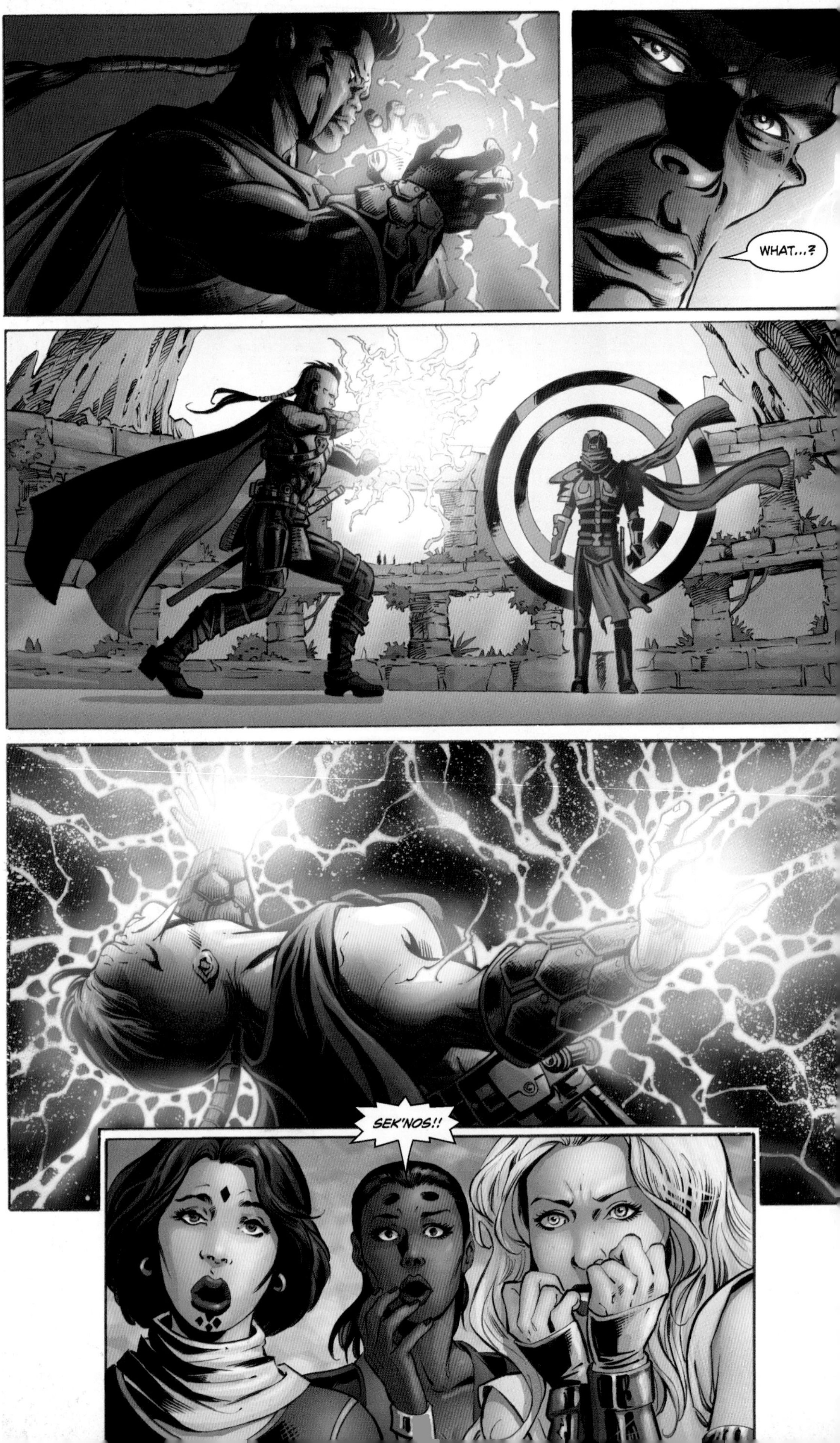
WHAT...?
SEK'NOS!!

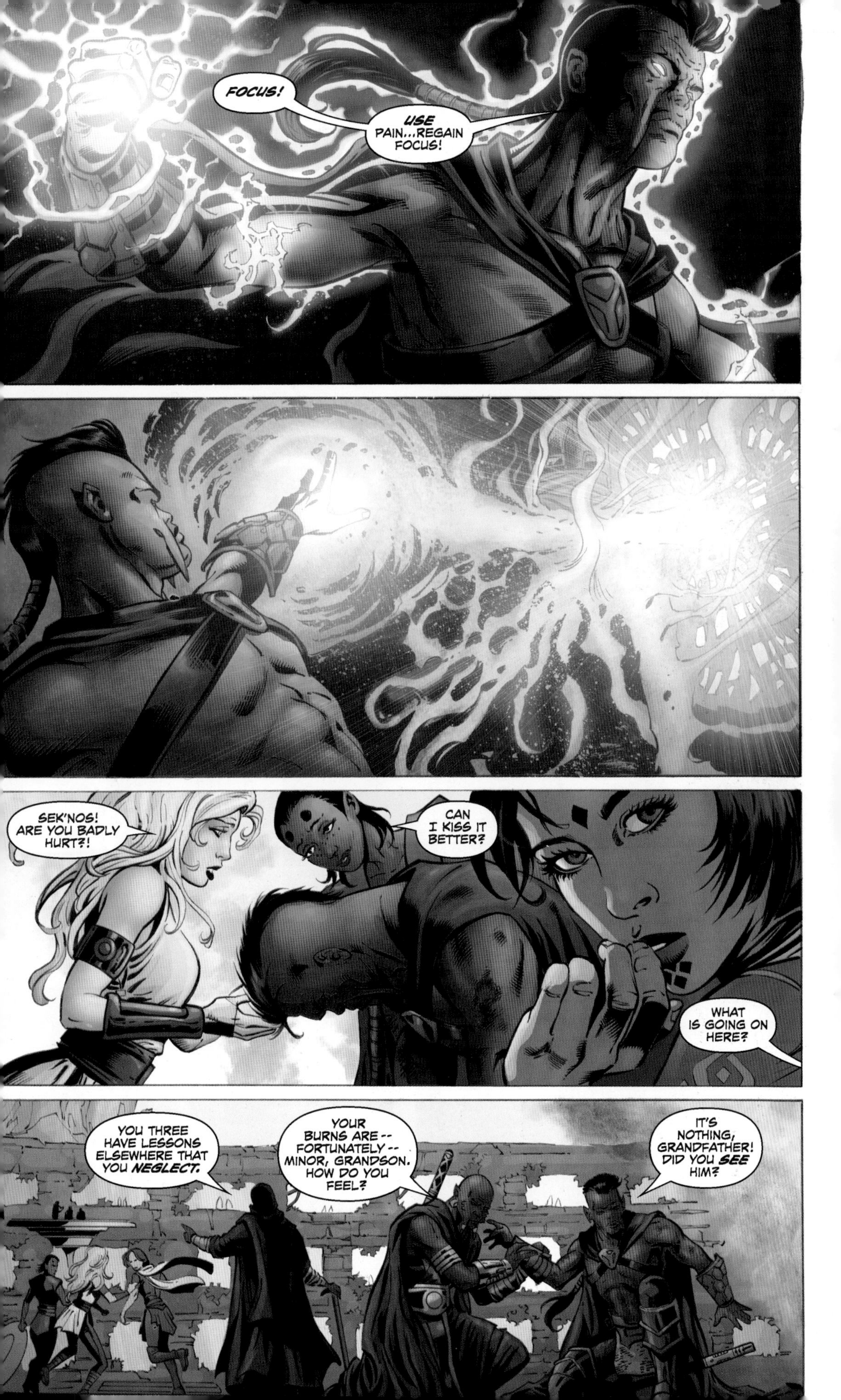
FOCUS!
USE PAIN...REGAIN FOCUS!
SEK'NOS! ARE YOU BADLY HURT?!
CAN I KISS IT BETTER?
WHAT IS GOING ON HERE?
YOU THREE HAVE LESSONS ELSEWHERE THAT YOU NEGLECT.
YOUR BURNS ARE-- FORTUNATELY-- MINOR, GRANDSON. HOW DO YOU FEEL?
IT'S NOTHING, GRANDFATHER! DID YOU SEE HIM?

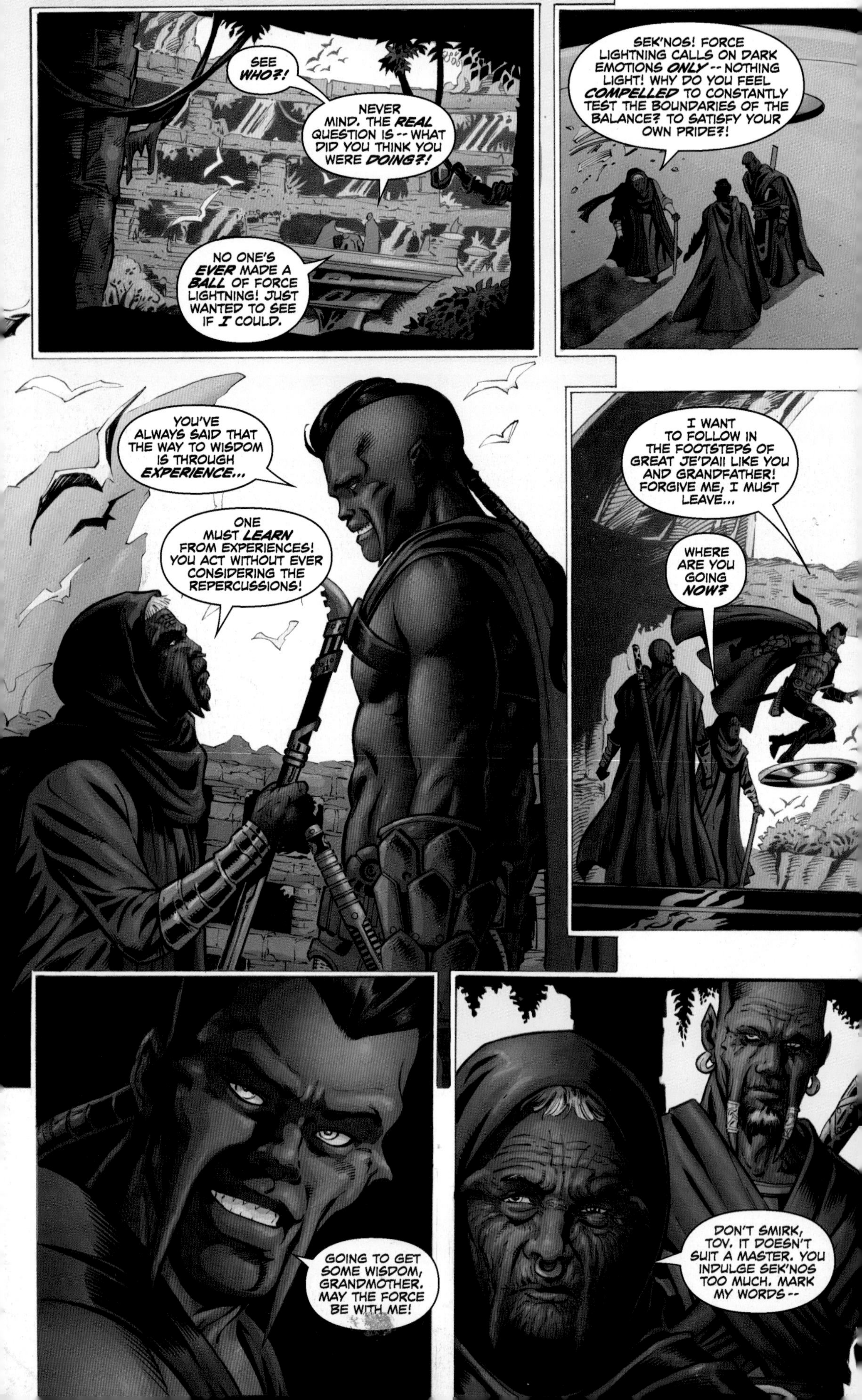
SEE WHO?!
NEVER MIND. THE REAL QUESTION IS -- WHAT DID YOU THINK YOU WERE DOING?!
NO ONE'S EVER MADE A BALL OF FORCE LIGHTNING! JUST WANTED TO SEE IF I COULD.
SEK'NOS! FORCE LIGHTNING CALLS ON DARK EMOTIONS ONLY -- NOTHING LIGHT! WHY DO YOU FEEL COMPELLED TO CONSTANTLY TEST THE BOUNDARIES OF THE BALANCE? TO SATISFY YOUR OWN PRIDE?!
YOU'VE ALWAYS SAID THAT THE WAY TO WISDOM IS THROUGH EXPERIENCE...
ONE MUST LEARN FROM EXPERIENCES! YOU ACT WITHOUT EVER CONSIDERING THE REPERCUSSIONS!
I WANT TO FOLLOW IN THE FOOTSTEPS OF GREAT JE'DAII LIKE YOU AND GRANDFATHER! FORGIVE ME, I MUST LEAVE...
WHERE ARE YOU GOING NOW?
GOING TO GET SOME WISDOM, GRANDMOTHER. MAY THE FORCE BE WITH ME!
DON'T SMIRK, TOV. IT DOESN'T SUIT A MASTER. YOU INDULGE SEK'NOS TOO MUCH. MARK MY WORDS --

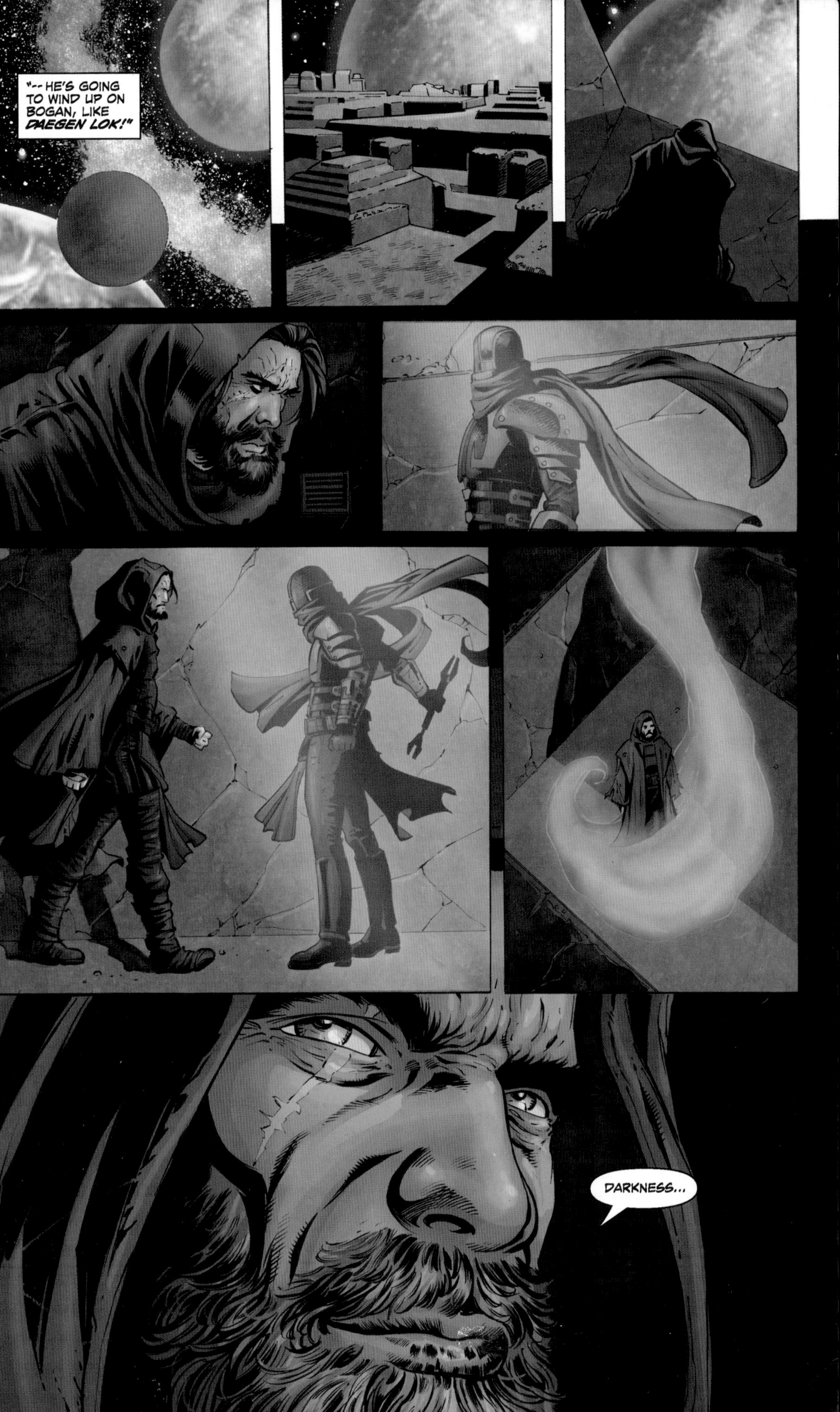
"-- HE'S GOING TO WIND UP ON BOGAN, LIKE *DAEGEN LOK!*"
DARKNESS...

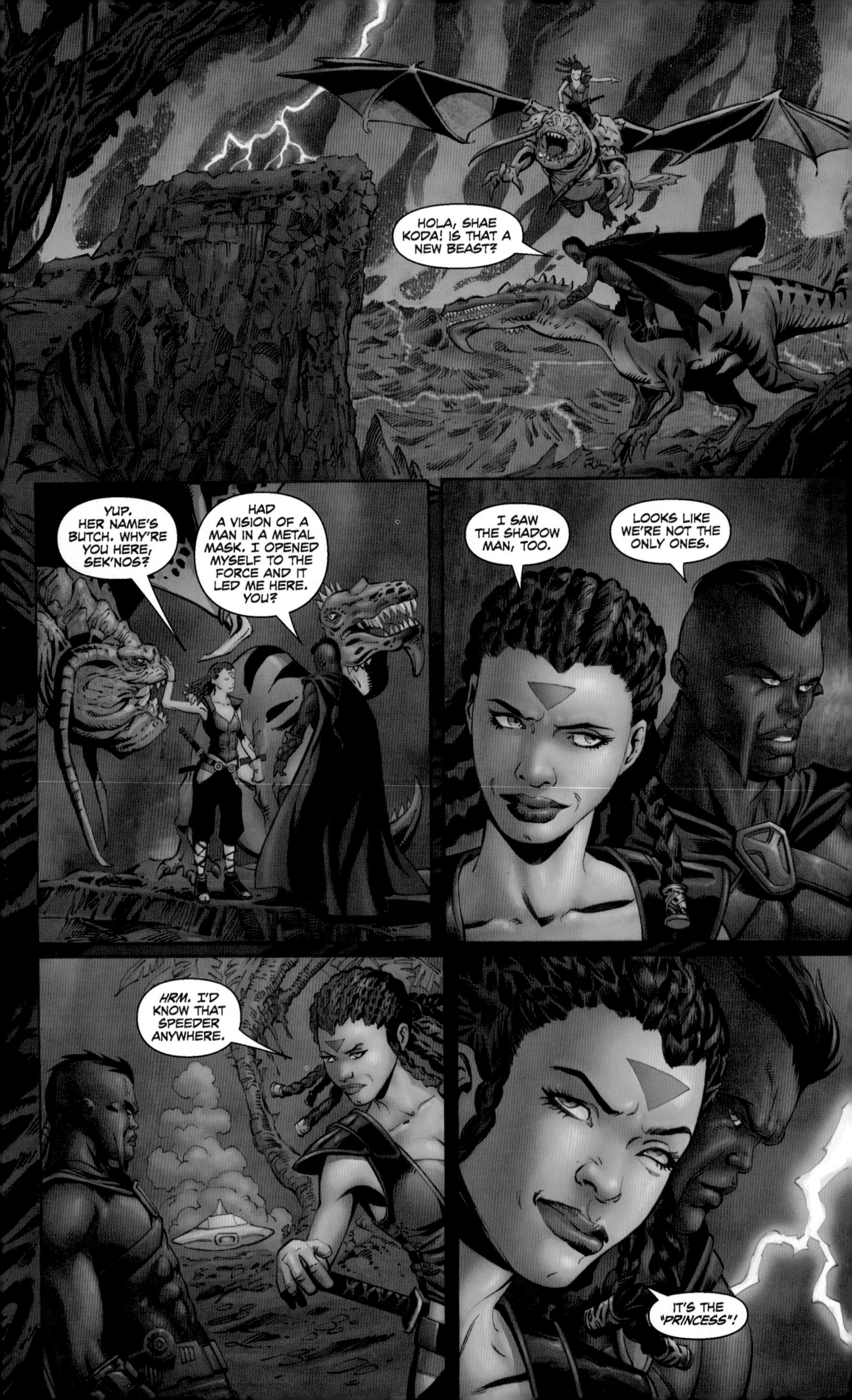
HOLA, SHAE KODA! IS THAT A NEW BEAST?
YUP. HER NAME'S BUTCH. WHY'RE YOU HERE, SEK'NOS?
HAD A VISION OF A MAN IN A METAL MASK. I OPENED MYSELF TO THE FORCE AND IT LED ME HERE. YOU?
I SAW THE SHADOW MAN, TOO.
LOOKS LIKE WE'RE NOT THE ONLY ONES.
HRM. I'D KNOW THAT SPEEDER ANYWHERE.
IT'S THE *"PRINCESS"*!

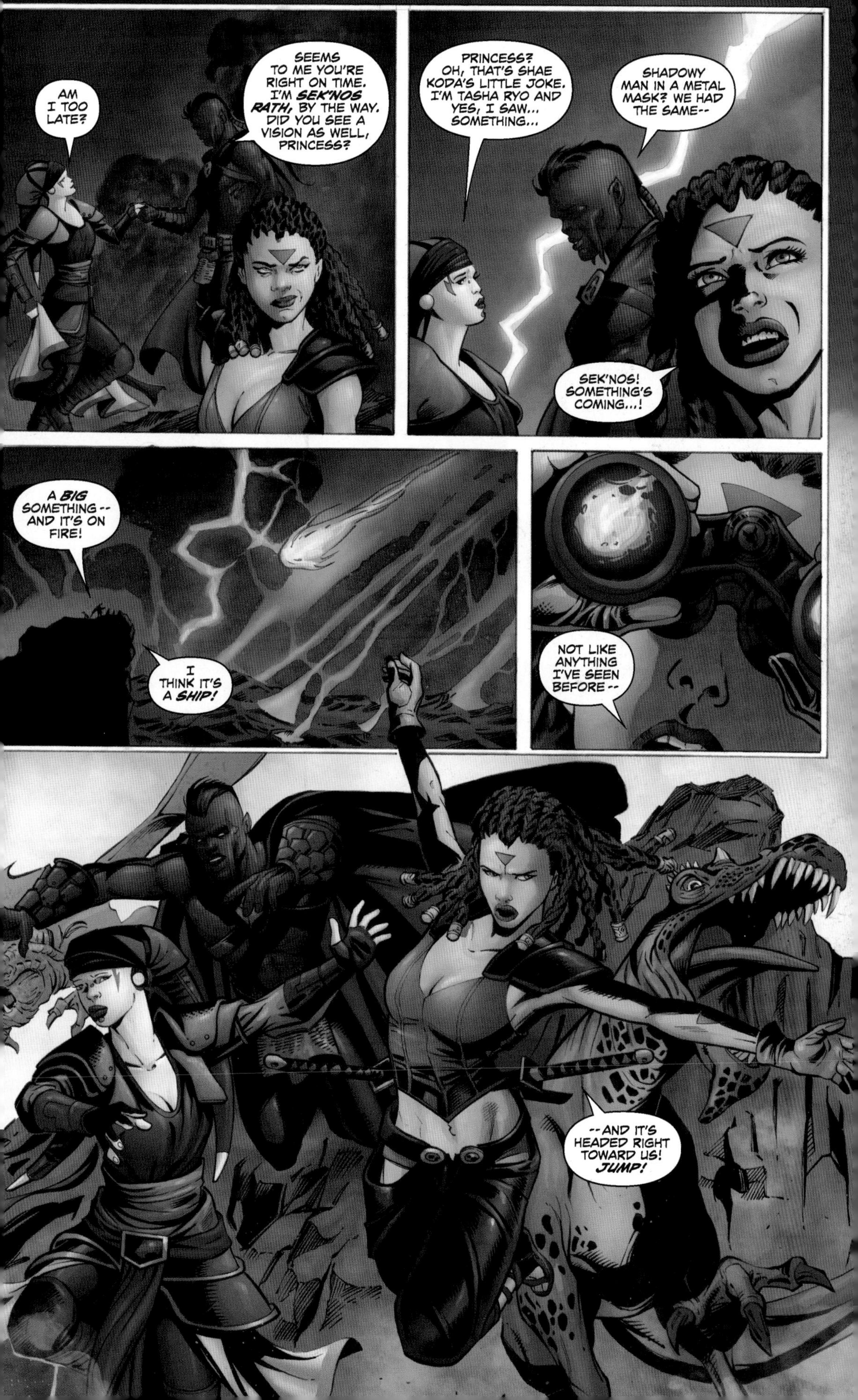
AM I TOO LATE?
SEEMS TO ME YOU'RE RIGHT ON TIME. I'M SEK'NOS RATH, BY THE WAY. DID YOU SEE A VISION AS WELL, PRINCESS?
PRINCESS? OH, THAT'S SHAE KODA'S LITTLE JOKE. I'M TASHA RYO AND YES, I SAW... SOMETHING...
SHADOWY MAN IN A METAL MASK? WE HAD THE SAME--
SEK'NOS! SOMETHING'S COMING...!
A BIG SOMETHING -- AND IT'S ON FIRE!
I THINK IT'S A SHIP!
NOT LIKE ANYTHING I'VE SEEN BEFORE --
--AND IT'S HEADED RIGHT TOWARD US! JUMP!

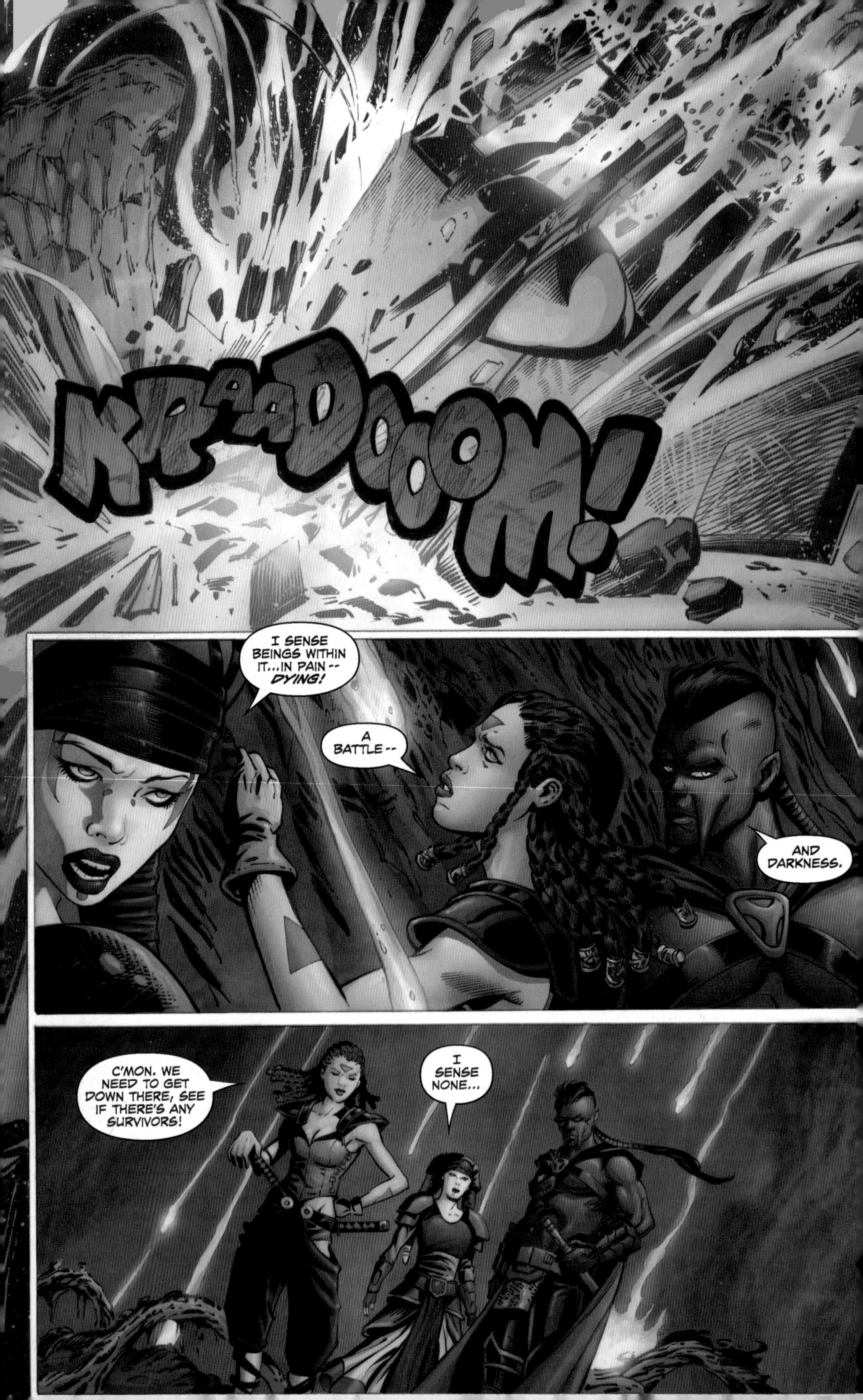
KRAADOOOOM!
I SENSE BEINGS WITHIN IT...IN PAIN -- DYING!
A BATTLE --
AND DARKNESS.
C'MON. WE NEED TO GET DOWN THERE, SEE IF THERE'S ANY SURVIVORS!
I SENSE NONE...

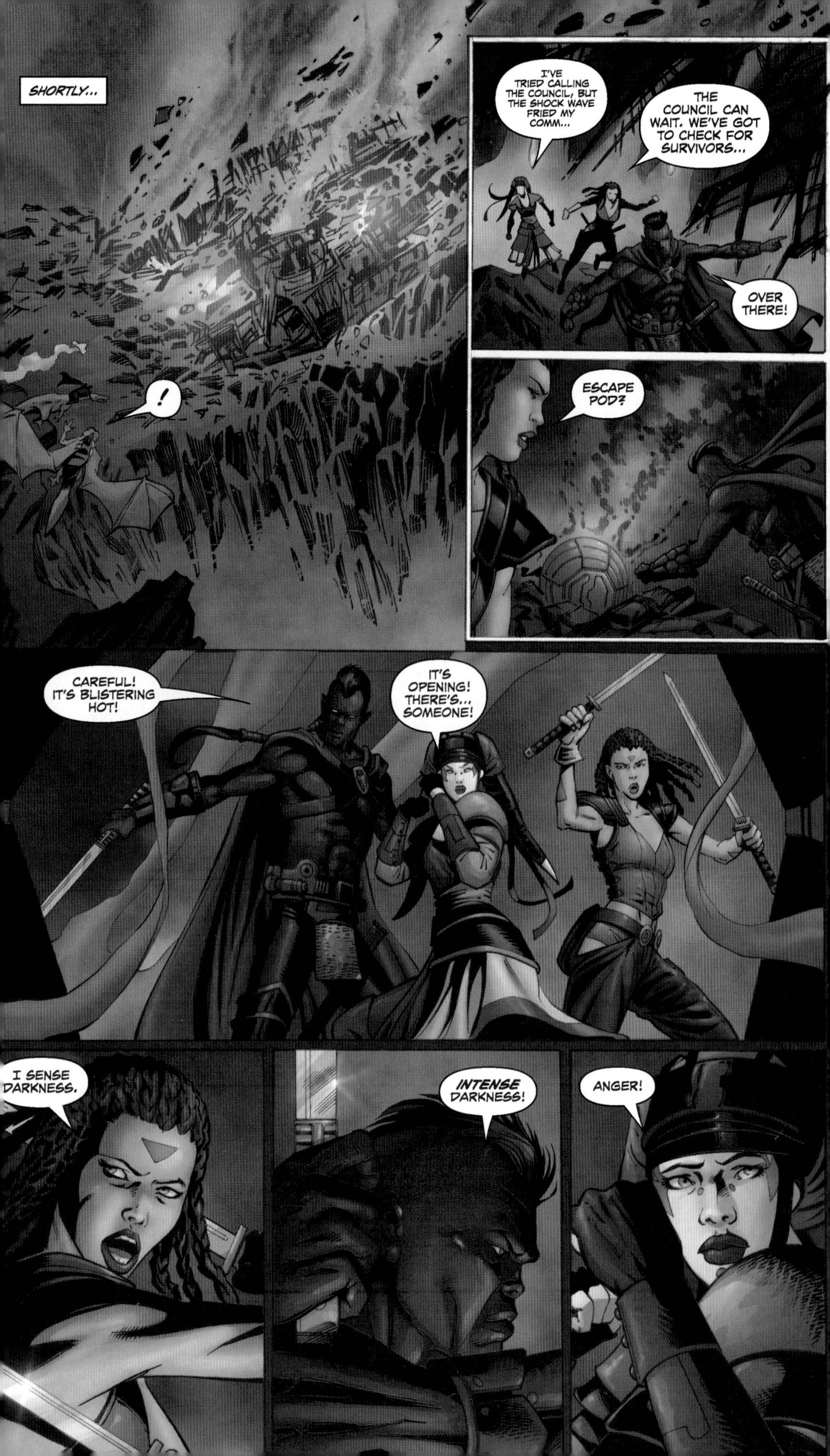
SHORTLY...
!
I'VE TRIED CALLING THE COUNCIL, BUT THE SHOCK WAVE FRIED MY COMM...
THE COUNCIL CAN WAIT. WE'VE GOT TO CHECK FOR SURVIVORS...
OVER THERE!
ESCAPE POD?
CAREFUL! IT'S BLISTERING HOT!
IT'S OPENING! THERE'S... SOMEONE!
I SENSE DARKNESS.
INTENSE DARKNESS!
ANGER!

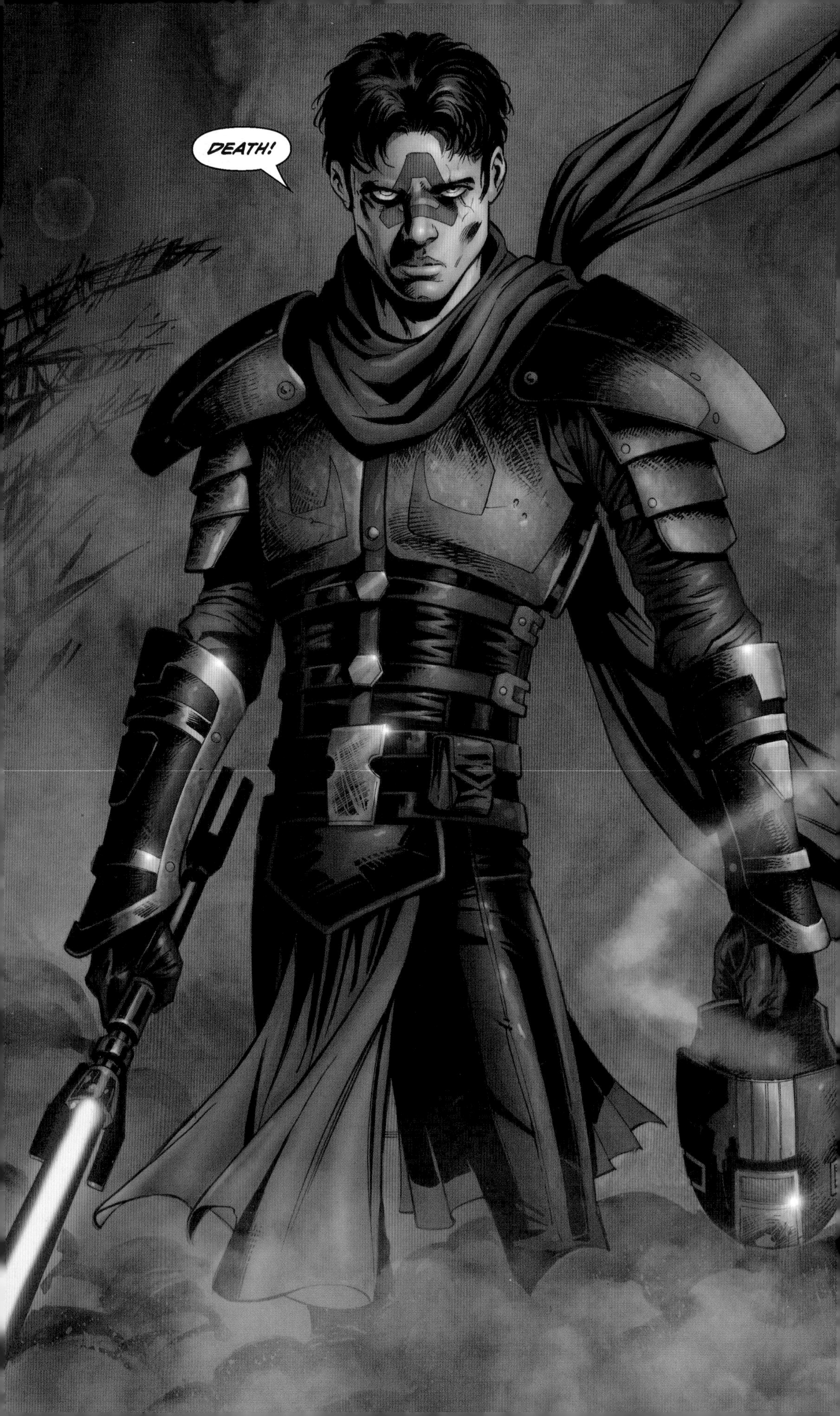
DEATH!

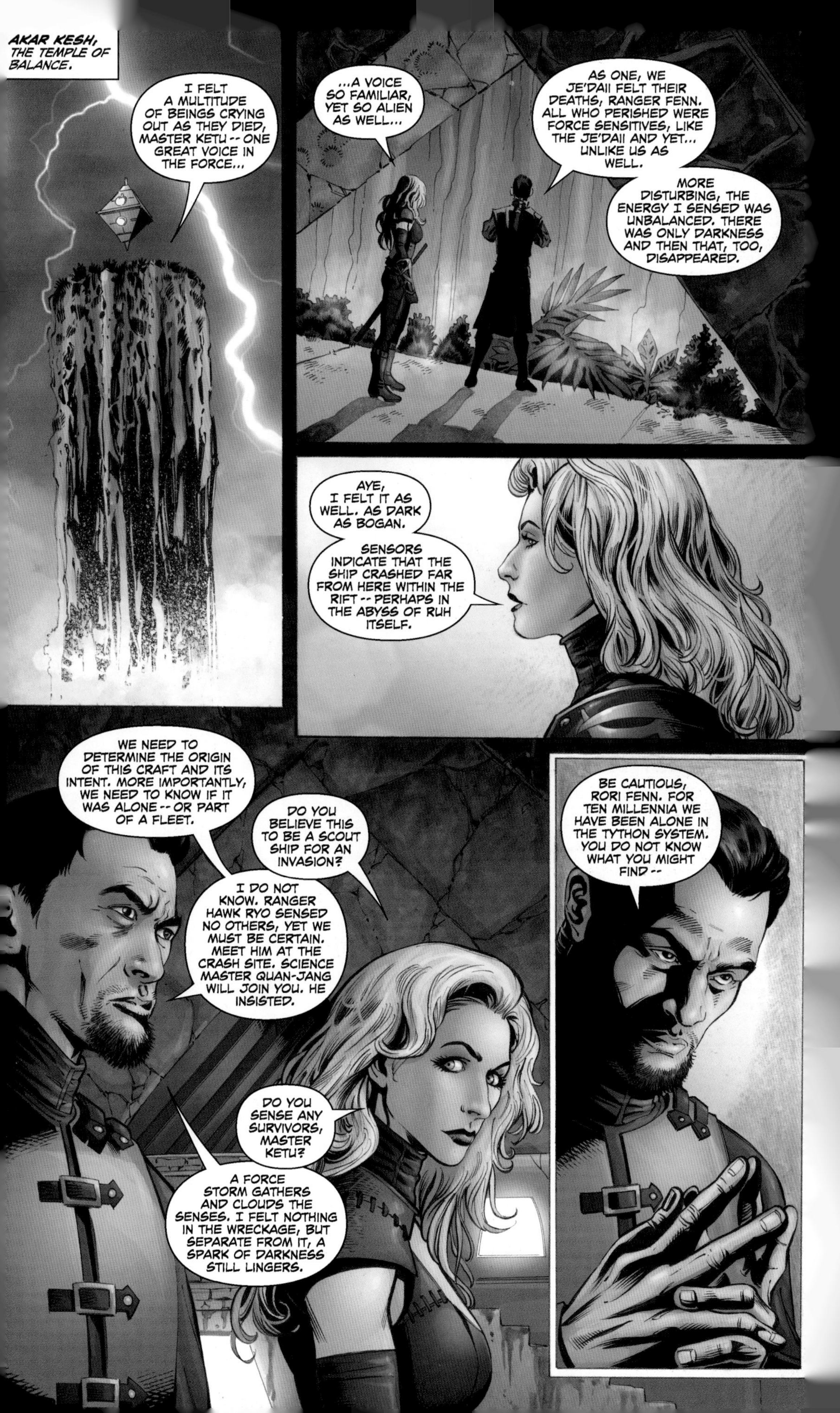
AKAR KESH, THE TEMPLE OF BALANCE.
I FELT A MULTITUDE OF BEINGS CRYING OUT AS THEY DIED, MASTER KETU -- ONE GREAT VOICE IN THE FORCE...
...A VOICE SO FAMILIAR, YET SO ALIEN AS WELL...
AS ONE, WE JE'DAII FELT THEIR DEATHS, RANGER FENN. ALL WHO PERISHED WERE FORCE SENSITIVES, LIKE THE JE'DAII AND YET... UNLIKE US AS WELL.
MORE DISTURBING, THE ENERGY I SENSED WAS UNBALANCED. THERE WAS ONLY DARKNESS AND THEN THAT, TOO, DISAPPEARED.
AYE, I FELT IT AS WELL. AS DARK AS BOGAN.
SENSORS INDICATE THAT THE SHIP CRASHED FAR FROM HERE WITHIN THE RIFT -- PERHAPS IN THE ABYSS OF RUH ITSELF.
WE NEED TO DETERMINE THE ORIGIN OF THIS CRAFT AND ITS INTENT. MORE IMPORTANTLY, WE NEED TO KNOW IF IT WAS ALONE -- OR PART OF A FLEET.
DO YOU BELIEVE THIS TO BE A SCOUT SHIP FOR AN INVASION?
I DO NOT KNOW. RANGER HAWK RYO SENSED NO OTHERS, YET WE MUST BE CERTAIN. MEET HIM AT THE CRASH SITE. SCIENCE MASTER QUAN-JANG WILL JOIN YOU. HE INSISTED.
DO YOU SENSE ANY SURVIVORS, MASTER KETU?
A FORCE STORM GATHERS AND CLOUDS THE SENSES. I FELT NOTHING IN THE WRECKAGE, BUT SEPARATE FROM IT, A SPARK OF DARKNESS STILL LINGERS.
BE CAUTIOUS, RORI FENN. FOR TEN MILLENNIA WE HAVE BEEN ALONE IN THE TYTHON SYSTEM. YOU DO NOT KNOW WHAT YOU MIGHT FIND --

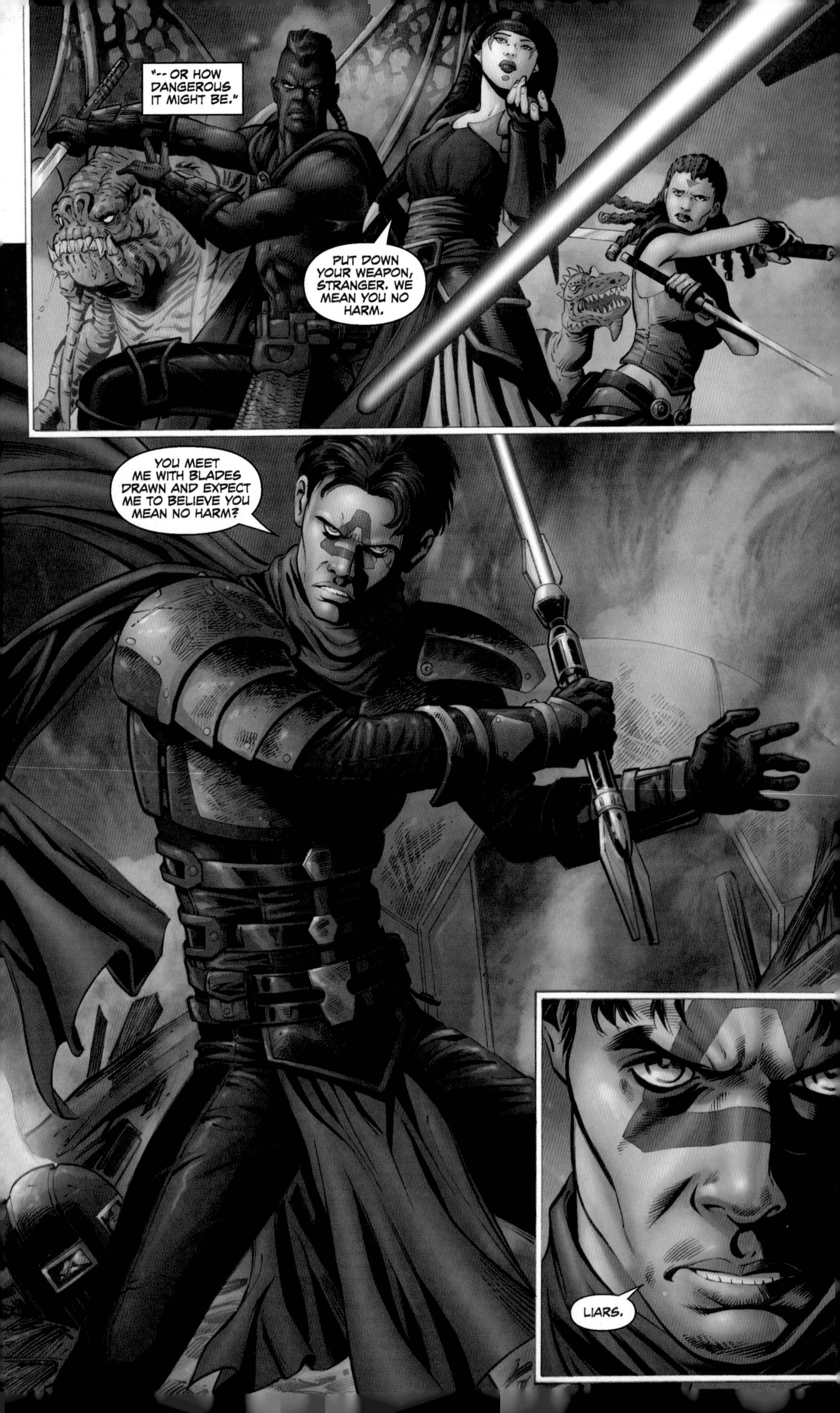
"-- OR HOW DANGEROUS IT MIGHT BE."
PUT DOWN YOUR WEAPON, STRANGER. WE MEAN YOU NO HARM.
YOU MEET ME WITH BLADES DRAWN AND EXPECT ME TO BELIEVE YOU MEAN NO HARM?
LIARS.

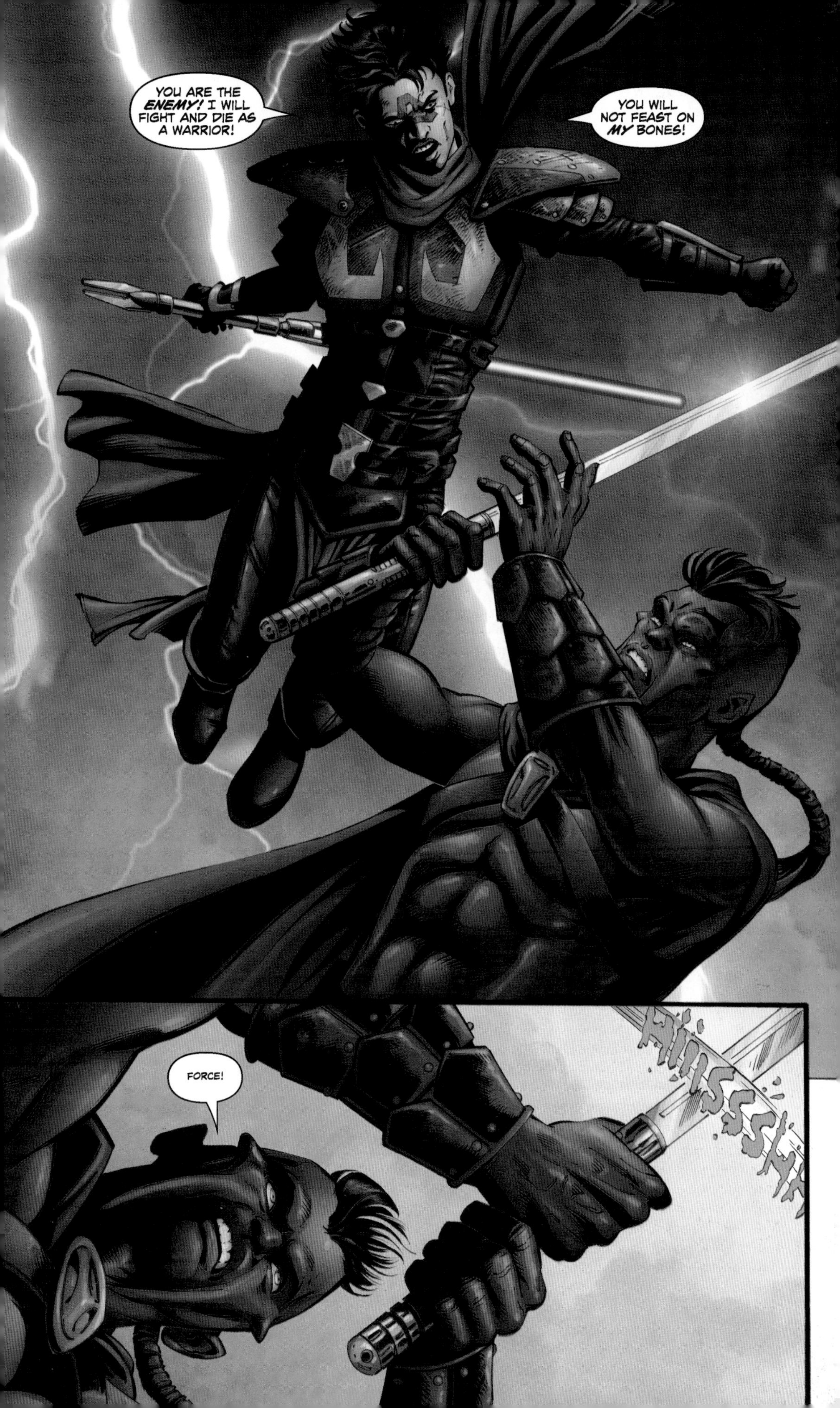
YOU ARE THE ENEMY! I WILL FIGHT AND DIE AS A WARRIOR!
YOU WILL NOT FEAST ON MY BONES!
FORCE!

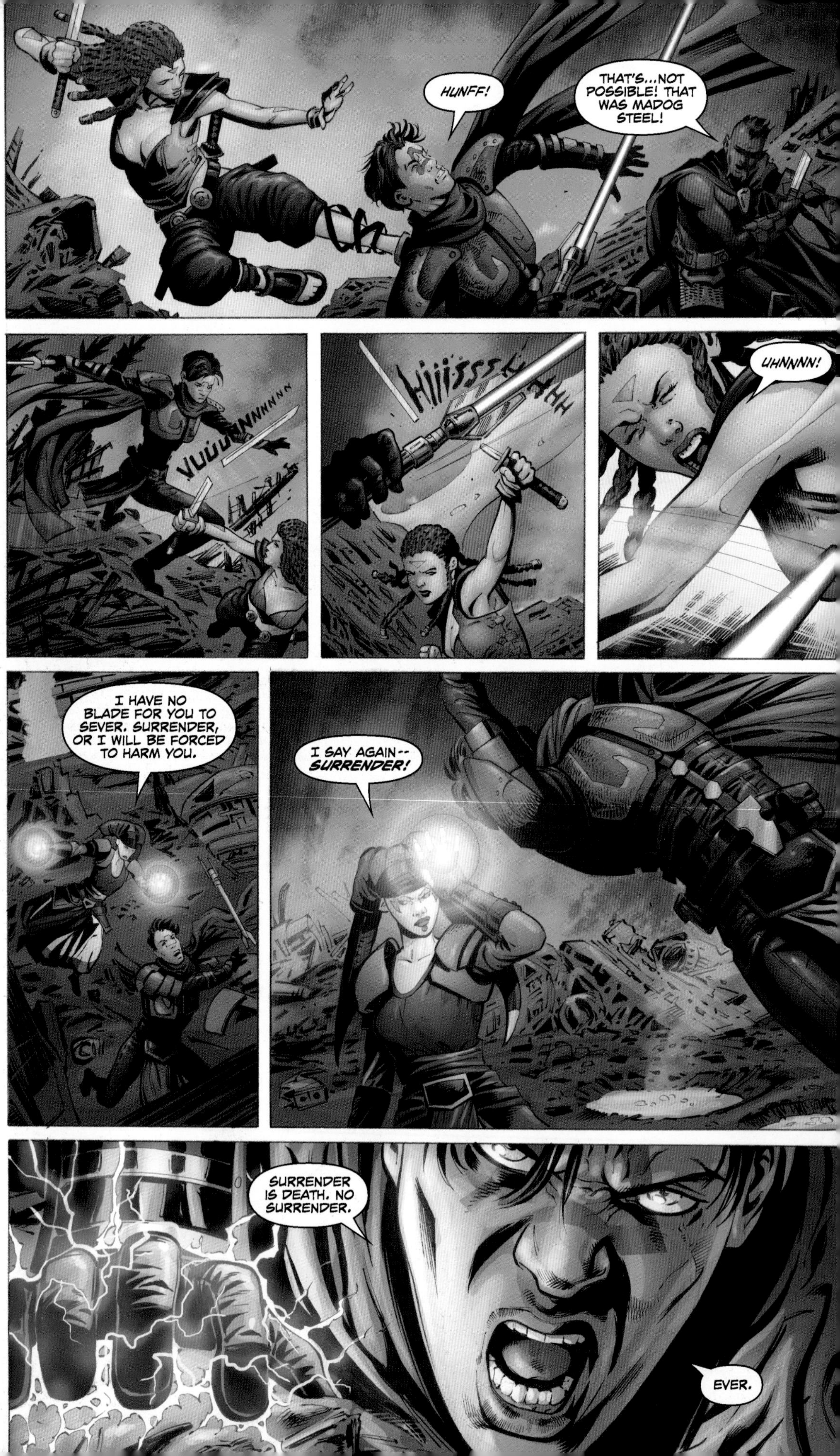
HUNFF!
THAT'S...NOT POSSIBLE! THAT WAS MADOG STEEL!
VUUUMNNNNNN
HIIISSSHHH
UHNNNN!
I HAVE NO BLADE FOR YOU TO SEVER. SURRENDER, OR I WILL BE FORCED TO HARM YOU.
I SAY AGAIN-- SURRENDER!
SURRENDER IS DEATH. NO SURRENDER.
EVER.

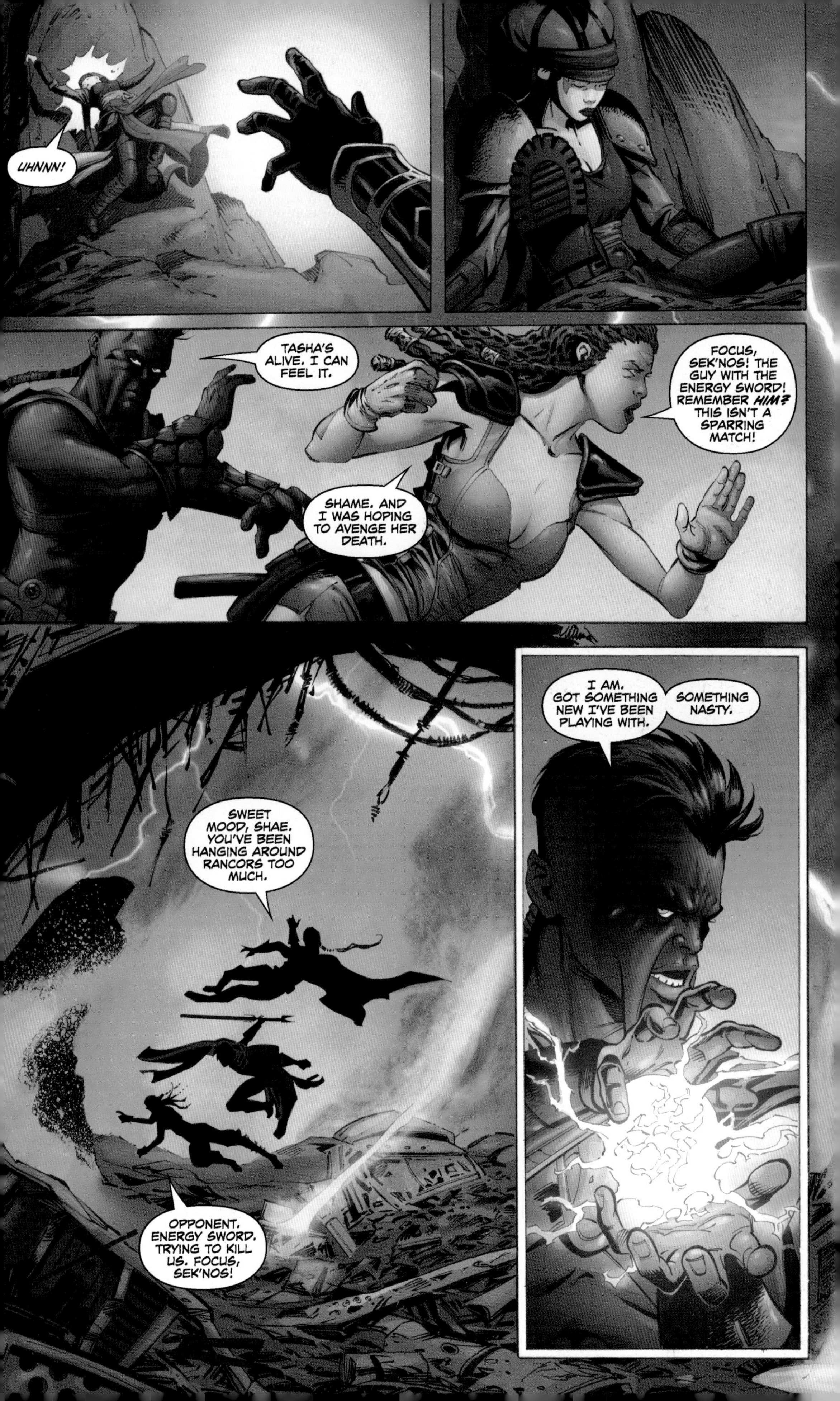
UHNNN!
TASHA'S ALIVE. I CAN FEEL IT.
FOCUS, SEK'NOS! THE GUY WITH THE ENERGY SWORD! REMEMBER *HIM?* THIS ISN'T A SPARRING MATCH!
SHAME. AND I WAS HOPING TO AVENGE HER DEATH.
SWEET MOOD, SHAE. YOU'VE BEEN HANGING AROUND RANCORS TOO MUCH.
OPPONENT. ENERGY SWORD. TRYING TO KILL US. FOCUS, SEK'NOS!
I AM. GOT SOMETHING NEW I'VE BEEN PLAYING WITH.
SOMETHING NASTY.

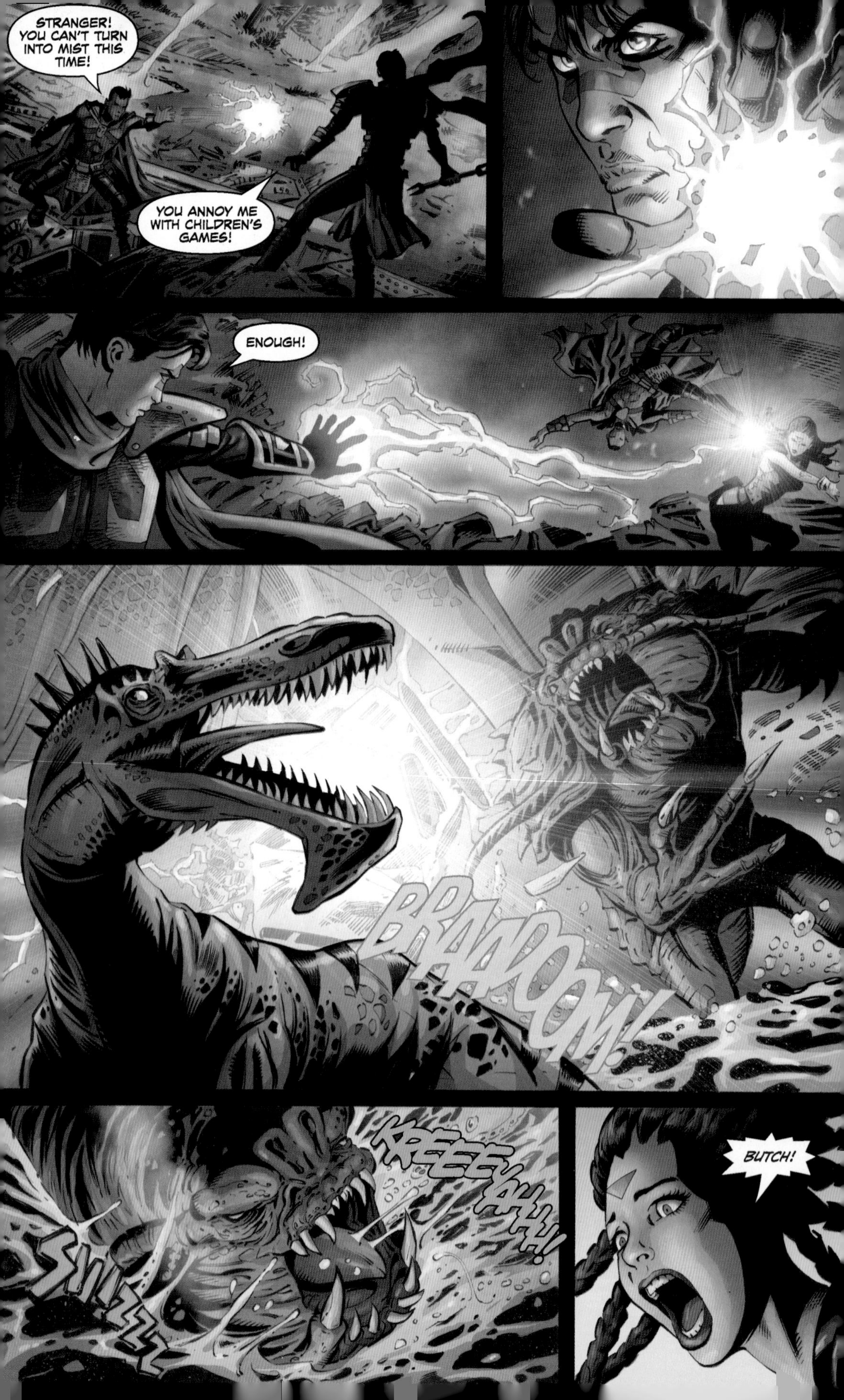
STRANGER! YOU CAN'T TURN INTO MIST THIS TIME!
YOU ANNOY ME WITH CHILDREN'S GAMES!
ENOUGH!
BRAAOOM!
KREEEYAHH!!
SHZZZZ
BUTCH!

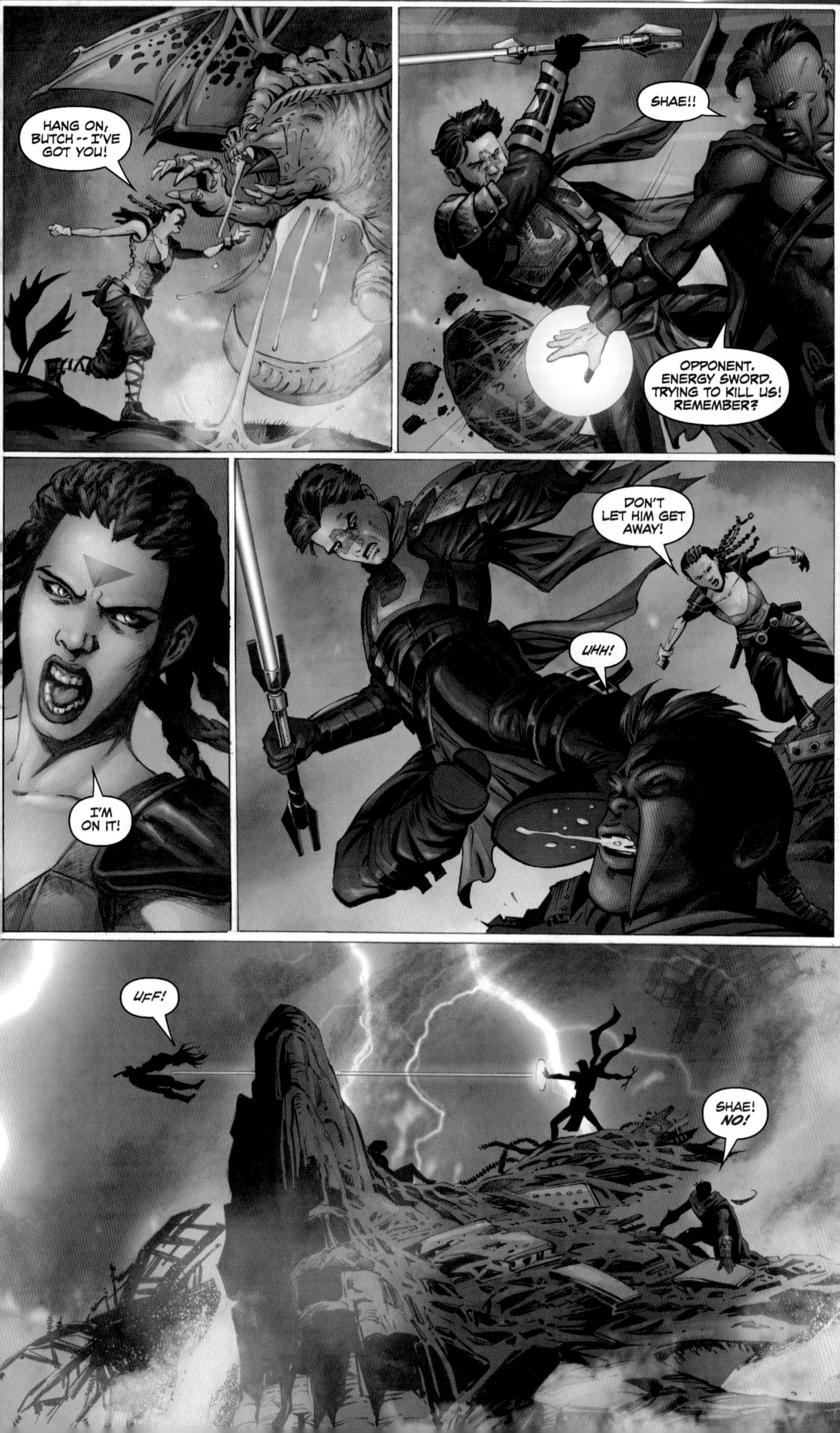
HANG ON, BUTCH -- I'VE GOT YOU!
SHAE!!
OPPONENT. ENERGY SWORD. TRYING TO KILL US! REMEMBER?
I'M ON IT!
DON'T LET HIM GET AWAY!
UHH!
UFF!
SHAE! NO!

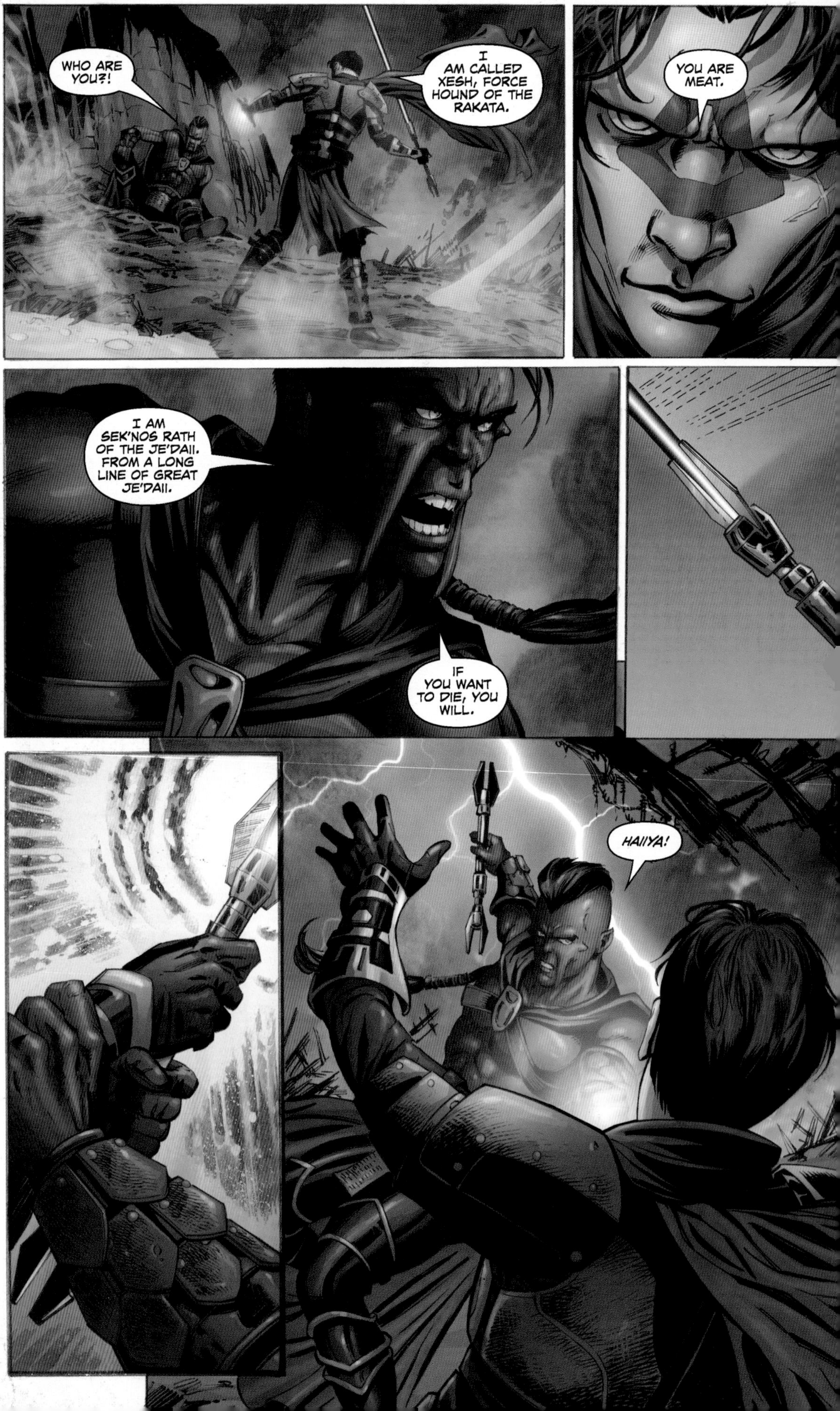
WHO ARE YOU?!
I AM CALLED XESH, FORCE HOUND OF THE RAKATA.
YOU ARE MEAT.
I AM SEK'NOS RATH OF THE JE'DAII. FROM A LONG LINE OF GREAT JE'DAII.
IF YOU WANT TO DIE, YOU WILL.
HAIIYA!

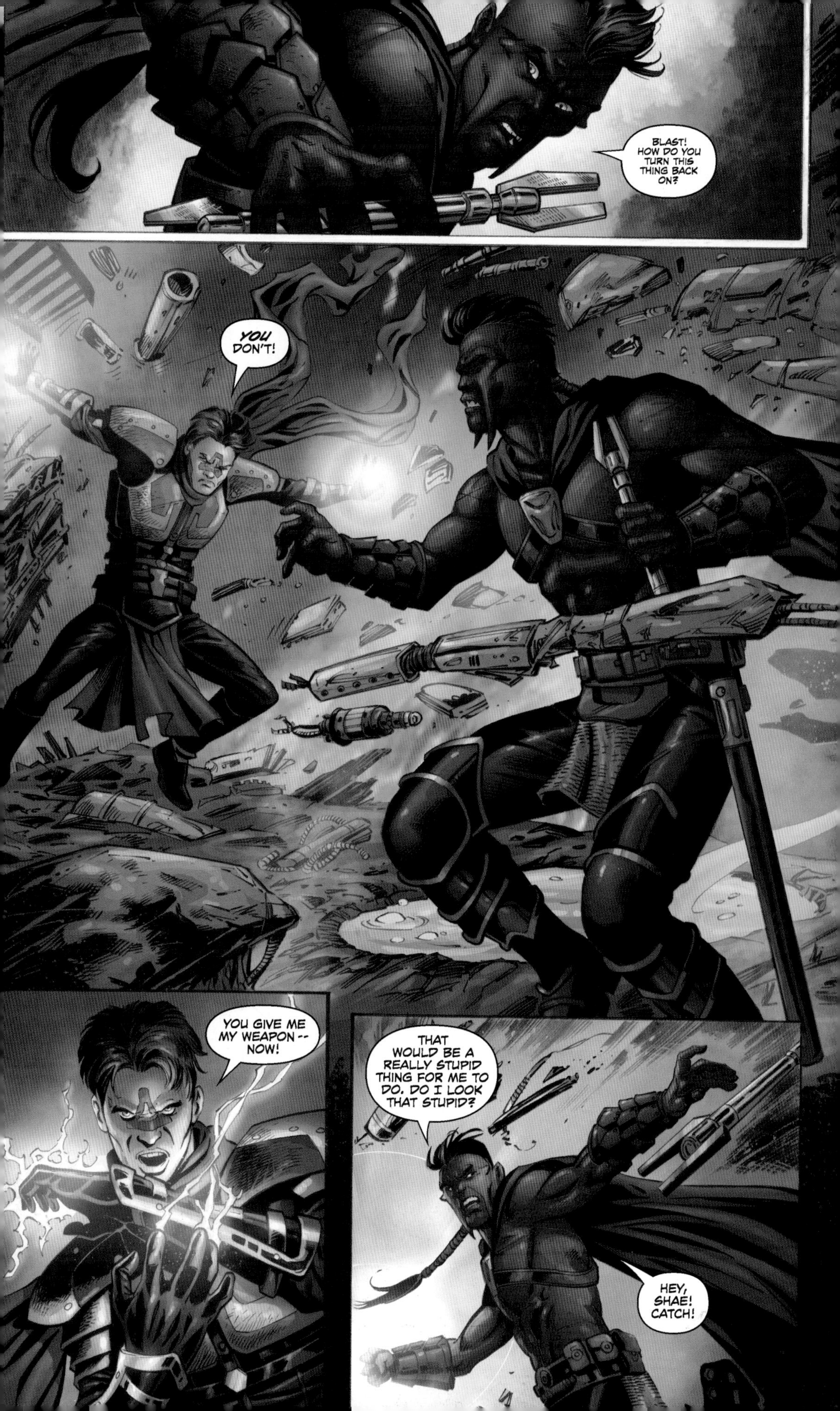
BLAST! HOW DO YOU TURN THIS THING BACK ON?
YOU DON'T!
YOU GIVE ME MY WEAPON -- NOW!
THAT WOULD BE A REALLY STUPID THING FOR ME TO DO. DO I LOOK THAT STUPID?
HEY, SHAE! CATCH!

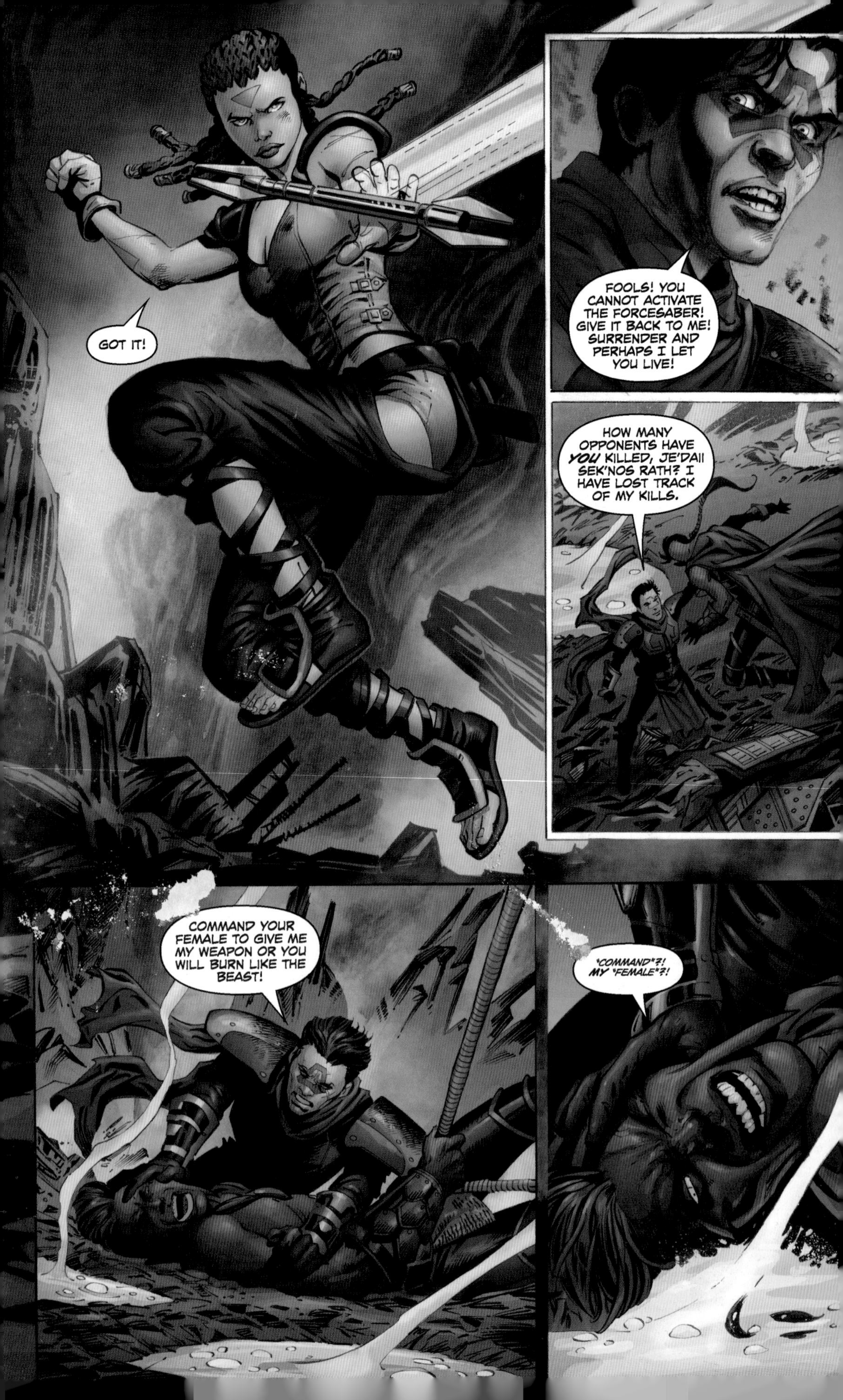
GOT IT!
FOOLS! YOU CANNOT ACTIVATE THE FORCESABER! GIVE IT BACK TO ME! SURRENDER AND PERHAPS I LET YOU LIVE!
HOW MANY OPPONENTS HAVE YOU KILLED, JE'DAII SEK'NOS RATH? I HAVE LOST TRACK OF MY KILLS.
COMMAND YOUR FEMALE TO GIVE ME MY WEAPON OR YOU WILL BURN LIKE THE BEAST!
"COMMAND"?! MY "FEMALE"?!

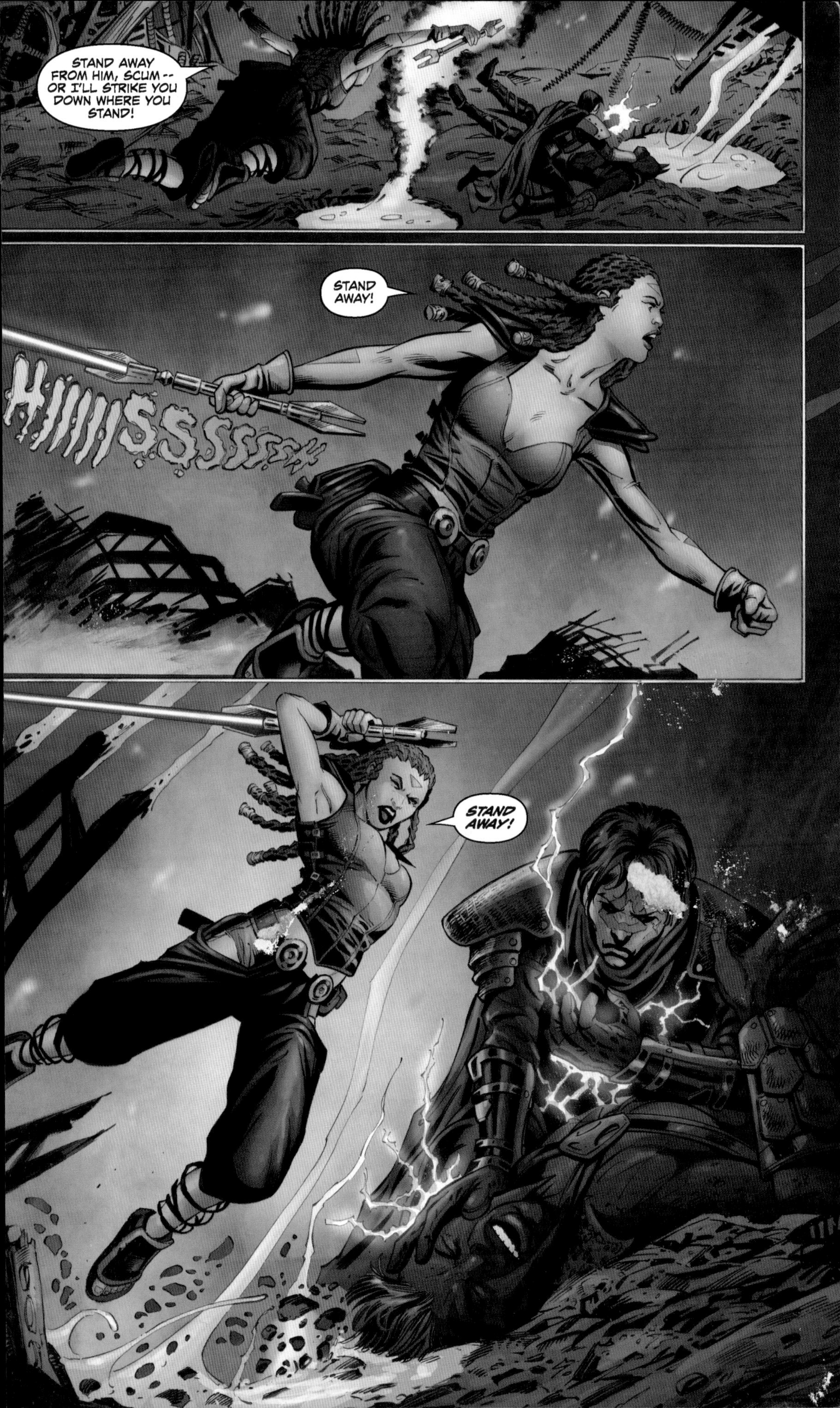
STAND AWAY FROM HIM, SCUM -- OR I'LL STRIKE YOU DOWN WHERE YOU STAND!
STAND AWAY!
HIIIISSSSSSSH
STAND AWAY!

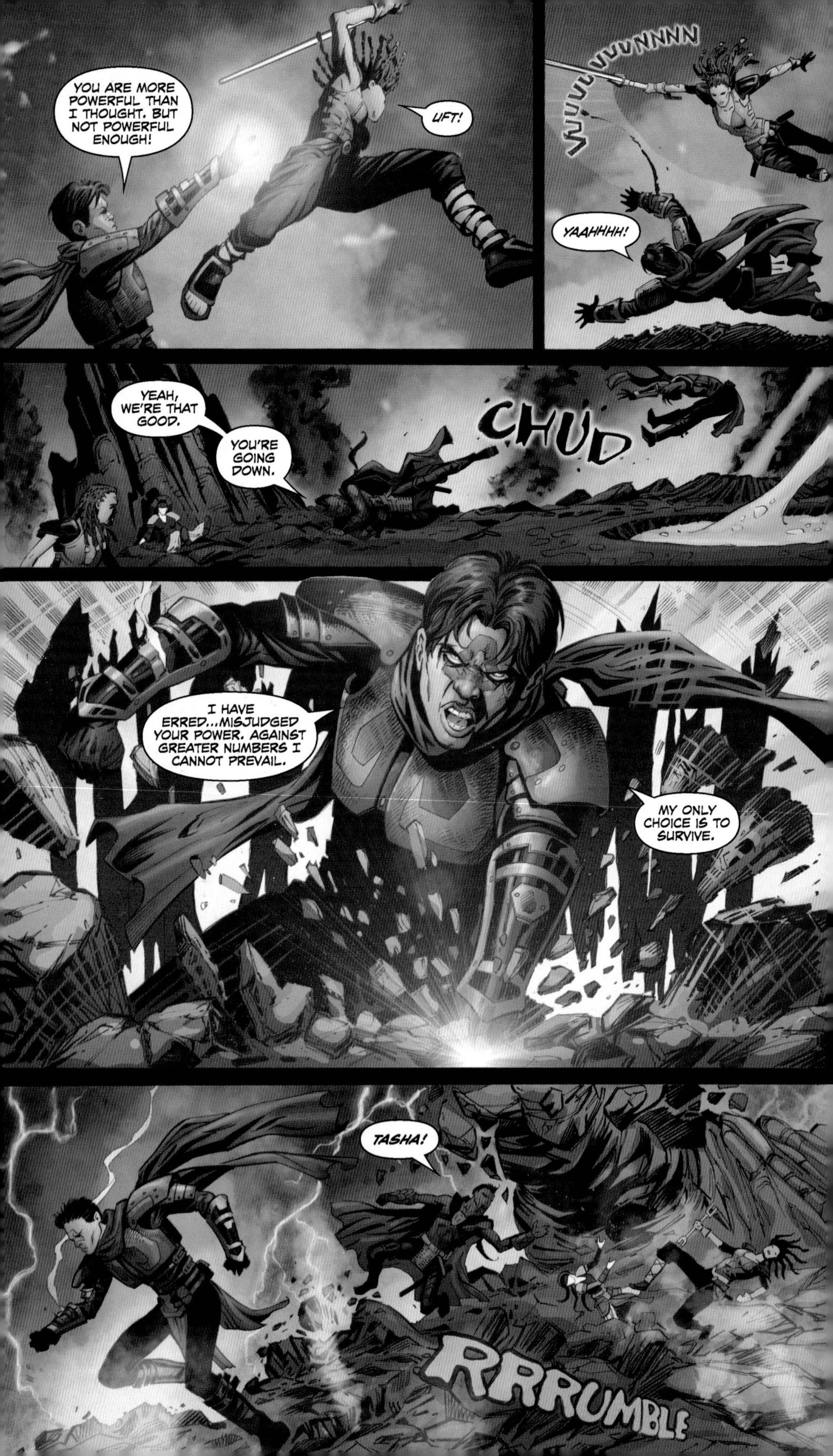
YOU ARE MORE POWERFUL THAN I THOUGHT. BUT NOT POWERFUL ENOUGH!
UFT!
VVUUUUUUUNNNN
YAAHHHH!
YEAH, WE'RE THAT GOOD.
YOU'RE GOING DOWN.
CHUD
I HAVE ERRED...MISJUDGED YOUR POWER. AGAINST GREATER NUMBERS I CANNOT PREVAIL.
MY ONLY CHOICE IS TO SURVIVE.
TASHA!
RRRUMBLE

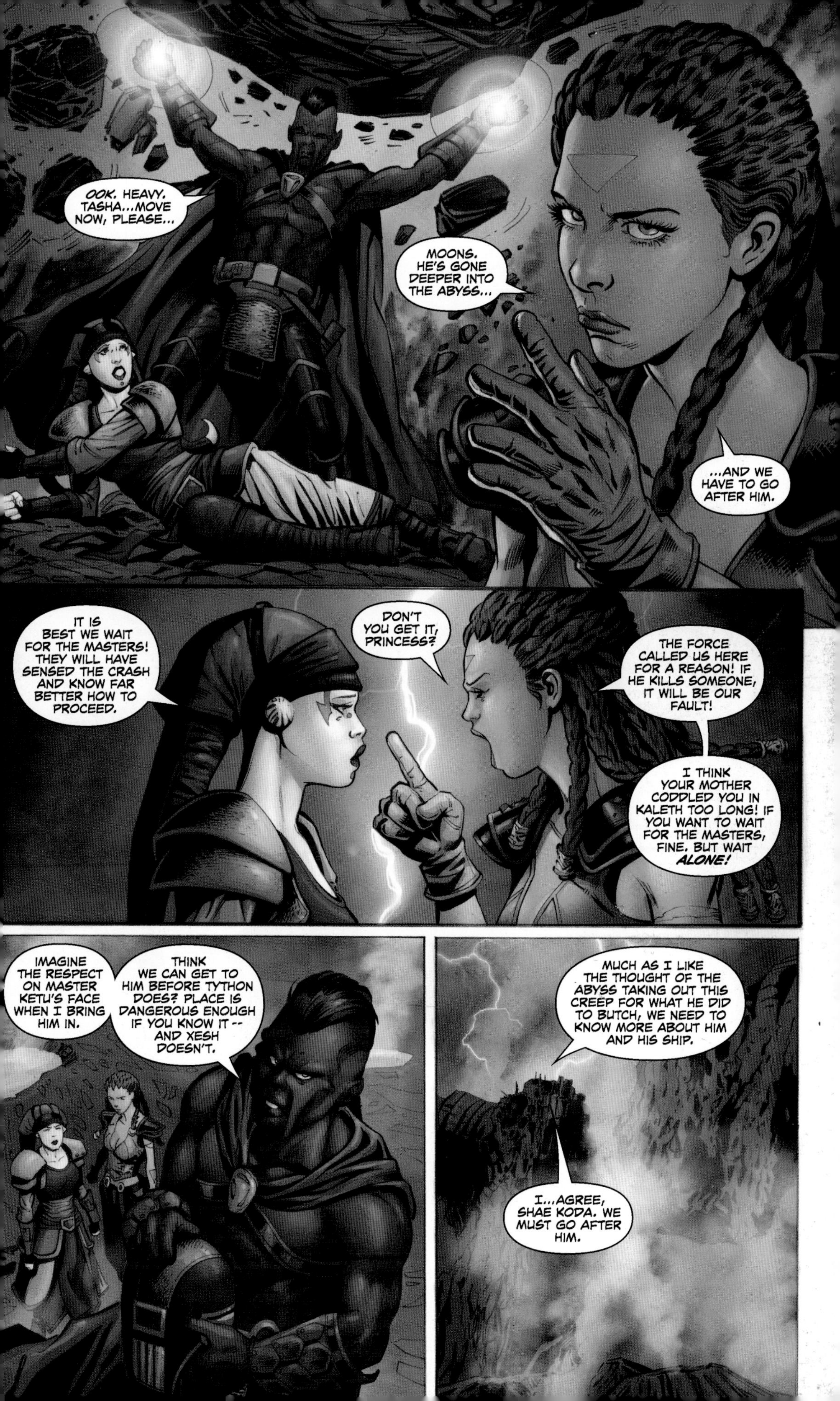
OOK. HEAVY. TASHA...MOVE NOW, PLEASE...
MOONS. HE'S GONE DEEPER INTO THE ABYSS...
...AND WE HAVE TO GO AFTER HIM.
IT IS BEST WE WAIT FOR THE MASTERS! THEY WILL HAVE SENSED THE CRASH AND KNOW FAR BETTER HOW TO PROCEED.
DON'T YOU GET IT, PRINCESS?
THE FORCE CALLED US HERE FOR A REASON! IF HE KILLS SOMEONE, IT WILL BE OUR FAULT!
I THINK YOUR MOTHER CODDLED YOU IN KALETH TOO LONG! IF YOU WANT TO WAIT FOR THE MASTERS, FINE. BUT WAIT ALONE!
IMAGINE THE RESPECT ON MASTER KETU'S FACE WHEN I BRING HIM IN.
THINK WE CAN GET TO HIM BEFORE TYTHON DOES? PLACE IS DANGEROUS ENOUGH IF YOU KNOW IT -- AND XESH DOESN'T.
MUCH AS I LIKE THE THOUGHT OF THE ABYSS TAKING OUT THIS CREEP FOR WHAT HE DID TO BUTCH, WE NEED TO KNOW MORE ABOUT HIM AND HIS SHIP.
I...AGREE, SHAE KODA. WE MUST GO AFTER HIM.

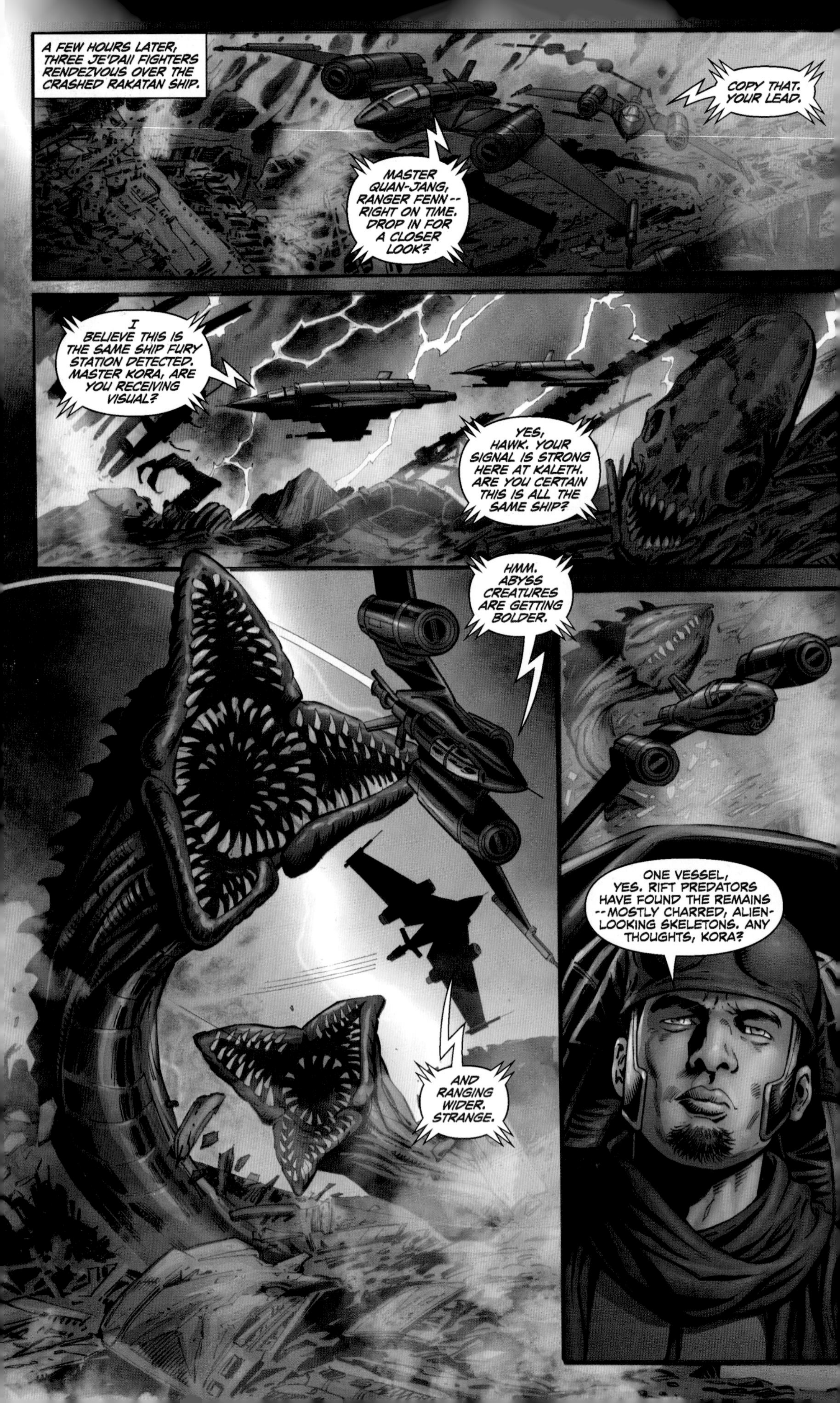
A FEW HOURS LATER, THREE JE'DAII FIGHTERS RENDEZVOUS OVER THE CRASHED RAKATAN SHIP.
MASTER QUAN-JANG, RANGER FENN-- RIGHT ON TIME. DROP IN FOR A CLOSER LOOK?
COPY THAT. YOUR LEAD.
I BELIEVE THIS IS THE SAME SHIP FURY STATION DETECTED. MASTER KORA, ARE YOU RECEIVING VISUAL?
YES, HAWK. YOUR SIGNAL IS STRONG HERE AT KALETH. ARE YOU CERTAIN THIS IS ALL THE SAME SHIP?
HMM. ABYSS CREATURES ARE GETTING BOLDER.
AND RANGING WIDER. STRANGE.
ONE VESSEL, YES. RIFT PREDATORS HAVE FOUND THE REMAINS --MOSTLY CHARRED, ALIEN-LOOKING SKELETONS. ANY THOUGHTS, KORA?

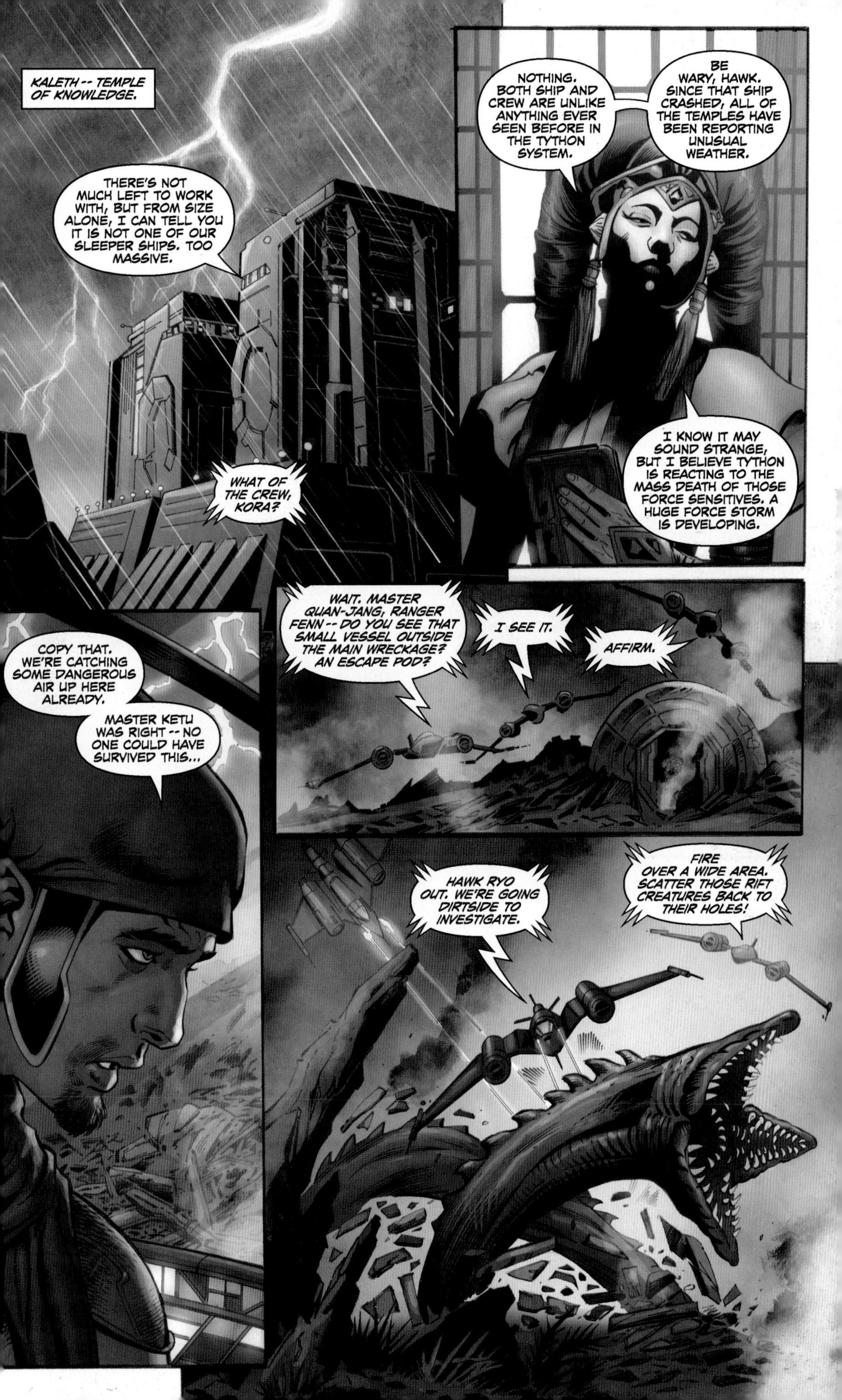
KALETH -- TEMPLE OF KNOWLEDGE.
THERE'S NOT MUCH LEFT TO WORK WITH, BUT FROM SIZE ALONE, I CAN TELL YOU IT IS NOT ONE OF OUR SLEEPER SHIPS. TOO MASSIVE.
WHAT OF THE CREW, KORA?
NOTHING. BOTH SHIP AND CREW ARE UNLIKE ANYTHING EVER SEEN BEFORE IN THE TYTHON SYSTEM.
BE WARY, HAWK. SINCE THAT SHIP CRASHED, ALL OF THE TEMPLES HAVE BEEN REPORTING UNUSUAL WEATHER.
I KNOW IT MAY SOUND STRANGE, BUT I BELIEVE TYTHON IS REACTING TO THE MASS DEATH OF THOSE FORCE SENSITIVES. A HUGE FORCE STORM IS DEVELOPING.
COPY THAT. WE'RE CATCHING SOME DANGEROUS AIR UP HERE ALREADY.
MASTER KETU WAS RIGHT -- NO ONE COULD HAVE SURVIVED THIS...
WAIT. MASTER QUAN-JANG, RANGER FENN -- DO YOU SEE THAT SMALL VESSEL OUTSIDE THE MAIN WRECKAGE? AN ESCAPE POD?
I SEE IT.
AFFIRM.
HAWK RYO OUT. WE'RE GOING DIRTSIDE TO INVESTIGATE.
FIRE OVER A WIDE AREA. SCATTER THOSE RIFT CREATURES BACK TO THEIR HOLES!

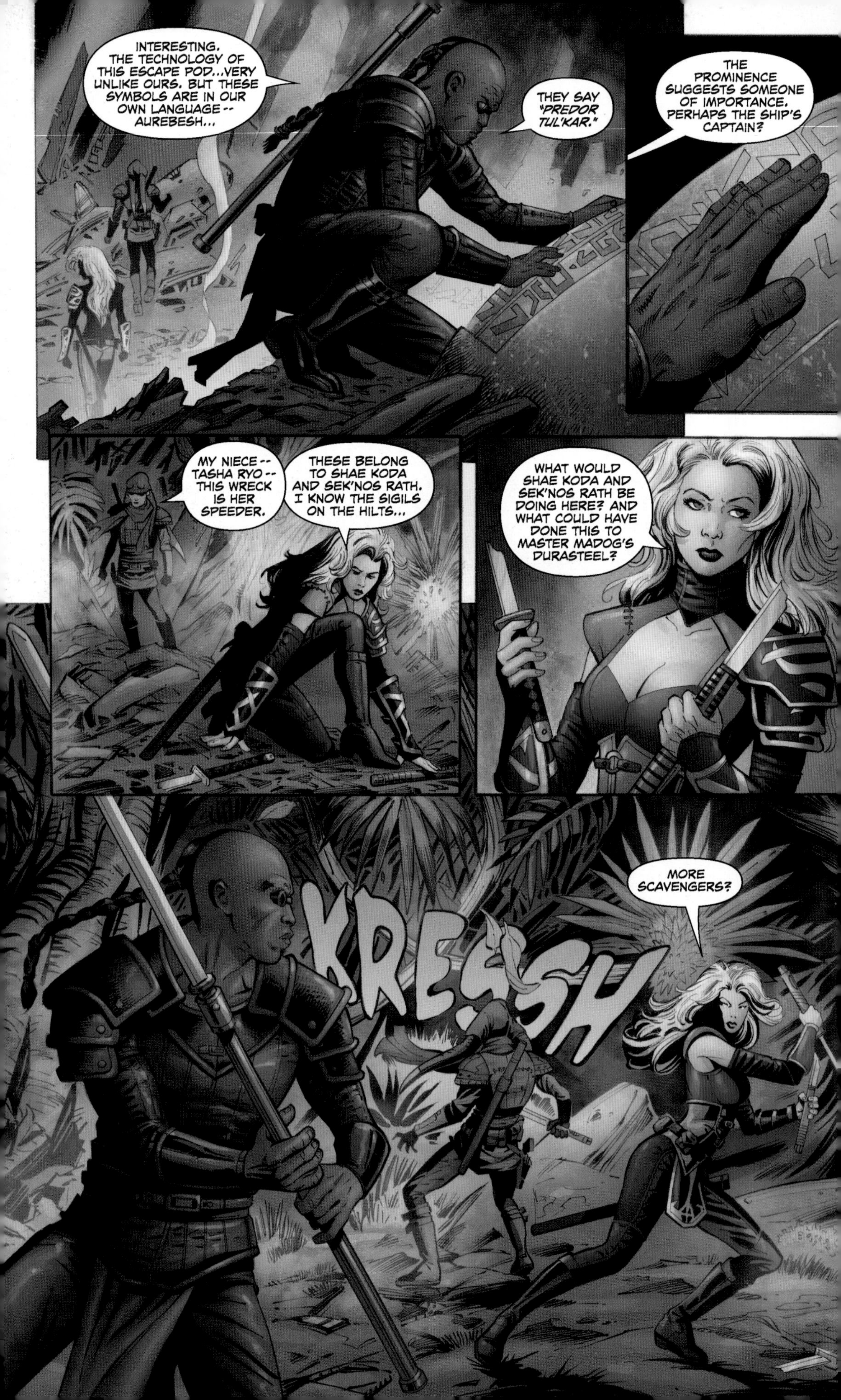

INTERESTING. THE TECHNOLOGY OF THIS ESCAPE POD...VERY UNLIKE OURS. BUT THESE SYMBOLS ARE IN OUR OWN LANGUAGE -- AUREBESH...
THEY SAY *"PREDOR TUL'KAR."*
THE PROMINENCE SUGGESTS SOMEONE OF IMPORTANCE. PERHAPS THE SHIP'S CAPTAIN?
MY NIECE -- TASHA RYO -- THIS WRECK IS HER SPEEDER.
THESE BELONG TO SHAE KODA AND SEK'NOS RATH. I KNOW THE SIGILS ON THE HILTS...
WHAT WOULD SHAE KODA AND SEK'NOS RATH BE DOING HERE? AND WHAT COULD HAVE DONE THIS TO MASTER MADOG'S DURASTEEL?
KRESSH
MORE SCAVENGERS?

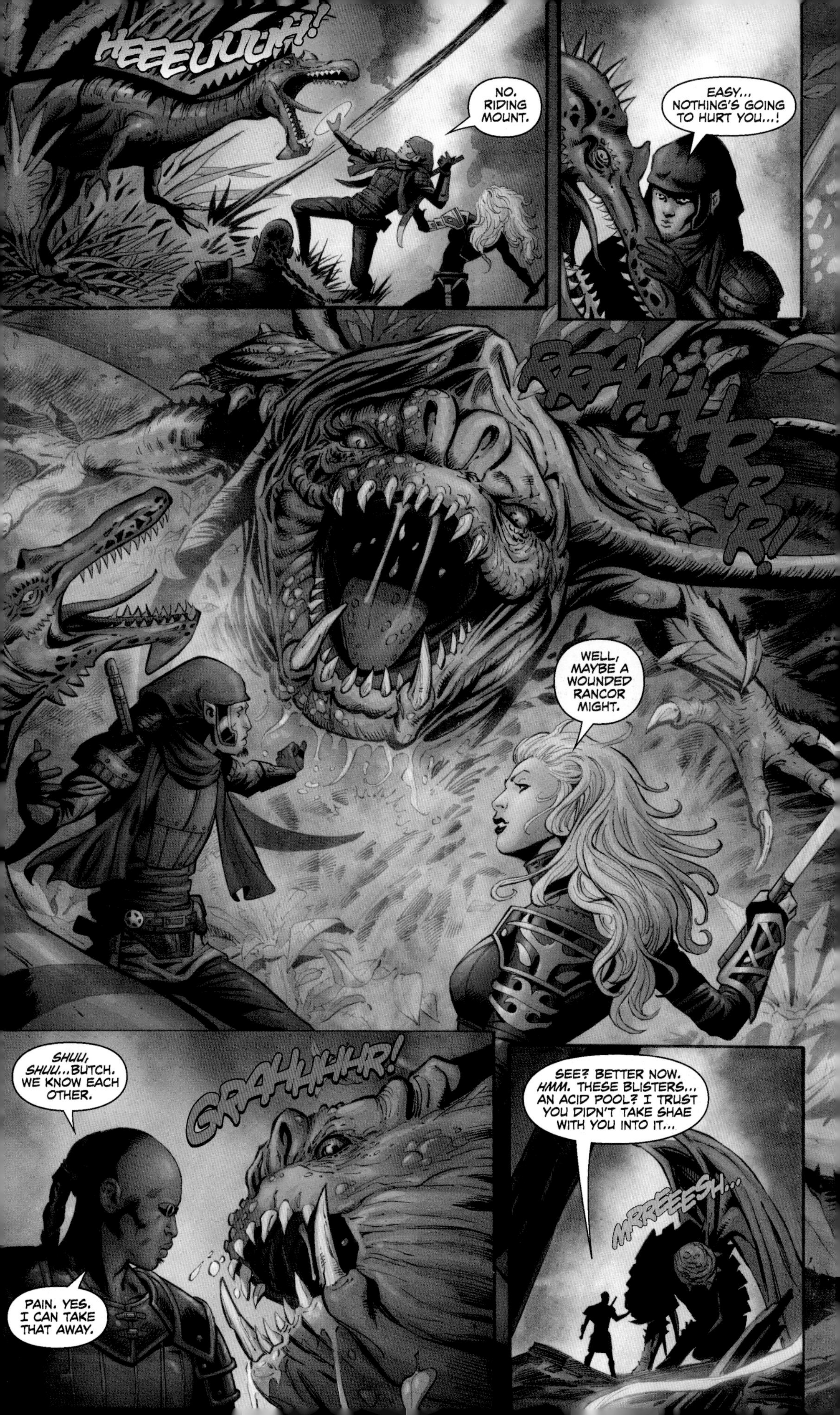
HEEEUUUH!
NO. RIDING MOUNT.
EASY... NOTHING'S GOING TO HURT YOU...!
RRAAHHRRR!
WELL, MAYBE A WOUNDED RANCOR MIGHT.
SHUU, SHUU...BUTCH. WE KNOW EACH OTHER.
GRAHHHHR!
PAIN. YES. I CAN TAKE THAT AWAY.
SEE? BETTER NOW. HMM. THESE BLISTERS... AN ACID POOL? I TRUST YOU DIDN'T TAKE SHAE WITH YOU INTO IT...
MRREEESH...

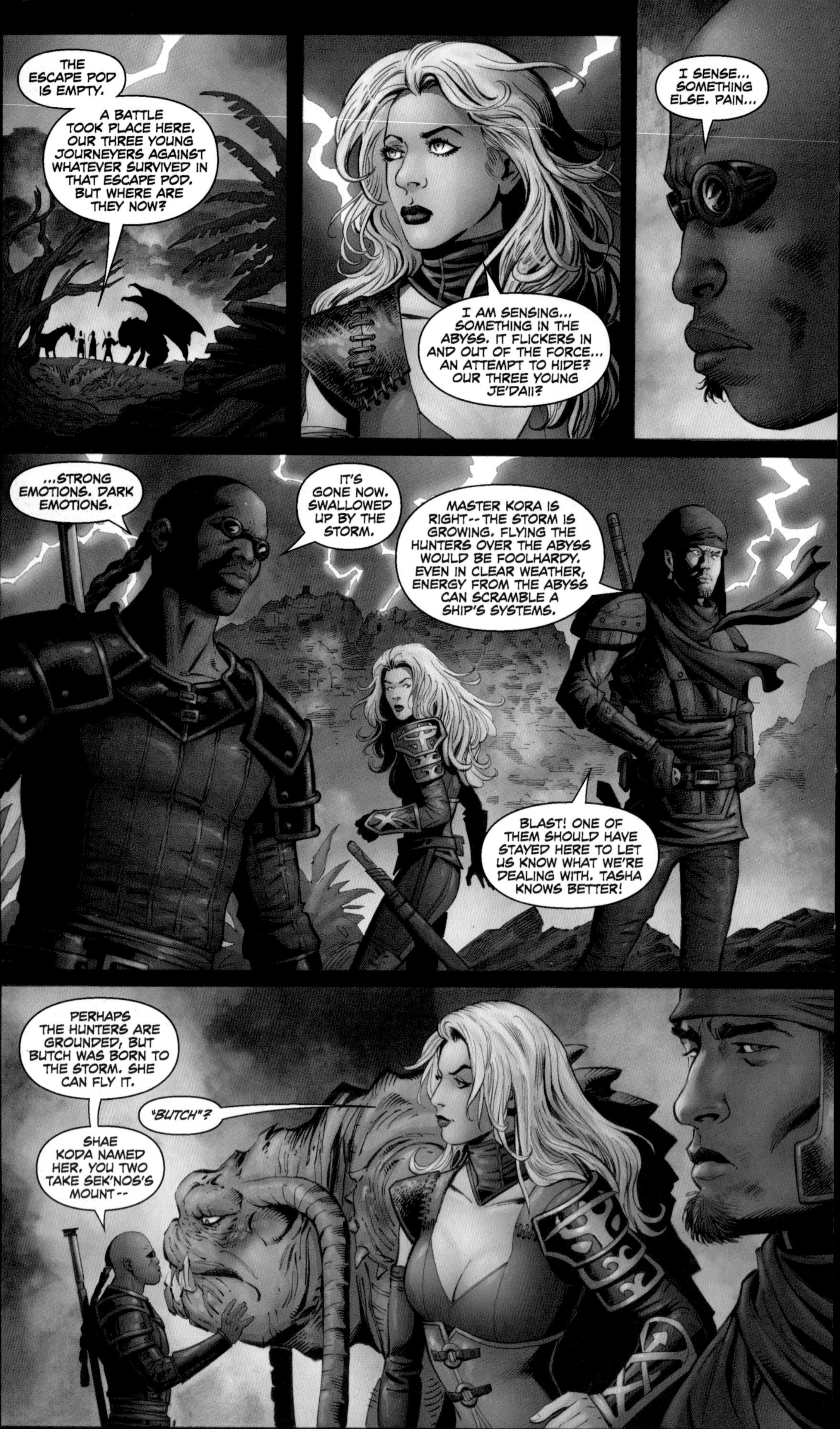
THE ESCAPE POD IS EMPTY.
A BATTLE TOOK PLACE HERE. OUR THREE YOUNG JOURNEYERS AGAINST WHATEVER SURVIVED IN THAT ESCAPE POD. BUT WHERE ARE THEY NOW?
I AM SENSING... SOMETHING IN THE ABYSS. IT FLICKERS IN AND OUT OF THE FORCE... AN ATTEMPT TO HIDE? OUR THREE YOUNG JE'DAII?
I SENSE... SOMETHING ELSE. PAIN...
...STRONG EMOTIONS. DARK EMOTIONS.
IT'S GONE NOW. SWALLOWED UP BY THE STORM.
MASTER KORA IS RIGHT--THE STORM IS GROWING. FLYING THE HUNTERS OVER THE ABYSS WOULD BE FOOLHARDY. EVEN IN CLEAR WEATHER, ENERGY FROM THE ABYSS CAN SCRAMBLE A SHIP'S SYSTEMS.
BLAST! ONE OF THEM SHOULD HAVE STAYED HERE TO LET US KNOW WHAT WE'RE DEALING WITH. TASHA KNOWS BETTER!
PERHAPS THE HUNTERS ARE GROUNDED, BUT BUTCH WAS BORN TO THE STORM. SHE CAN FLY IT.
"BUTCH"?
SHAE KODA NAMED HER. YOU TWO TAKE SEK'NOS'S MOUNT--

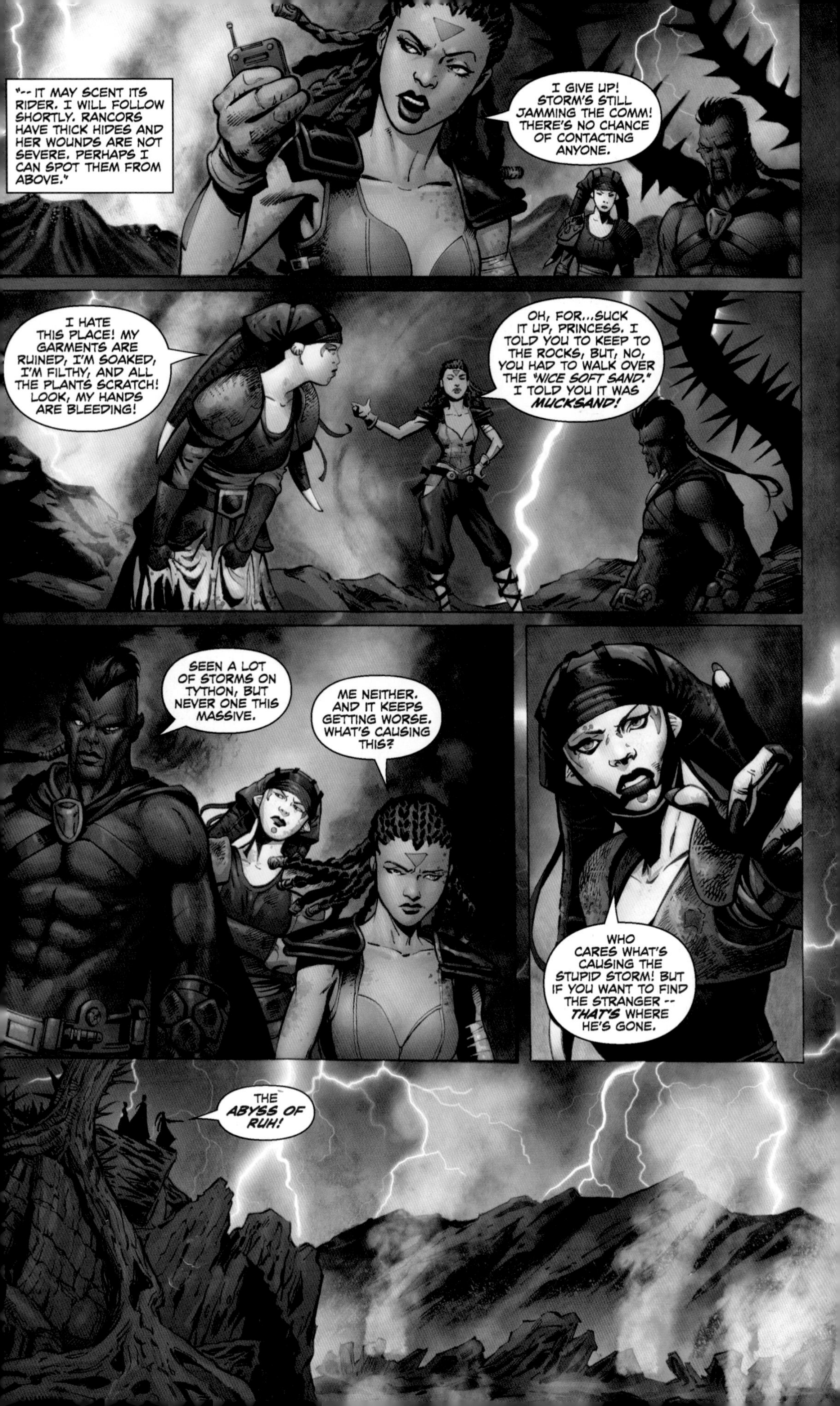

"-- IT MAY SCENT ITS RIDER. I WILL FOLLOW SHORTLY. RANCORS HAVE THICK HIDES AND HER WOUNDS ARE NOT SEVERE. PERHAPS I CAN SPOT THEM FROM ABOVE."
I GIVE UP! STORM'S STILL JAMMING THE COMM! THERE'S NO CHANCE OF CONTACTING ANYONE.
I HATE THIS PLACE! MY GARMENTS ARE RUINED, I'M SOAKED, I'M FILTHY, AND ALL THE PLANTS SCRATCH! LOOK, MY HANDS ARE BLEEDING!
OH, FOR...SUCK IT UP, PRINCESS. I TOLD YOU TO KEEP TO THE ROCKS, BUT, NO, YOU HAD TO WALK OVER THE "NICE SOFT SAND." I TOLD YOU IT WAS MUCKSAND!
SEEN A LOT OF STORMS ON TYTHON, BUT NEVER ONE THIS MASSIVE.
ME NEITHER. AND IT KEEPS GETTING WORSE. WHAT'S CAUSING THIS?
WHO CARES WHAT'S CAUSING THE STUPID STORM! BUT IF YOU WANT TO FIND THE STRANGER -- THAT'S WHERE HE'S GONE.
THE ABYSS OF RUH!

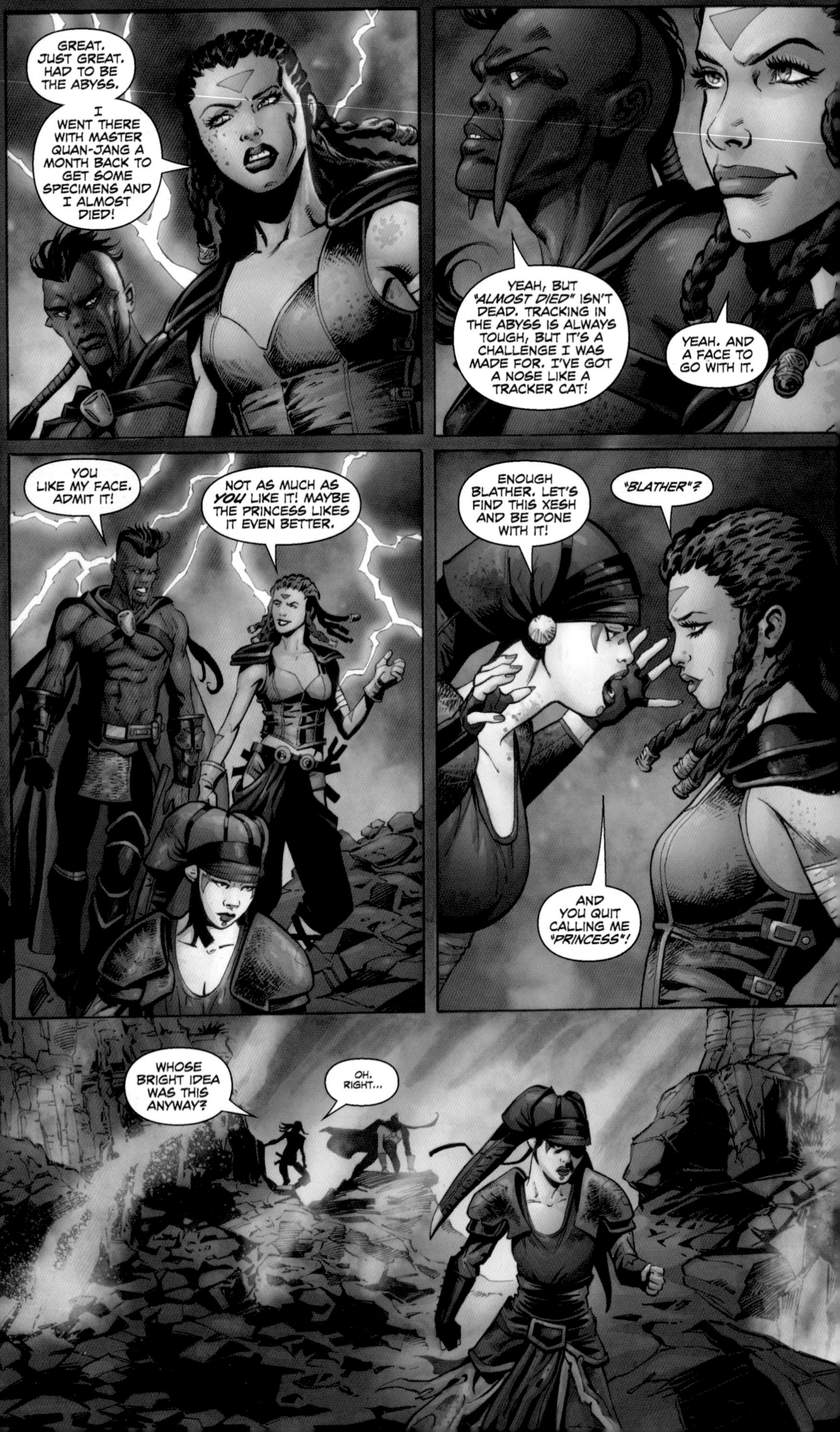
GREAT. JUST GREAT. HAD TO BE THE ABYSS.
I WENT THERE WITH MASTER QUAN-JANG A MONTH BACK TO GET SOME SPECIMENS AND I ALMOST DIED!
YEAH, BUT "ALMOST DIED" ISN'T DEAD. TRACKING IN THE ABYSS IS ALWAYS TOUGH, BUT IT'S A CHALLENGE I WAS MADE FOR. I'VE GOT A NOSE LIKE A TRACKER CAT!
YEAH. AND A FACE TO GO WITH IT.
YOU LIKE MY FACE. ADMIT IT!
NOT AS MUCH AS YOU LIKE IT! MAYBE THE PRINCESS LIKES IT EVEN BETTER.
ENOUGH BLATHER. LET'S FIND THIS XESH AND BE DONE WITH IT!
"BLATHER"?
AND YOU QUIT CALLING ME "PRINCESS"!
WHOSE BRIGHT IDEA WAS THIS ANYWAY?
OH. RIGHT...

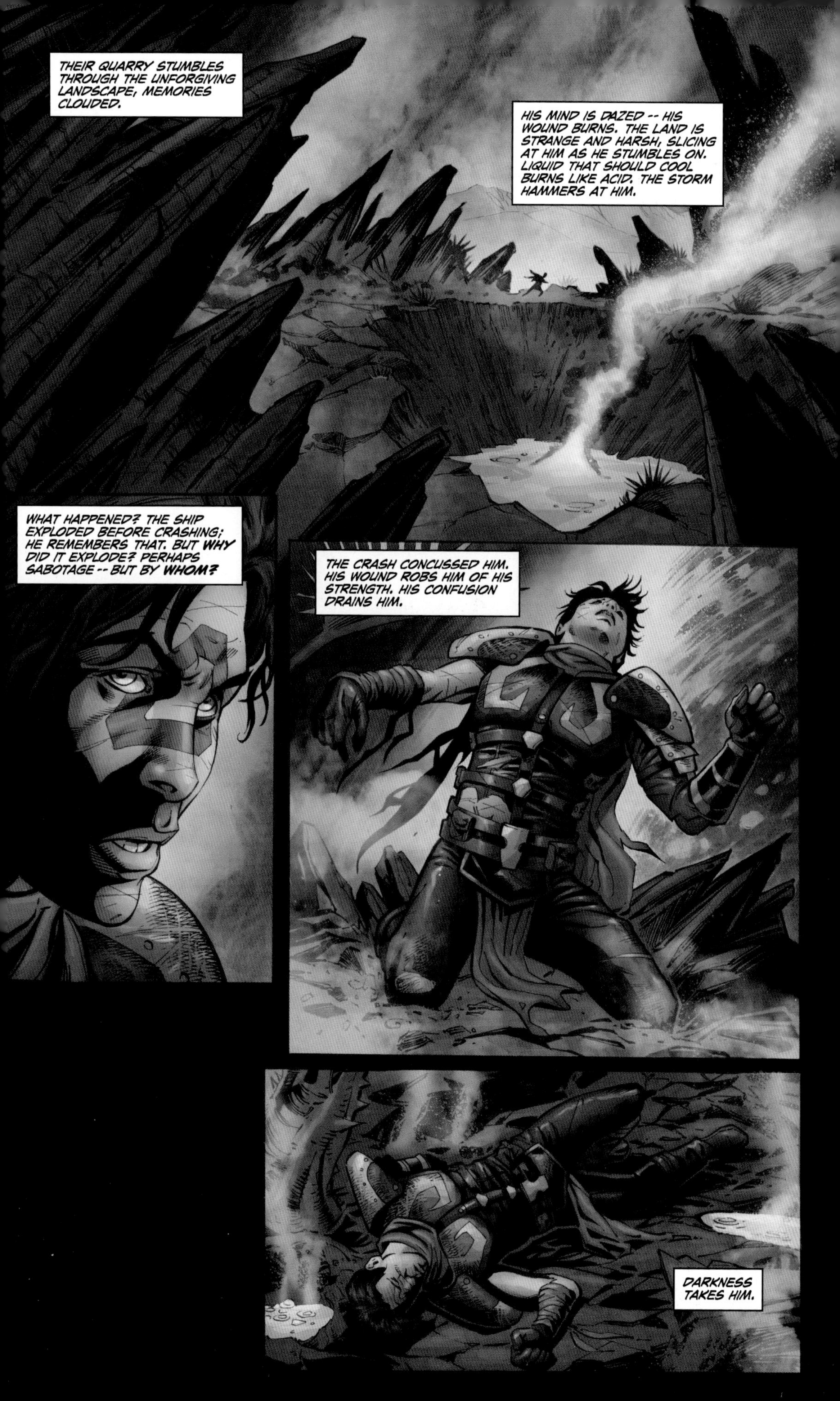
THEIR QUARRY STUMBLES THROUGH THE UNFORGIVING LANDSCAPE, MEMORIES CLOUDED.
HIS MIND IS DAZED -- HIS WOUND BURNS. THE LAND IS STRANGE AND HARSH, SLICING AT HIM AS HE STUMBLES ON. LIQUID THAT SHOULD COOL BURNS LIKE ACID. THE STORM HAMMERS AT HIM.
WHAT HAPPENED? THE SHIP EXPLODED BEFORE CRASHING; HE REMEMBERS THAT. BUT **WHY** DID IT EXPLODE? PERHAPS SABOTAGE -- BUT BY **WHOM**?
THE CRASH CONCUSSED HIM. HIS WOUND ROBS HIM OF HIS STRENGTH. HIS CONFUSION DRAINS HIM.
DARKNESS TAKES HIM.

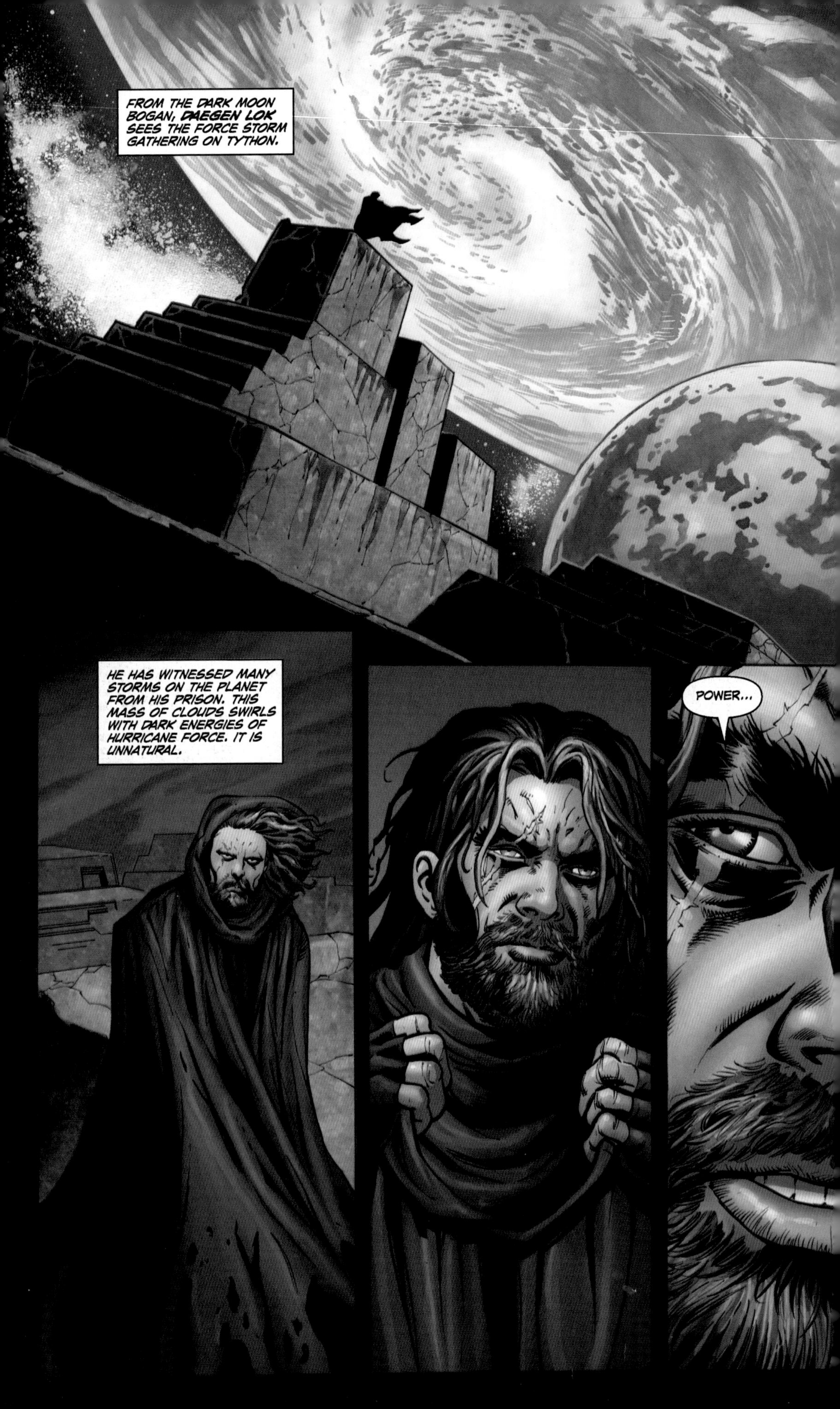
FROM THE DARK MOON BOGAN, DAEGEN LOK SEES THE FORCE STORM GATHERING ON TYTHON.
HE HAS WITNESSED MANY STORMS ON THE PLANET FROM HIS PRISON. THIS MASS OF CLOUDS SWIRLS WITH DARK ENERGIES OF HURRICANE FORCE. IT IS UNNATURAL.
POWER...

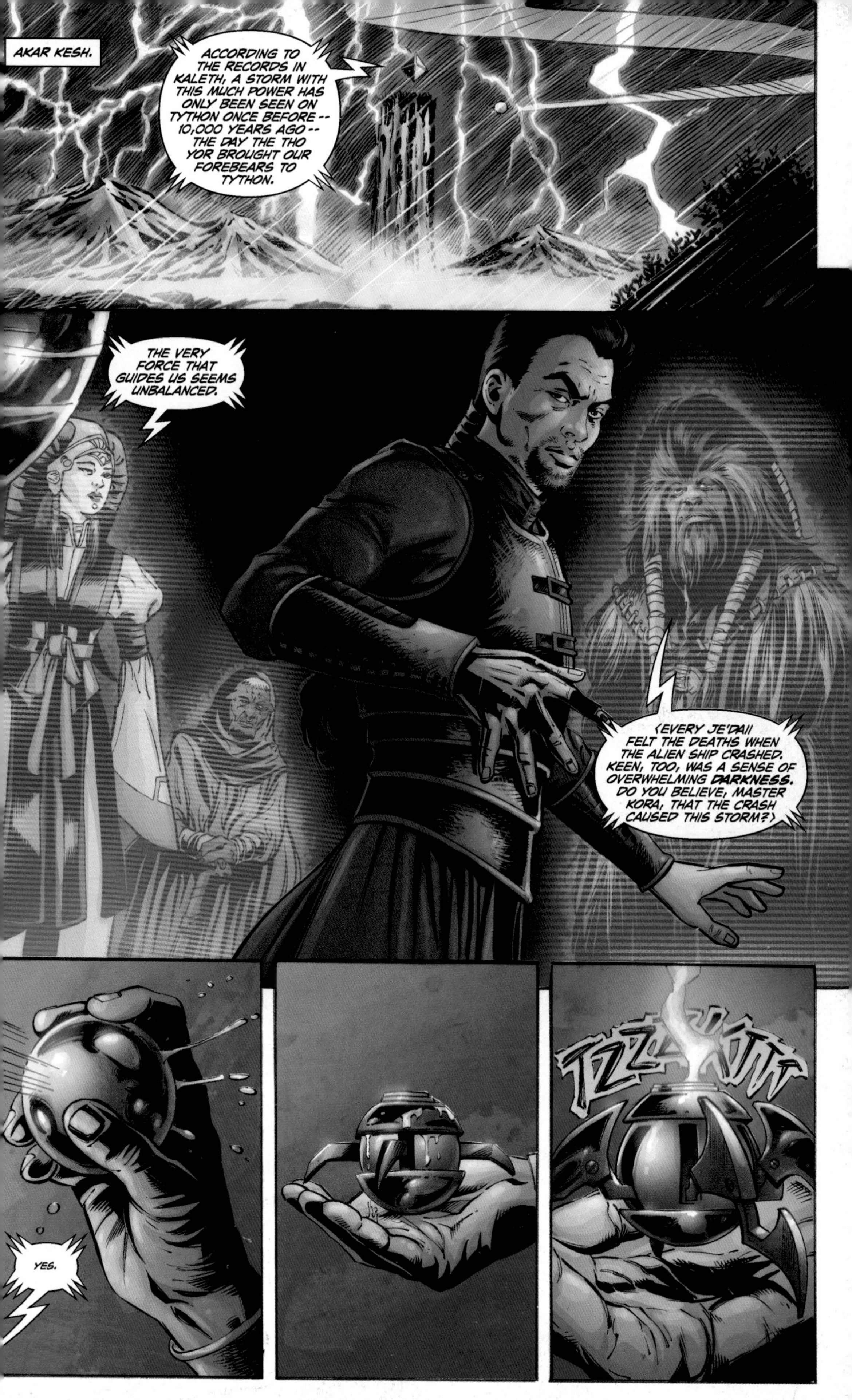
AKAR KESH.
ACCORDING TO THE RECORDS IN KALETH, A STORM WITH THIS MUCH POWER HAS ONLY BEEN SEEN ON TYTHON ONCE BEFORE -- 10,000 YEARS AGO -- THE DAY THE THO YOR BROUGHT OUR FOREBEARS TO TYTHON.
THE VERY FORCE THAT GUIDES US SEEMS UNBALANCED.
‹EVERY JE'DAII FELT THE DEATHS WHEN THE ALIEN SHIP CRASHED. KEEN, TOO, WAS A SENSE OF OVERWHELMING DARKNESS. DO YOU BELIEVE, MASTER KORA, THAT THE CRASH CAUSED THIS STORM?›
YES.
TZZZSSTTT

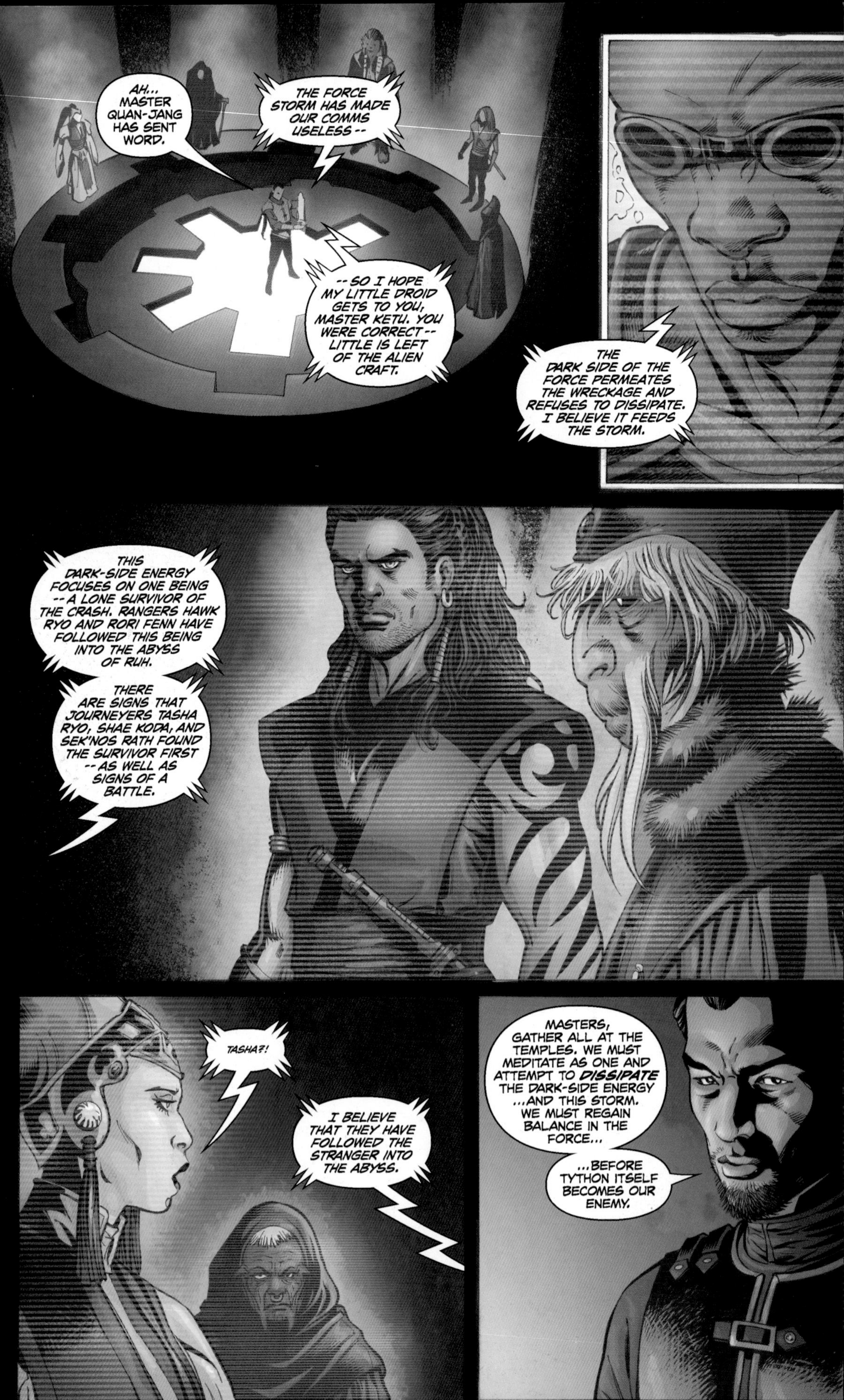
AH... MASTER QUAN-JANG HAS SENT WORD.
THE FORCE STORM HAS MADE OUR COMMS USELESS --
-- SO I HOPE MY LITTLE DROID GETS TO YOU, MASTER KETU. YOU WERE CORRECT -- LITTLE IS LEFT OF THE ALIEN CRAFT.
THE DARK SIDE OF THE FORCE PERMEATES THE WRECKAGE AND REFUSES TO DISSIPATE. I BELIEVE IT FEEDS THE STORM.
THIS DARK-SIDE ENERGY FOCUSES ON ONE BEING -- A LONE SURVIVOR OF THE CRASH. RANGERS HAWK RYO AND RORI FENN HAVE FOLLOWED THIS BEING INTO THE ABYSS OF RUH.
THERE ARE SIGNS THAT JOURNEYERS TASHA RYO, SHAE KODA, AND SEK'NOS RATH FOUND THE SURVIVOR FIRST -- AS WELL AS SIGNS OF A BATTLE.
TASHA?!
I BELIEVE THAT THEY HAVE FOLLOWED THE STRANGER INTO THE ABYSS.
MASTERS, GATHER ALL AT THE TEMPLES. WE MUST MEDITATE AS ONE AND ATTEMPT TO DISSIPATE THE DARK-SIDE ENERGY ...AND THIS STORM. WE MUST REGAIN BALANCE IN THE FORCE...
...BEFORE TYTHON ITSELF BECOMES OUR ENEMY.

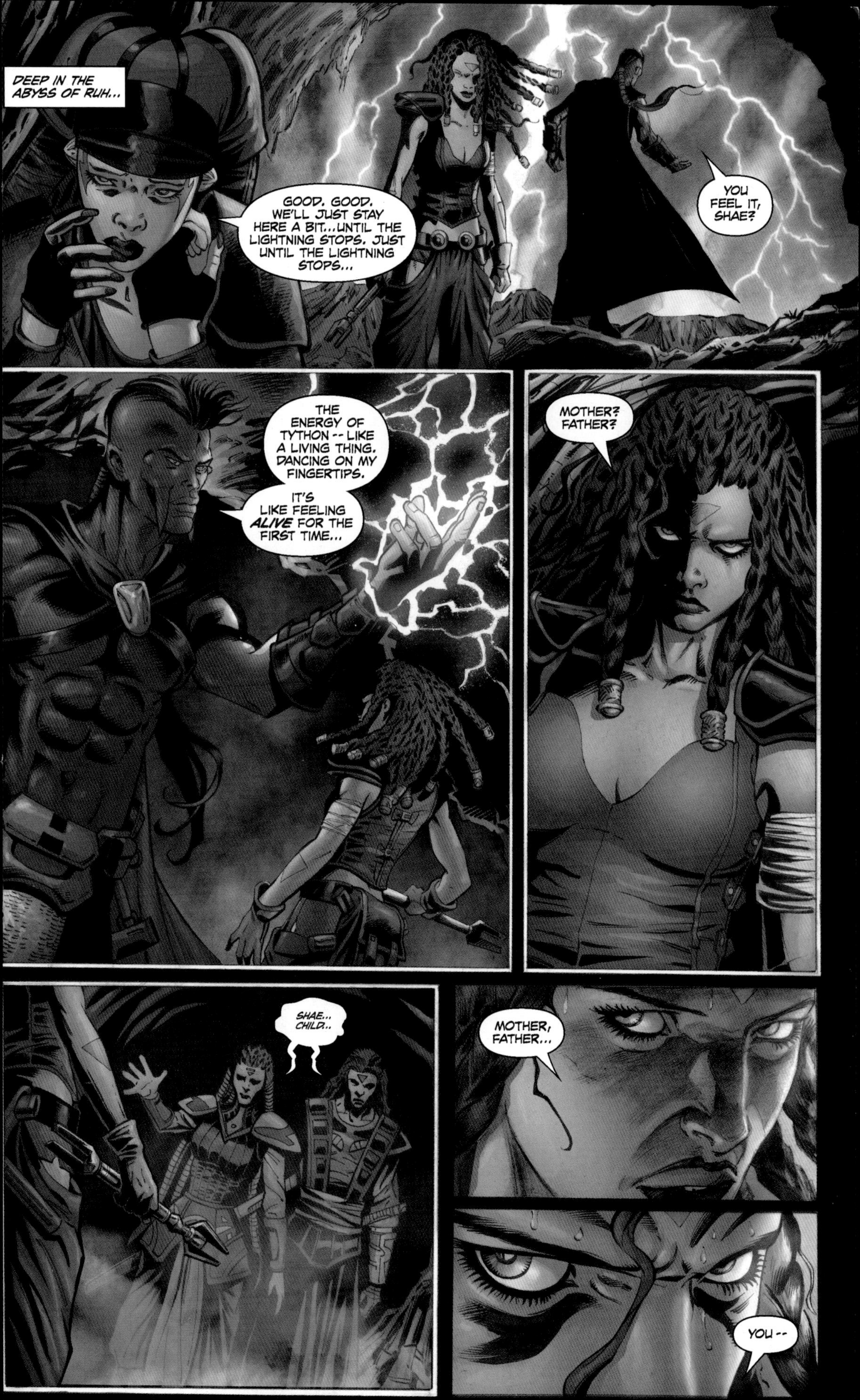
DEEP IN THE ABYSS OF RUH...
GOOD. GOOD. WE'LL JUST STAY HERE A BIT...UNTIL THE LIGHTNING STOPS. JUST UNTIL THE LIGHTNING STOPS...
YOU FEEL IT, SHAE?
THE ENERGY OF TYTHON -- LIKE A LIVING THING. DANCING ON MY FINGERTIPS.
IT'S LIKE FEELING ALIVE FOR THE FIRST TIME...
MOTHER? FATHER?
SHAE... CHILD...
MOTHER, FATHER...
YOU --

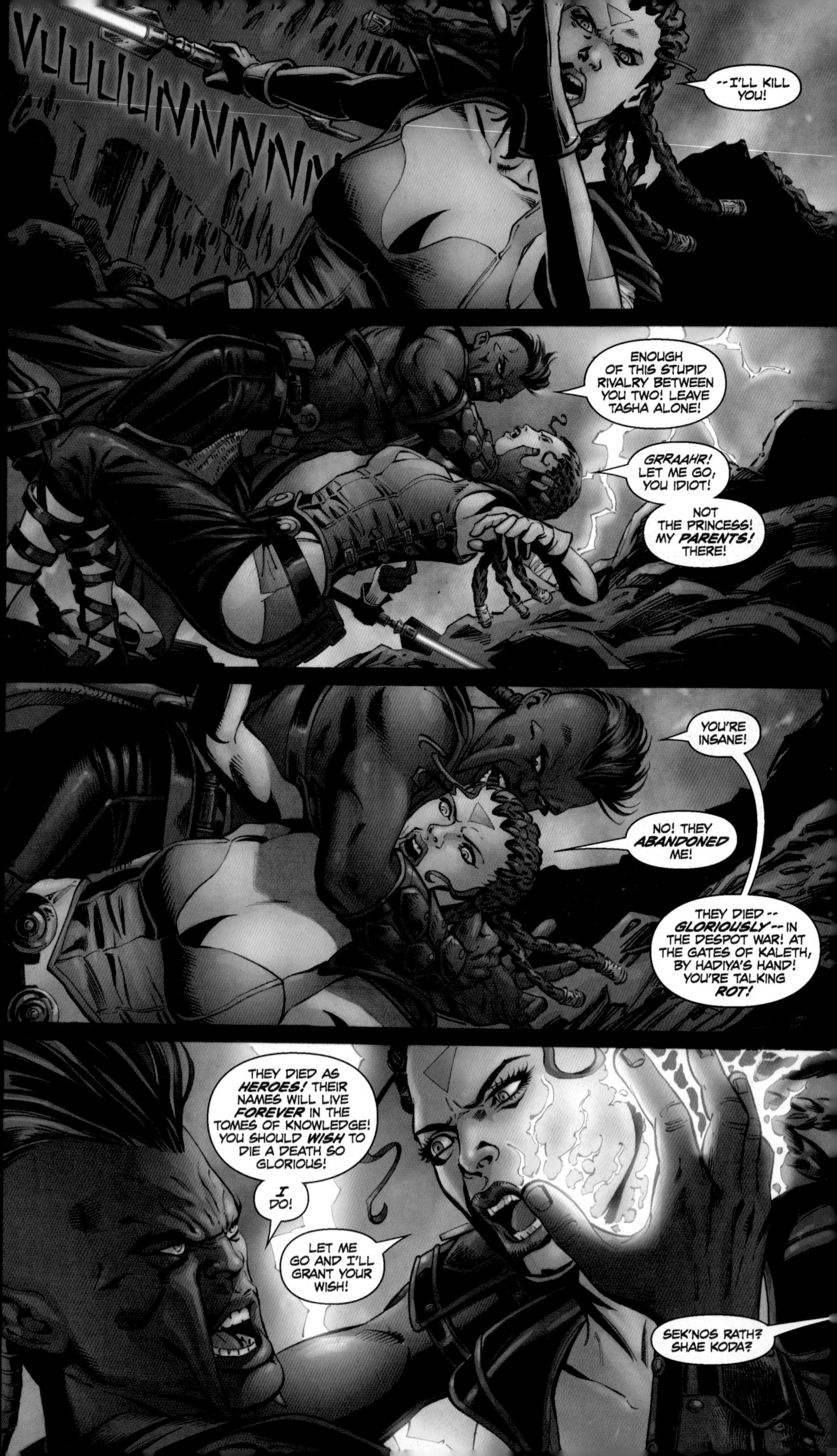
VUUUUNNNNNN
--I'LL KILL YOU!
ENOUGH OF THIS STUPID RIVALRY BETWEEN YOU TWO! LEAVE TASHA ALONE!
GRRAAHR! LET ME GO, YOU IDIOT!
NOT THE PRINCESS! MY PARENTS! THERE!
YOU'RE INSANE!
NO! THEY ABANDONED ME!
THEY DIED -- GLORIOUSLY -- IN THE DESPOT WAR! AT THE GATES OF KALETH, BY HADIYA'S HAND! YOU'RE TALKING ROT!
THEY DIED AS HEROES! THEIR NAMES WILL LIVE FOREVER IN THE TOMES OF KNOWLEDGE! YOU SHOULD WISH TO DIE A DEATH SO GLORIOUS!
I DO!
LET ME GO AND I'LL GRANT YOUR WISH!
SEK'NOS RATH? SHAE KODA?

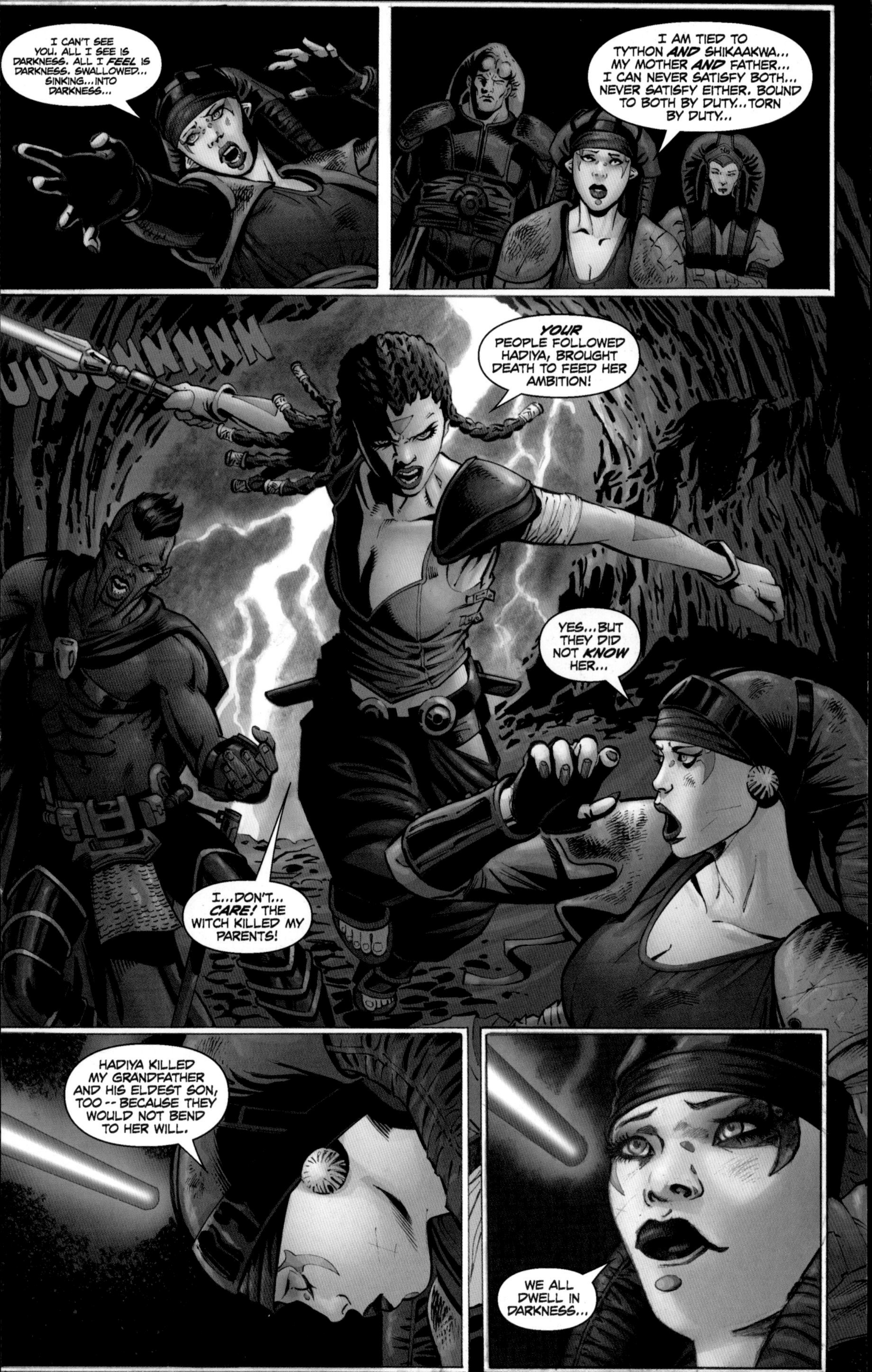
I CAN'T SEE YOU. ALL I SEE IS DARKNESS. ALL I FEEL IS DARKNESS. SWALLOWED... SINKING...INTO DARKNESS...
I AM TIED TO TYTHON AND SHIKAAKWA... MY MOTHER AND FATHER... I CAN NEVER SATISFY BOTH... NEVER SATISFY EITHER. BOUND TO BOTH BY DUTY...TORN BY DUTY...
GUUUHNNNNN
YOUR PEOPLE FOLLOWED HADIYA, BROUGHT DEATH TO FEED HER AMBITION!
YES...BUT THEY DID NOT KNOW HER...
I...DON'T... CARE! THE WITCH KILLED MY PARENTS!
HADIYA KILLED MY GRANDFATHER AND HIS ELDEST SON, TOO -- BECAUSE THEY WOULD NOT BEND TO HER WILL.
WE ALL DWELL IN DARKNESS...

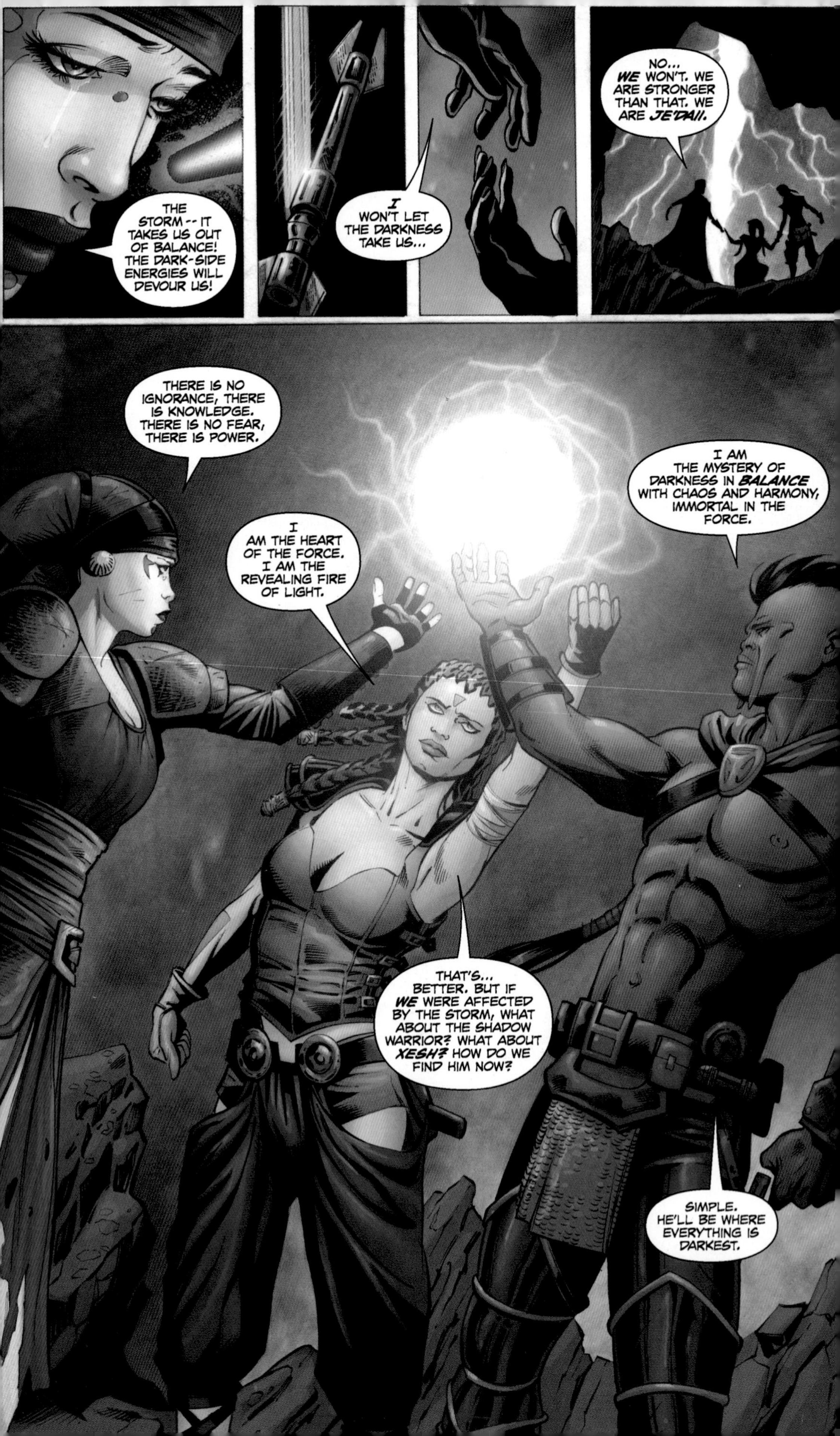
THE STORM -- IT TAKES US OUT OF BALANCE! THE DARK-SIDE ENERGIES WILL DEVOUR US!
I WON'T LET THE DARKNESS TAKE US...
NO... WE WON'T. WE ARE STRONGER THAN THAT. WE ARE JE'DAII.
THERE IS NO IGNORANCE, THERE IS KNOWLEDGE. THERE IS NO FEAR, THERE IS POWER.
I AM THE HEART OF THE FORCE. I AM THE REVEALING FIRE OF LIGHT.
I AM THE MYSTERY OF DARKNESS IN BALANCE WITH CHAOS AND HARMONY, IMMORTAL IN THE FORCE.
THAT'S... BETTER. BUT IF WE WERE AFFECTED BY THE STORM, WHAT ABOUT THE SHADOW WARRIOR? WHAT ABOUT XESH? HOW DO WE FIND HIM NOW?
SIMPLE. HE'LL BE WHERE EVERYTHING IS DARKEST.

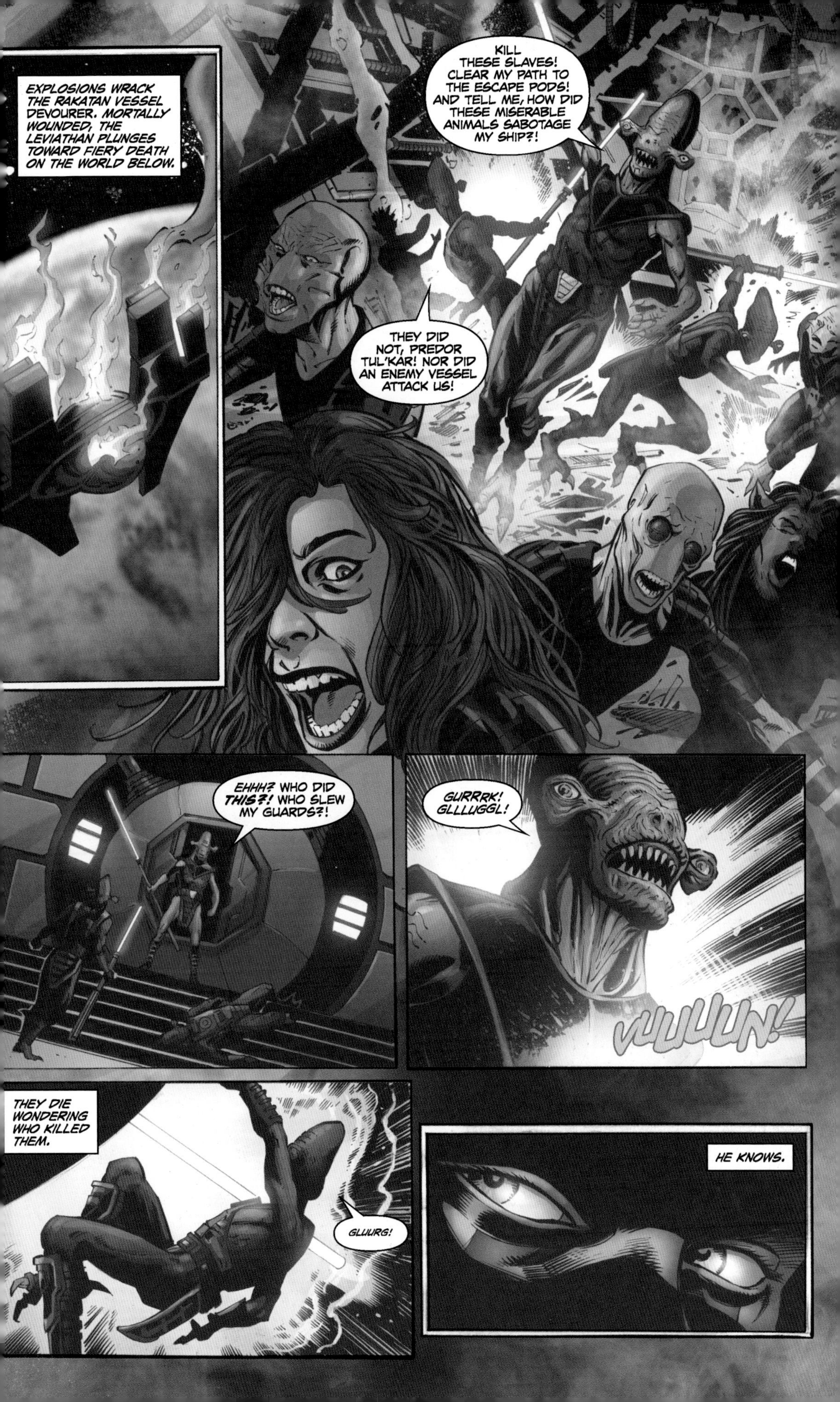
EXPLOSIONS WRACK THE RAKATAN VESSEL DEVOURER. MORTALLY WOUNDED, THE LEVIATHAN PLUNGES TOWARD FIERY DEATH ON THE WORLD BELOW.
KILL THESE SLAVES! CLEAR MY PATH TO THE ESCAPE PODS! AND TELL ME, HOW DID THESE MISERABLE ANIMALS SABOTAGE MY SHIP?!
THEY DID NOT, PREDOR TUL'KAR! NOR DID AN ENEMY VESSEL ATTACK US!
EHHH? WHO DID THIS?! WHO SLEW MY GUARDS?!
GURRRK! GLLLUGGL!
VUUUUN!
THEY DIE WONDERING WHO KILLED THEM.
GLUURG!
HE KNOWS.

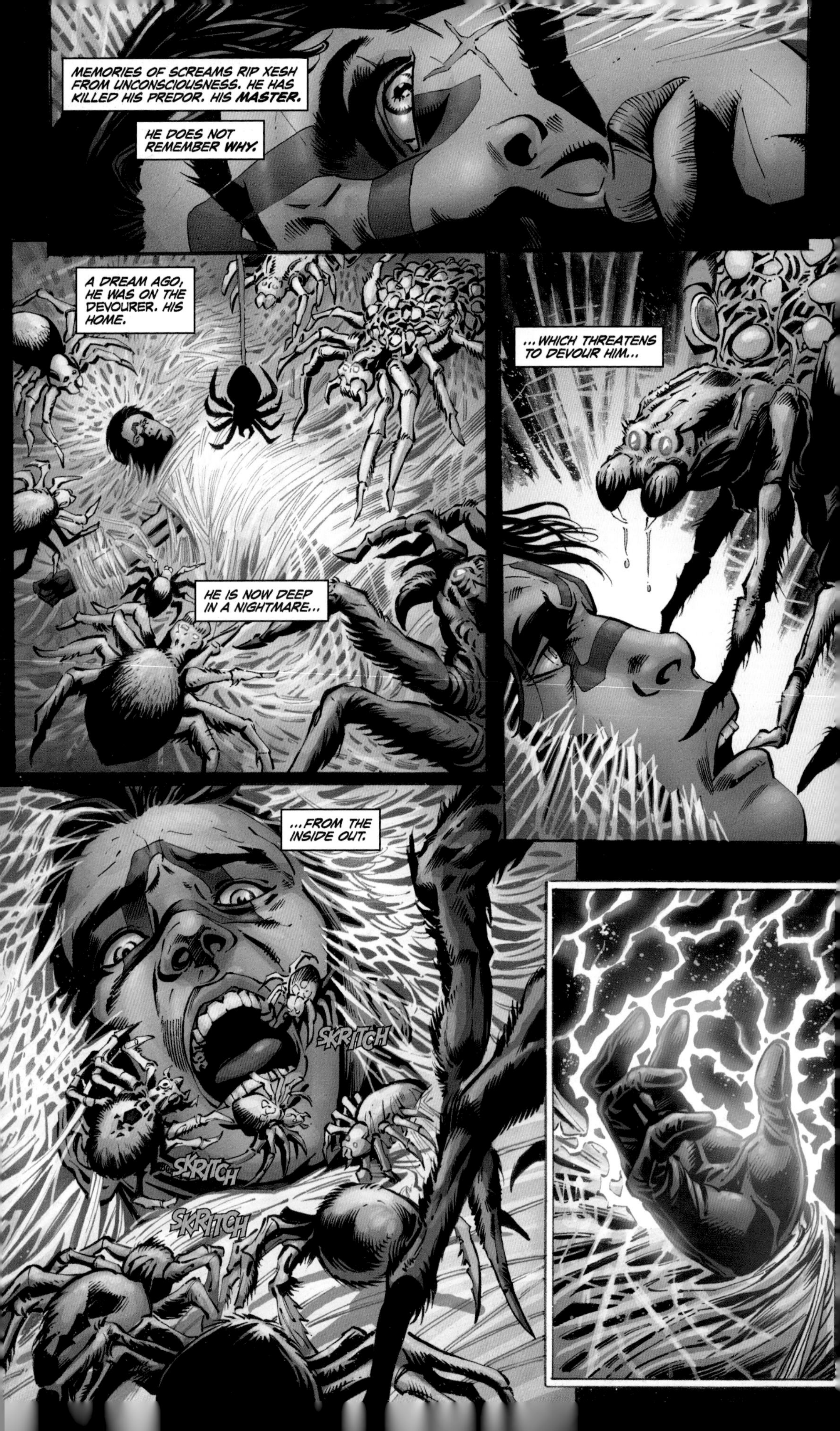
MEMORIES OF SCREAMS RIP XESH FROM UNCONSCIOUSNESS. HE HAS KILLED HIS PREDOR. HIS MASTER.
HE DOES NOT REMEMBER WHY.
A DREAM AGO, HE WAS ON THE DEVOURER. HIS HOME.
HE IS NOW DEEP IN A NIGHTMARE...
...WHICH THREATENS TO DEVOUR HIM...
...FROM THE INSIDE OUT.
SKRITCH
SKRITCH
SKRITCH

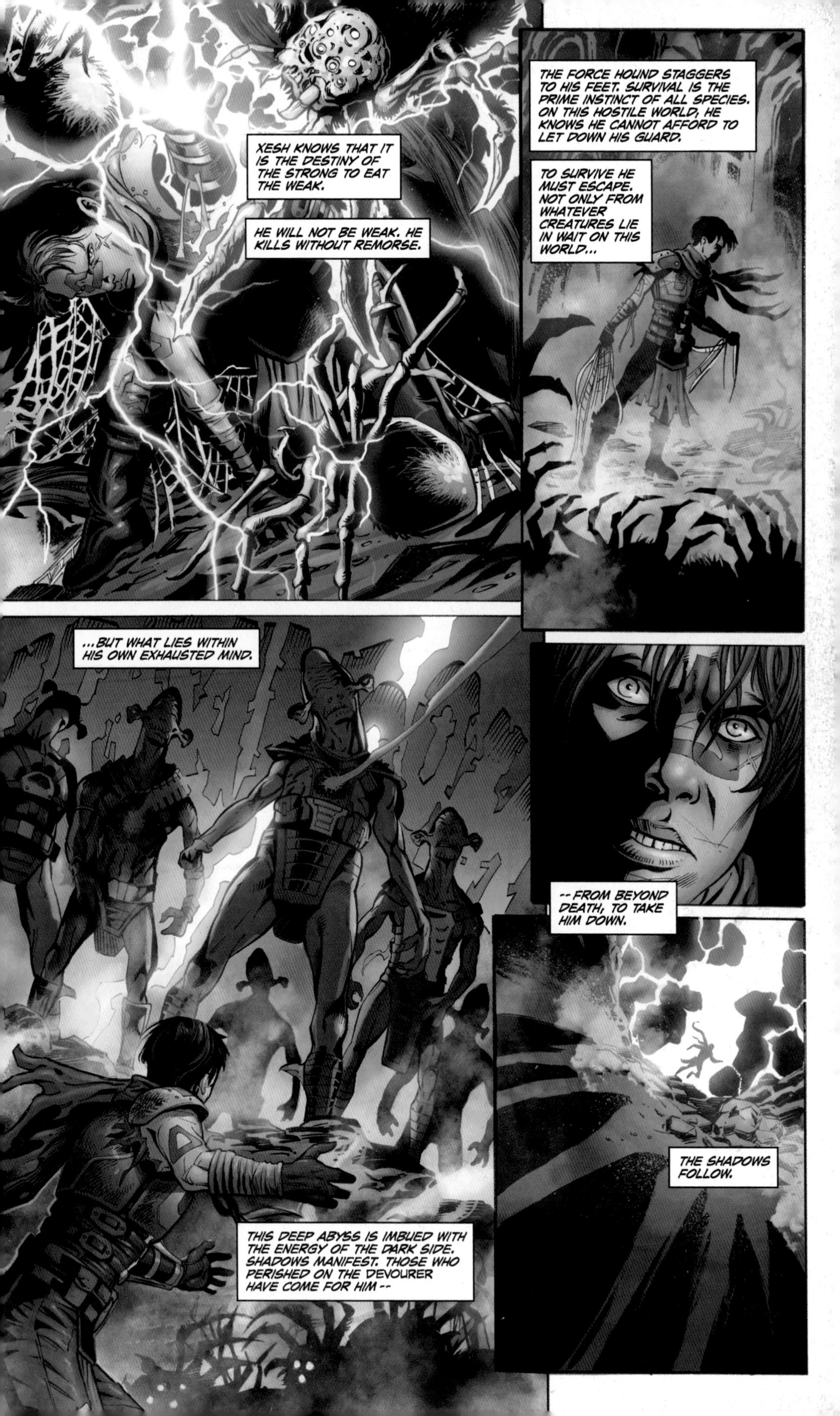
XESH KNOWS THAT IT IS THE DESTINY OF THE STRONG TO EAT THE WEAK.
HE WILL NOT BE WEAK. HE KILLS WITHOUT REMORSE.
THE FORCE HOUND STAGGERS TO HIS FEET. SURVIVAL IS THE PRIME INSTINCT OF ALL SPECIES. ON THIS HOSTILE WORLD, HE KNOWS HE CANNOT AFFORD TO LET DOWN HIS GUARD.
TO SURVIVE HE MUST ESCAPE. NOT ONLY FROM WHATEVER CREATURES LIE IN WAIT ON THIS WORLD...
...BUT WHAT LIES WITHIN HIS OWN EXHAUSTED MIND.
THIS DEEP ABYSS IS IMBUED WITH THE ENERGY OF THE DARK SIDE. SHADOWS MANIFEST. THOSE WHO PERISHED ON THE DEVOURER HAVE COME FOR HIM--
--FROM BEYOND DEATH, TO TAKE HIM DOWN.
THE SHADOWS FOLLOW.

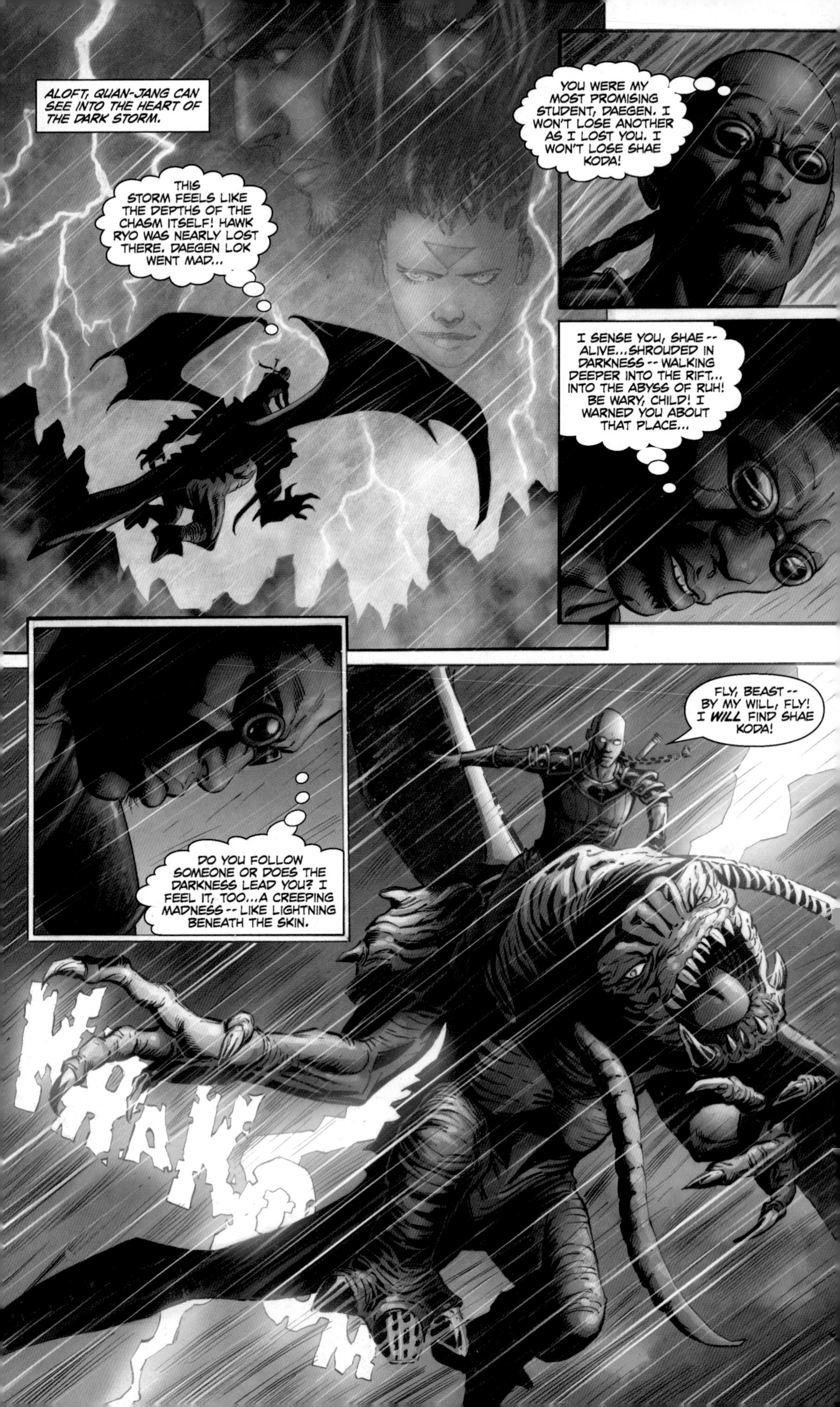

ALOFT, QUAN-JANG CAN SEE INTO THE HEART OF THE DARK STORM.
THIS STORM FEELS LIKE THE DEPTHS OF THE CHASM ITSELF! HAWK RYO WAS NEARLY LOST THERE. DAEGEN LOK WENT MAD...
YOU WERE MY MOST PROMISING STUDENT, DAEGEN. I WON'T LOSE ANOTHER AS I LOST YOU. I WON'T LOSE SHAE KODA!
I SENSE YOU, SHAE -- ALIVE...SHROUDED IN DARKNESS -- WALKING DEEPER INTO THE RIFT... INTO THE ABYSS OF RUH! BE WARY, CHILD! I WARNED YOU ABOUT THAT PLACE...
DO YOU FOLLOW SOMEONE OR DOES THE DARKNESS LEAD YOU? I FEEL IT, TOO...A CREEPING MADNESS -- LIKE LIGHTNING BENEATH THE SKIN.
FLY, BEAST -- BY MY WILL, FLY! I *WILL* FIND SHAE KODA!

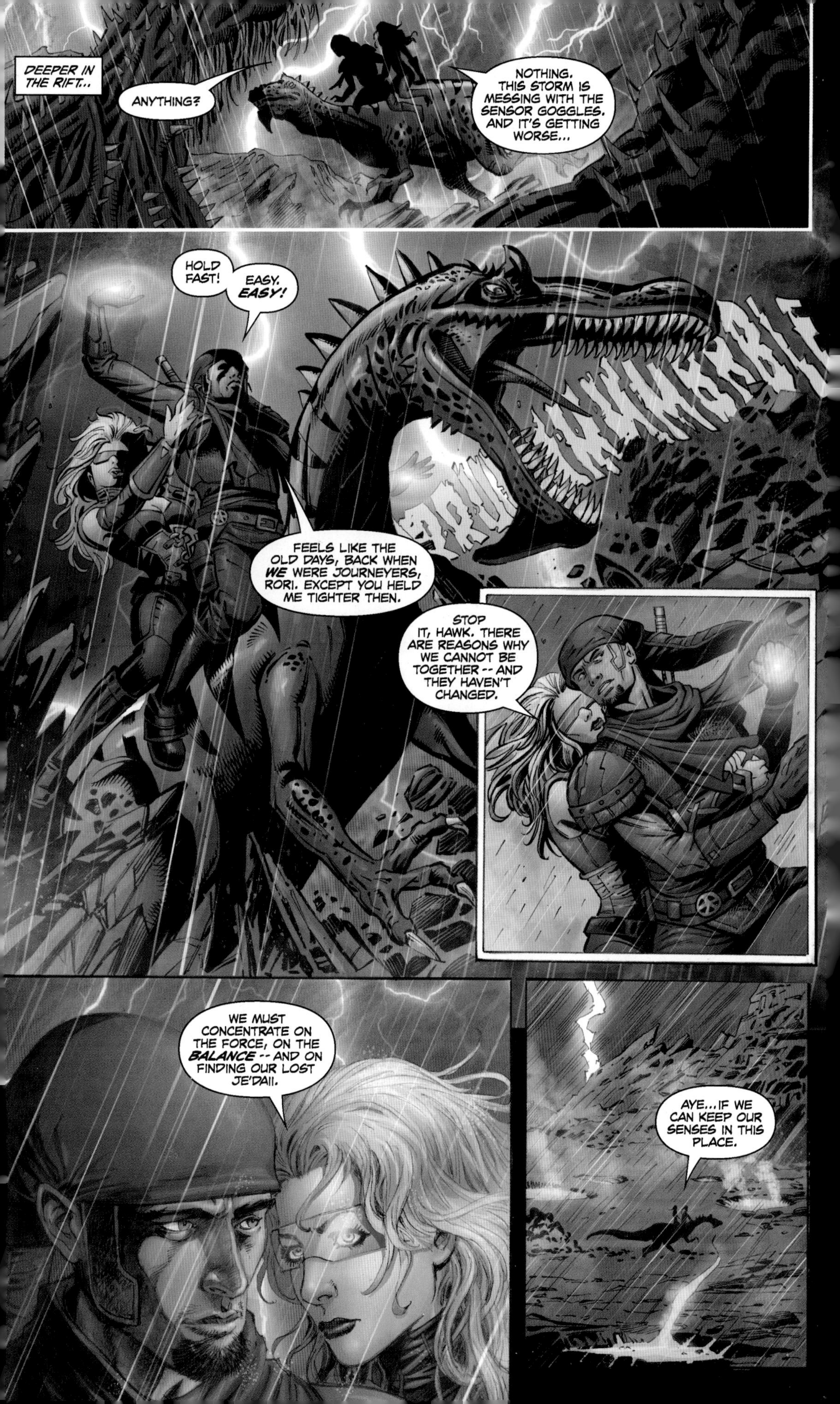

DEEPER IN THE RIFT...
ANYTHING?
NOTHING. THIS STORM IS MESSING WITH THE SENSOR GOGGLES. AND IT'S GETTING WORSE...
HOLD FAST!
EASY. EASY!
RRRUMMMBLE
FEELS LIKE THE OLD DAYS, BACK WHEN WE WERE JOURNEYERS, RORI. EXCEPT YOU HELD ME TIGHTER THEN.
STOP IT, HAWK. THERE ARE REASONS WHY WE CANNOT BE TOGETHER -- AND THEY HAVEN'T CHANGED.
WE MUST CONCENTRATE ON THE FORCE, ON THE BALANCE -- AND ON FINDING OUR LOST JE'DAII.
AYE...IF WE CAN KEEP OUR SENSES IN THIS PLACE.

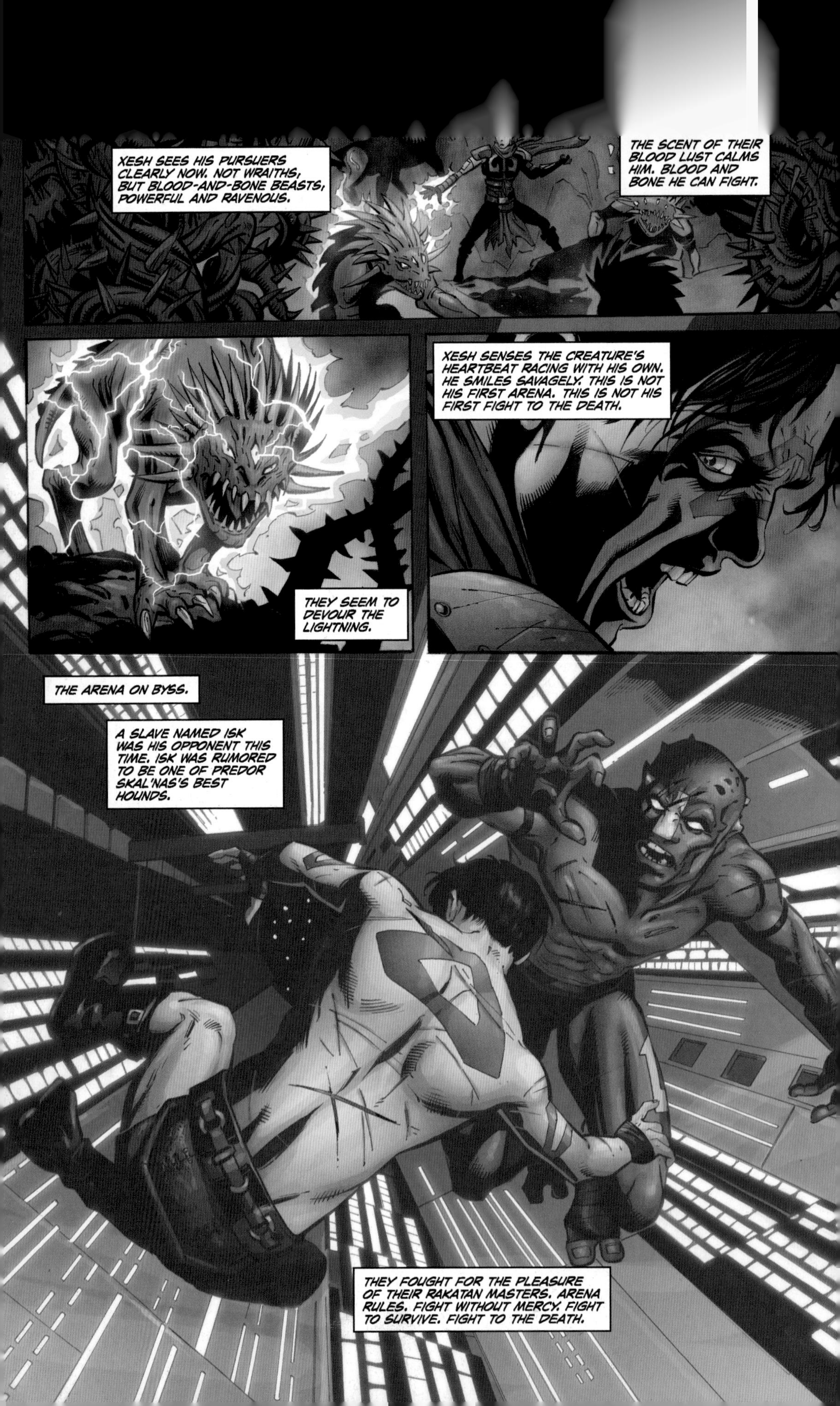
XESH SEES HIS PURSUERS CLEARLY NOW. NOT WRAITHS, BUT BLOOD-AND-BONE BEASTS, POWERFUL AND RAVENOUS.
THE SCENT OF THEIR BLOOD LUST CALMS HIM. BLOOD AND BONE HE CAN FIGHT.
THEY SEEM TO DEVOUR THE LIGHTNING.
XESH SENSES THE CREATURE'S HEARTBEAT RACING WITH HIS OWN. HE SMILES SAVAGELY. THIS IS NOT HIS FIRST ARENA. THIS IS NOT HIS FIRST FIGHT TO THE DEATH.
THE ARENA ON BYSS.
A SLAVE NAMED ISK WAS HIS OPPONENT THIS TIME. ISK WAS RUMORED TO BE ONE OF PREDOR SKAL'NAS'S BEST HOUNDS.
THEY FOUGHT FOR THE PLEASURE OF THEIR RAKATAN MASTERS. ARENA RULES. FIGHT WITHOUT MERCY. FIGHT TO SURVIVE. FIGHT TO THE DEATH.

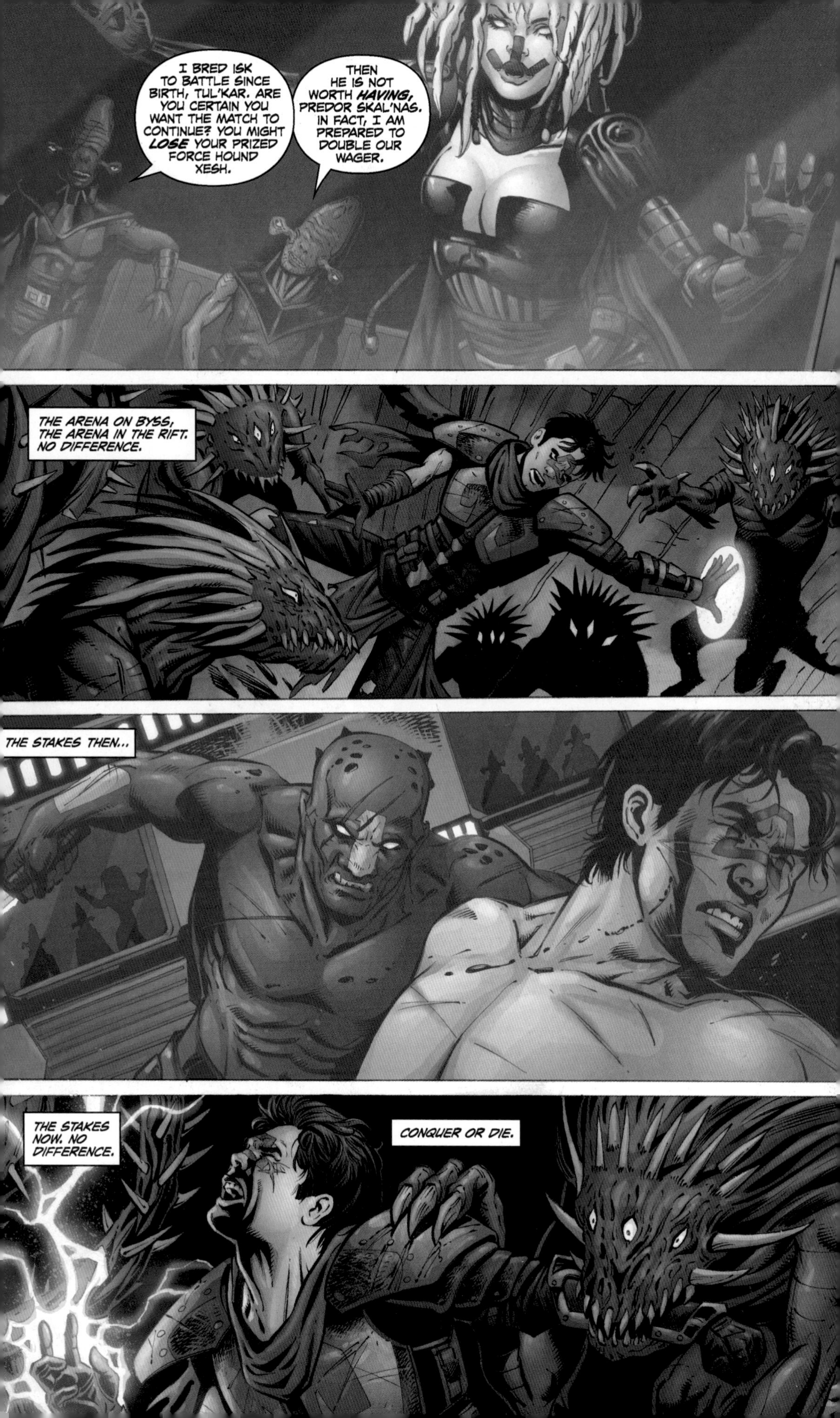
I BRED ISK TO BATTLE SINCE BIRTH, TUL'KAR. ARE YOU CERTAIN YOU WANT THE MATCH TO CONTINUE? YOU MIGHT *LOSE* YOUR PRIZED FORCE HOUND XESH.
THEN HE IS NOT WORTH *HAVING,* PREDOR SKAL'NAS. IN FACT, I AM PREPARED TO DOUBLE OUR WAGER.
THE ARENA ON BYSS, THE ARENA IN THE RIFT. NO DIFFERENCE.
THE STAKES THEN...
THE STAKES NOW. NO DIFFERENCE.
CONQUER OR DIE.

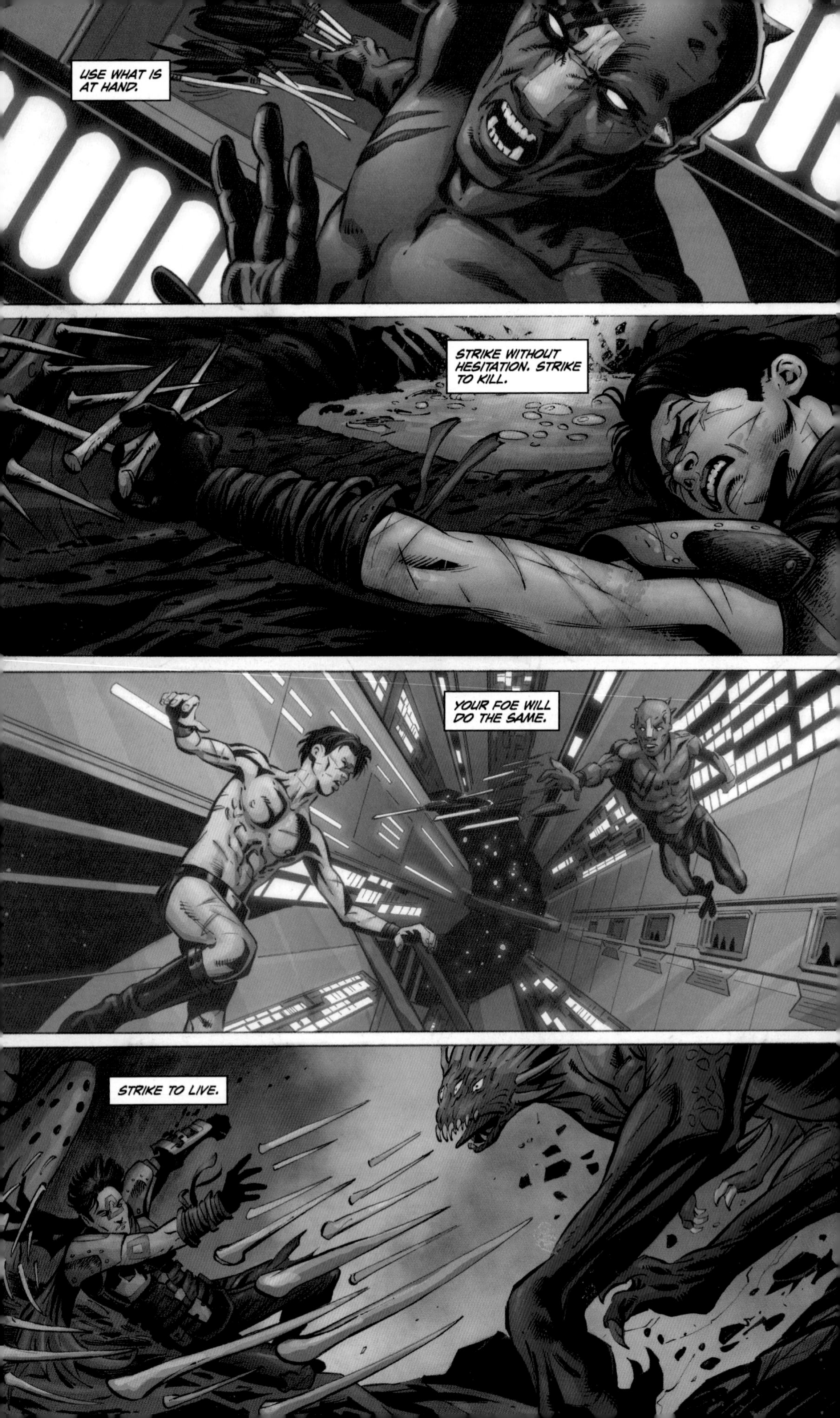
USE WHAT IS AT HAND.
STRIKE WITHOUT HESITATION. STRIKE TO KILL.
YOUR FOE WILL DO THE SAME.
STRIKE TO LIVE.

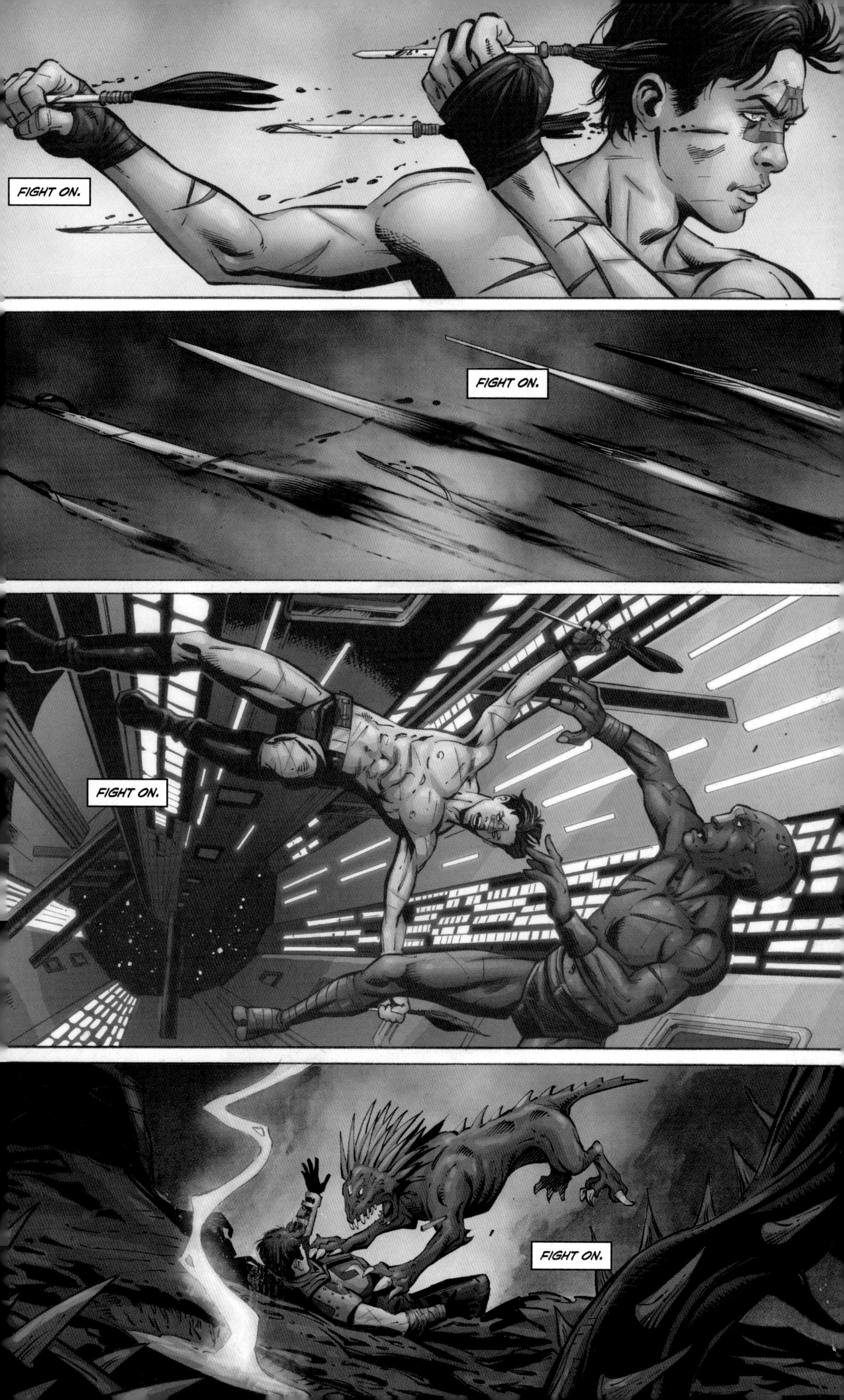
FIGHT ON.
FIGHT ON.
FIGHT ON.
FIGHT ON.

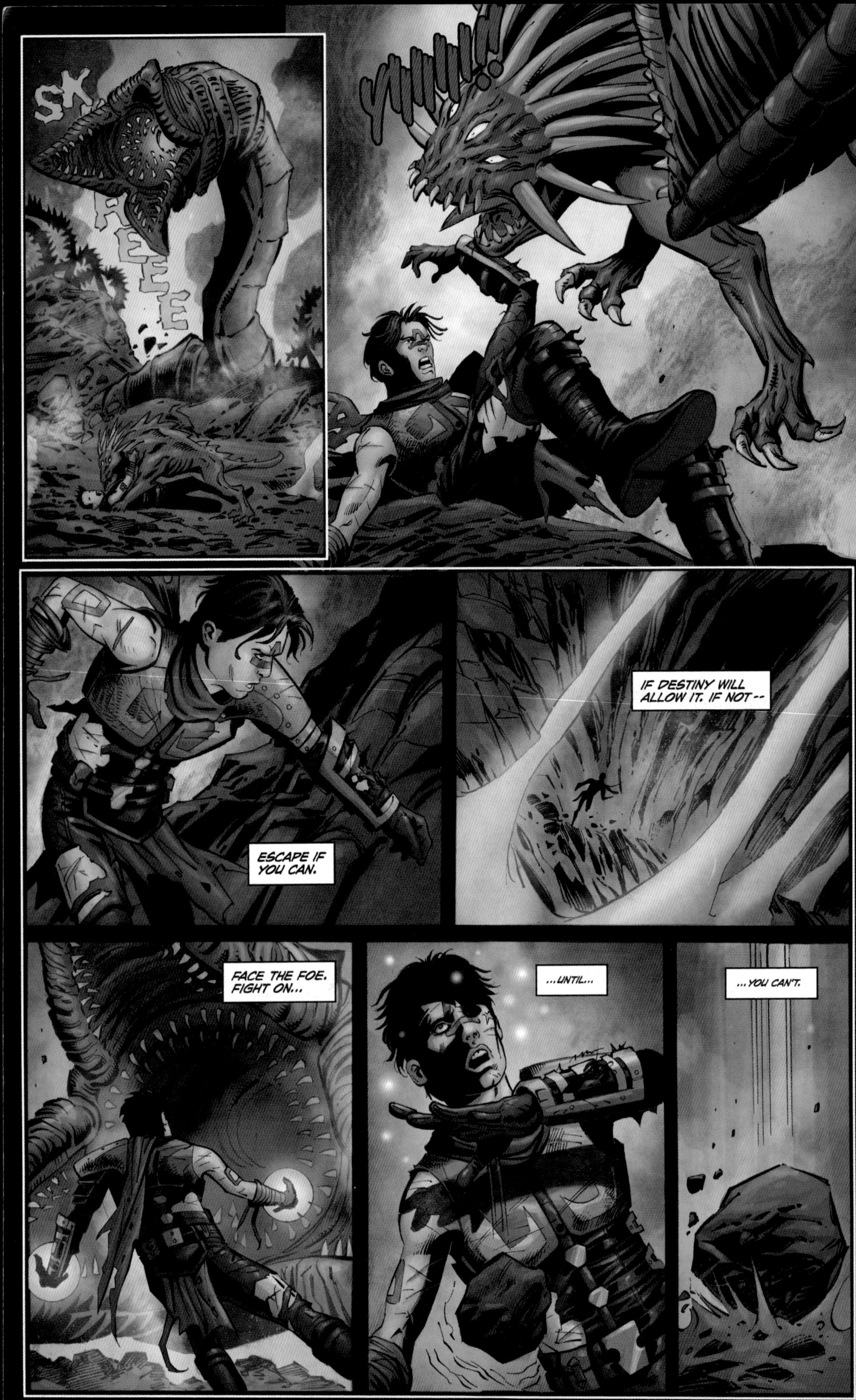
SKREEEE
YIIIIIII!!
ESCAPE IF YOU CAN.
IF DESTINY WILL ALLOW IT. IF NOT--
FACE THE FOE. FIGHT ON...
...UNTIL...
...YOU CAN'T.

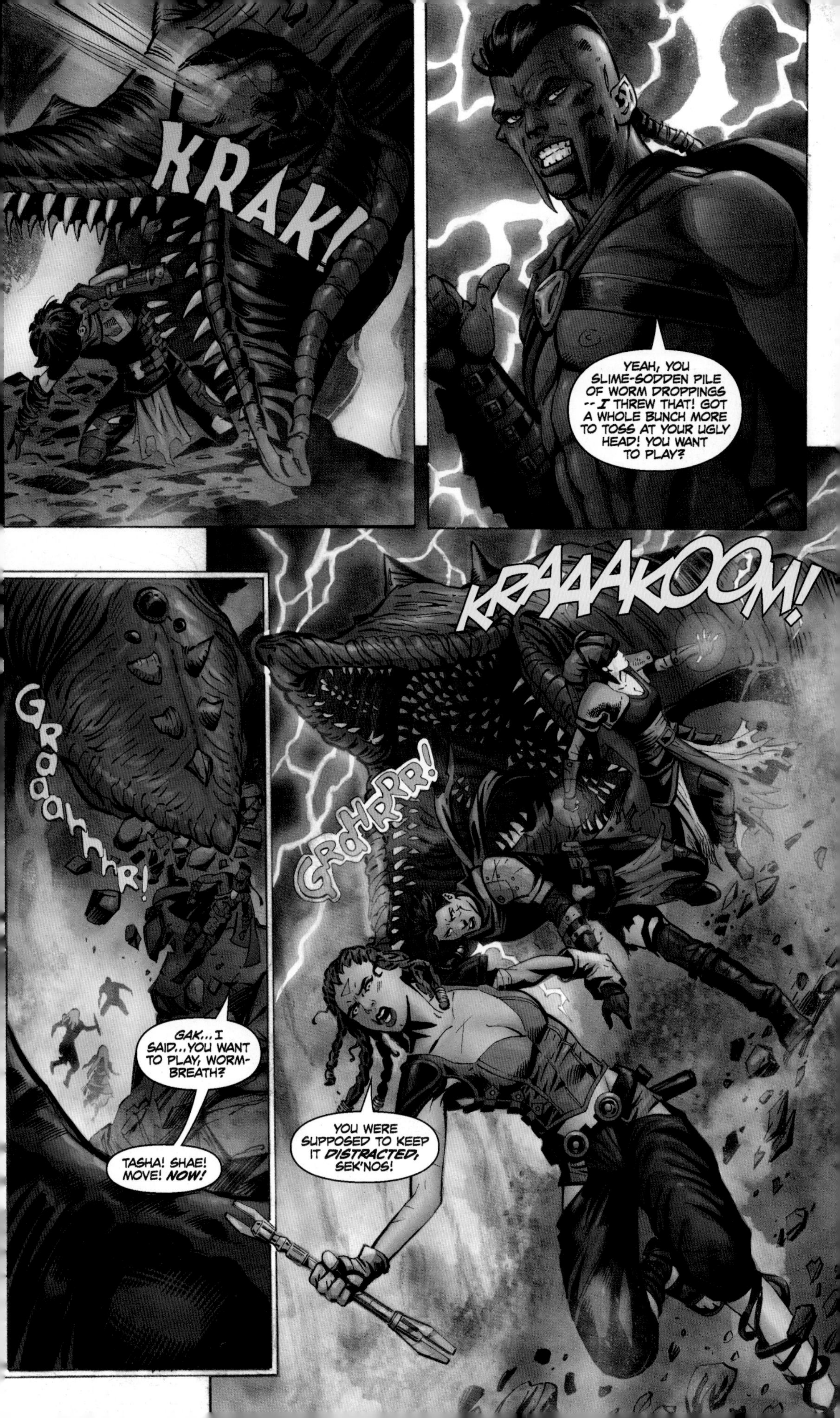
KRAK!
YEAH, YOU SLIME-SODDEN PILE OF WORM DROPPINGS -- I THREW THAT! GOT A WHOLE BUNCH MORE TO TOSS AT YOUR UGLY HEAD! YOU WANT TO PLAY?
Graaaarhhhr!
GAK... I SAID... YOU WANT TO PLAY, WORM-BREATH?
TASHA! SHAE! MOVE! NOW!
KRAAAKOOM!
GRAHRRR!
YOU WERE SUPPOSED TO KEEP IT DISTRACTED, SEK'NOS!

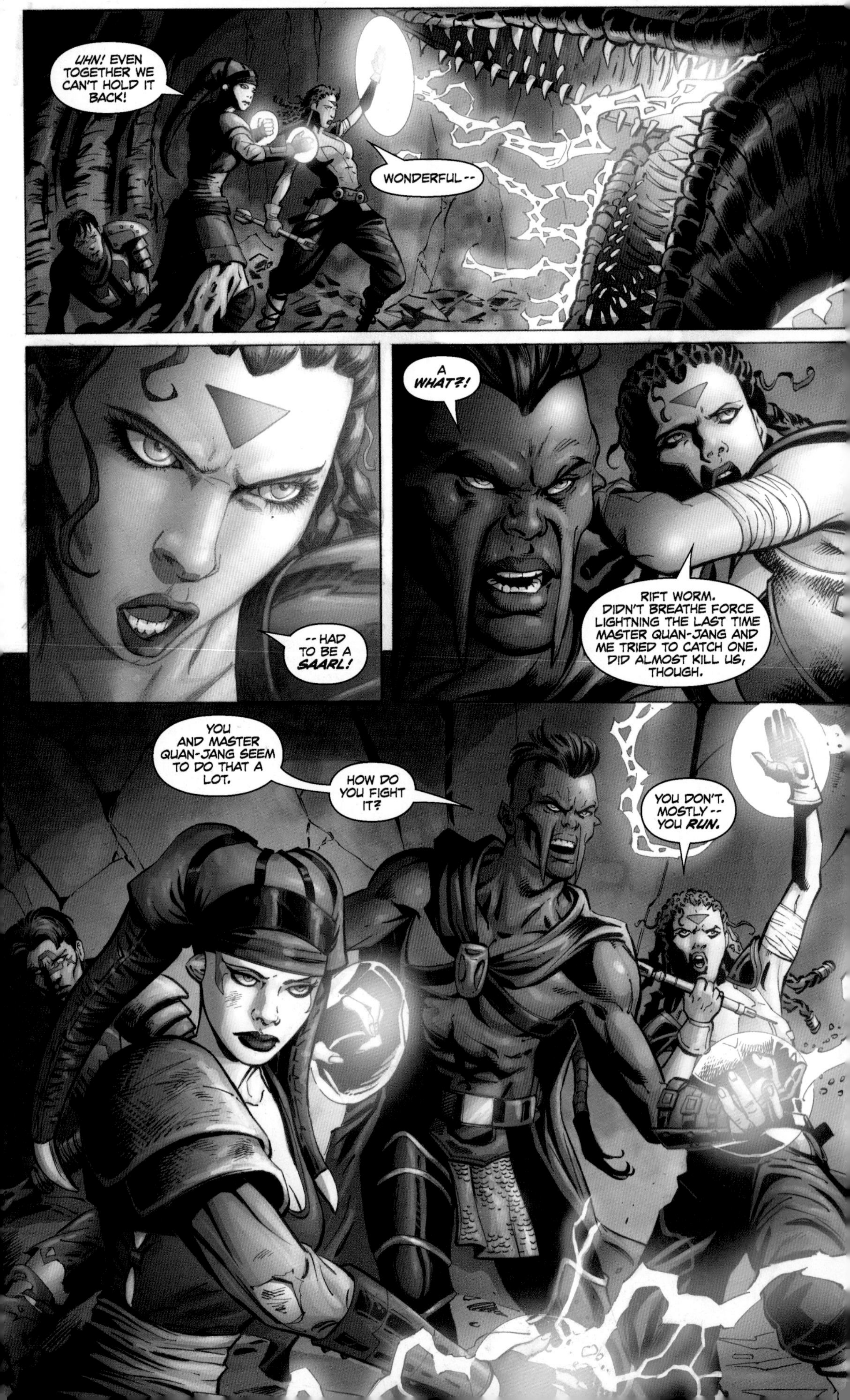
UHN! EVEN TOGETHER WE CAN'T HOLD IT BACK!
WONDERFUL--
--HAD TO BE A SAARL!
A WHAT?!
RIFT WORM. DIDN'T BREATHE FORCE LIGHTNING THE LAST TIME MASTER QUAN-JANG AND ME TRIED TO CATCH ONE. DID ALMOST KILL US, THOUGH.
YOU AND MASTER QUAN-JANG SEEM TO DO THAT A LOT.
HOW DO YOU FIGHT IT?
YOU DON'T. MOSTLY-- YOU RUN.

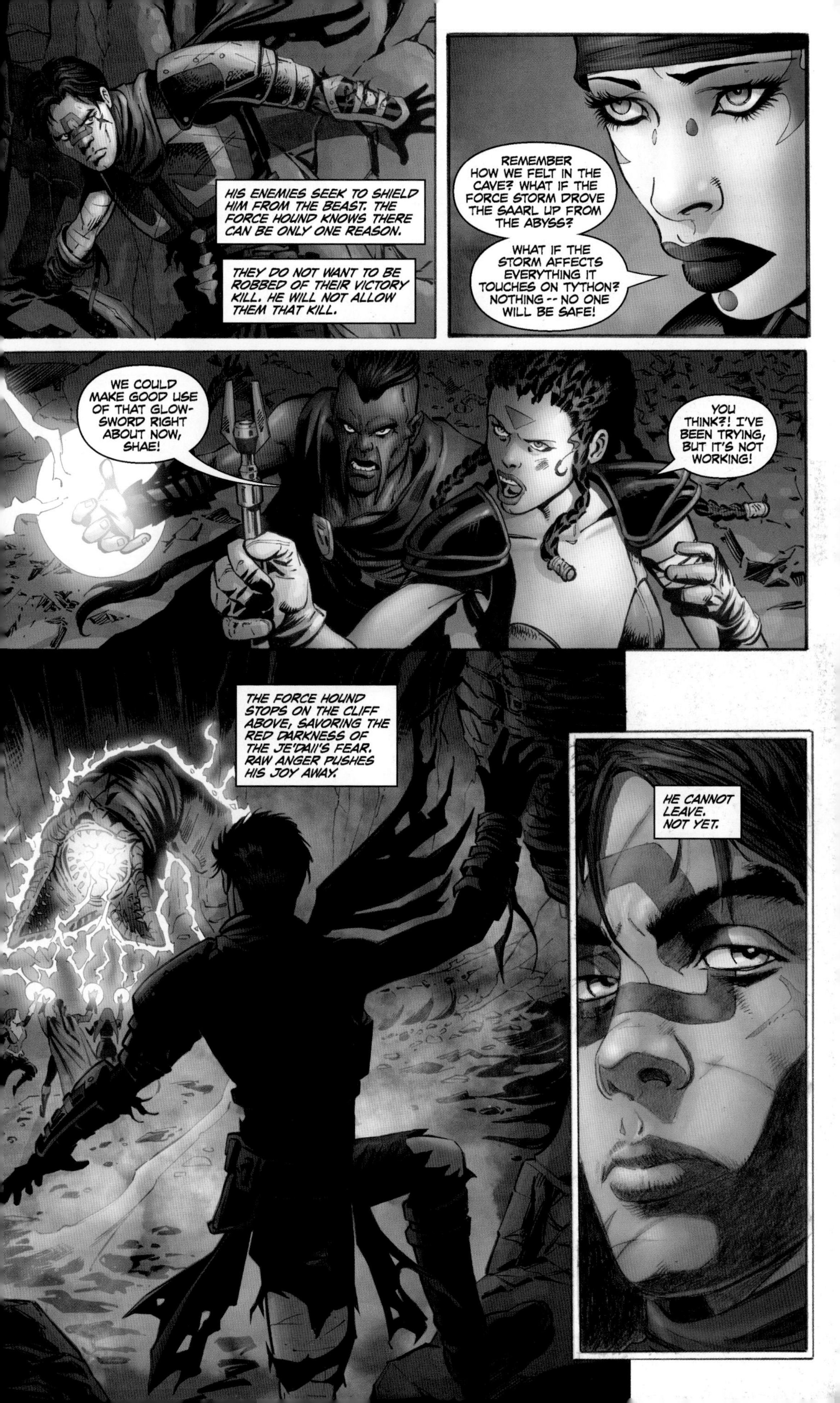
HIS ENEMIES SEEK TO SHIELD HIM FROM THE BEAST. THE FORCE HOUND KNOWS THERE CAN BE ONLY ONE REASON.
THEY DO NOT WANT TO BE ROBBED OF THEIR VICTORY KILL. HE WILL NOT ALLOW THEM THAT KILL.
REMEMBER HOW WE FELT IN THE CAVE? WHAT IF THE FORCE STORM DROVE THE SAARL UP FROM THE ABYSS?
WHAT IF THE STORM AFFECTS EVERYTHING IT TOUCHES ON TYTHON? NOTHING -- NO ONE WILL BE SAFE!
WE COULD MAKE GOOD USE OF THAT GLOW-SWORD RIGHT ABOUT NOW, SHAE!
YOU THINK?! I'VE BEEN TRYING, BUT IT'S NOT WORKING!
THE FORCE HOUND STOPS ON THE CLIFF ABOVE, SAVORING THE RED DARKNESS OF THE JE'DAII'S FEAR. RAW ANGER PUSHES HIS JOY AWAY.
HE CANNOT LEAVE. NOT YET.

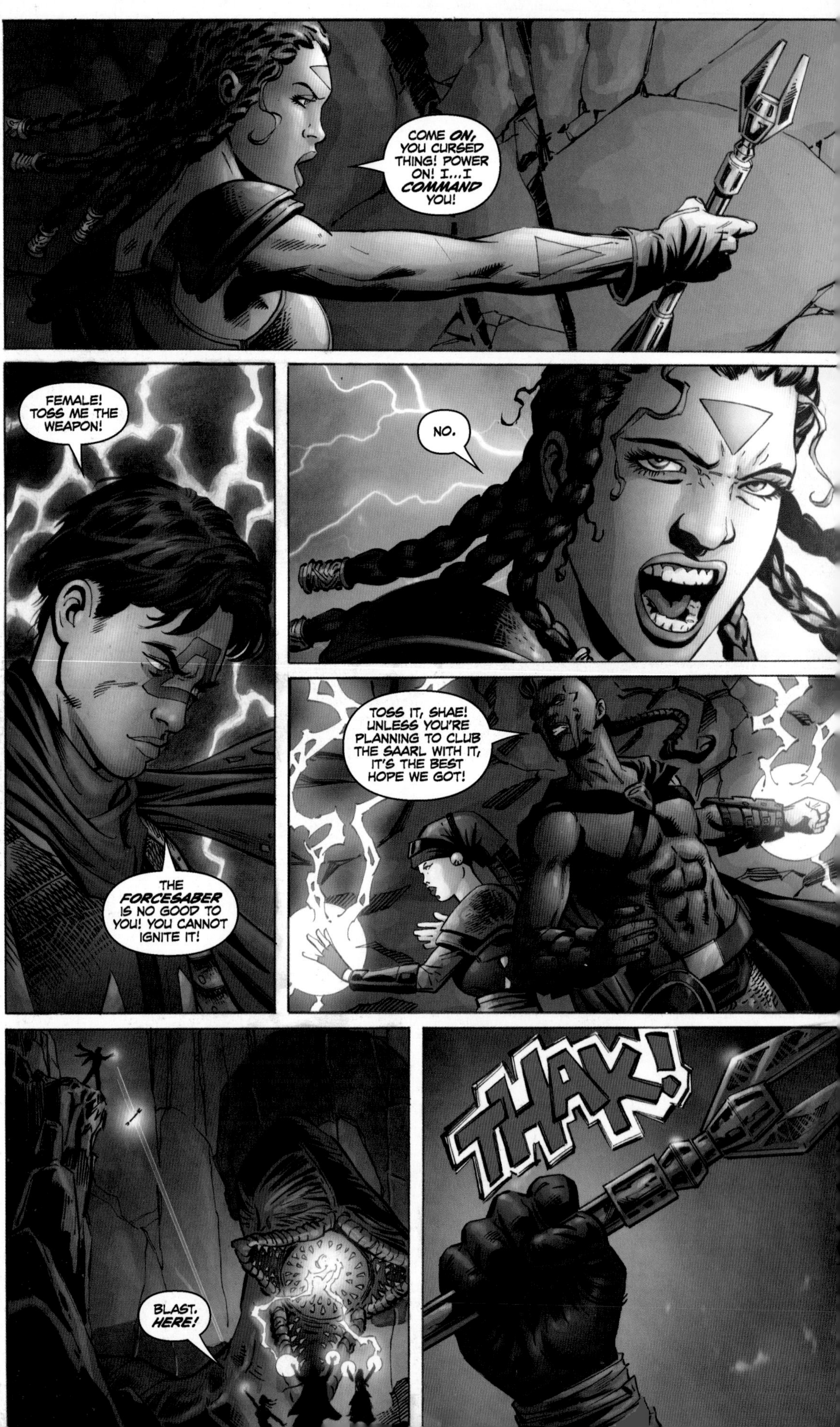
COME ON, YOU CURSED THING! POWER ON! I...I COMMAND YOU!
FEMALE! TOSS ME THE WEAPON!
NO.
THE FORCESABER IS NO GOOD TO YOU! YOU CANNOT IGNITE IT!
TOSS IT, SHAE! UNLESS YOU'RE PLANNING TO CLUB THE SAARL WITH IT, IT'S THE BEST HOPE WE GOT!
BLAST. HERE!
THAK!

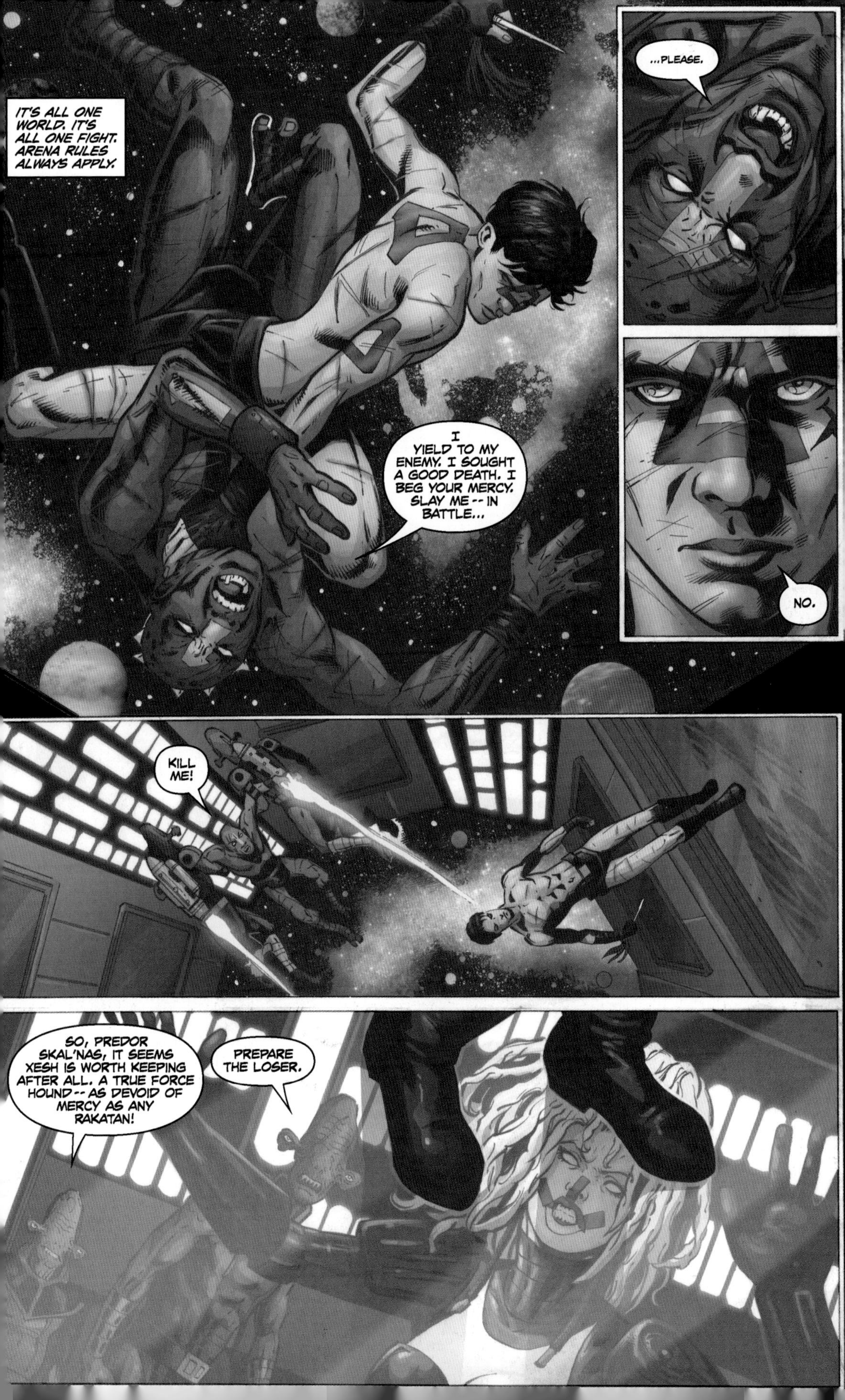
IT'S ALL ONE WORLD. IT'S ALL ONE FIGHT. ARENA RULES ALWAYS APPLY.
I YIELD TO MY ENEMY. I SOUGHT A GOOD DEATH. I BEG YOUR MERCY. SLAY ME -- IN BATTLE...
...PLEASE.
NO.
KILL ME!
SO, PREDOR SKAL'NAS, IT SEEMS XESH IS WORTH KEEPING AFTER ALL. A TRUE FORCE HOUND -- AS DEVOID OF MERCY AS ANY RAKATAN!
PREPARE THE LOSER.

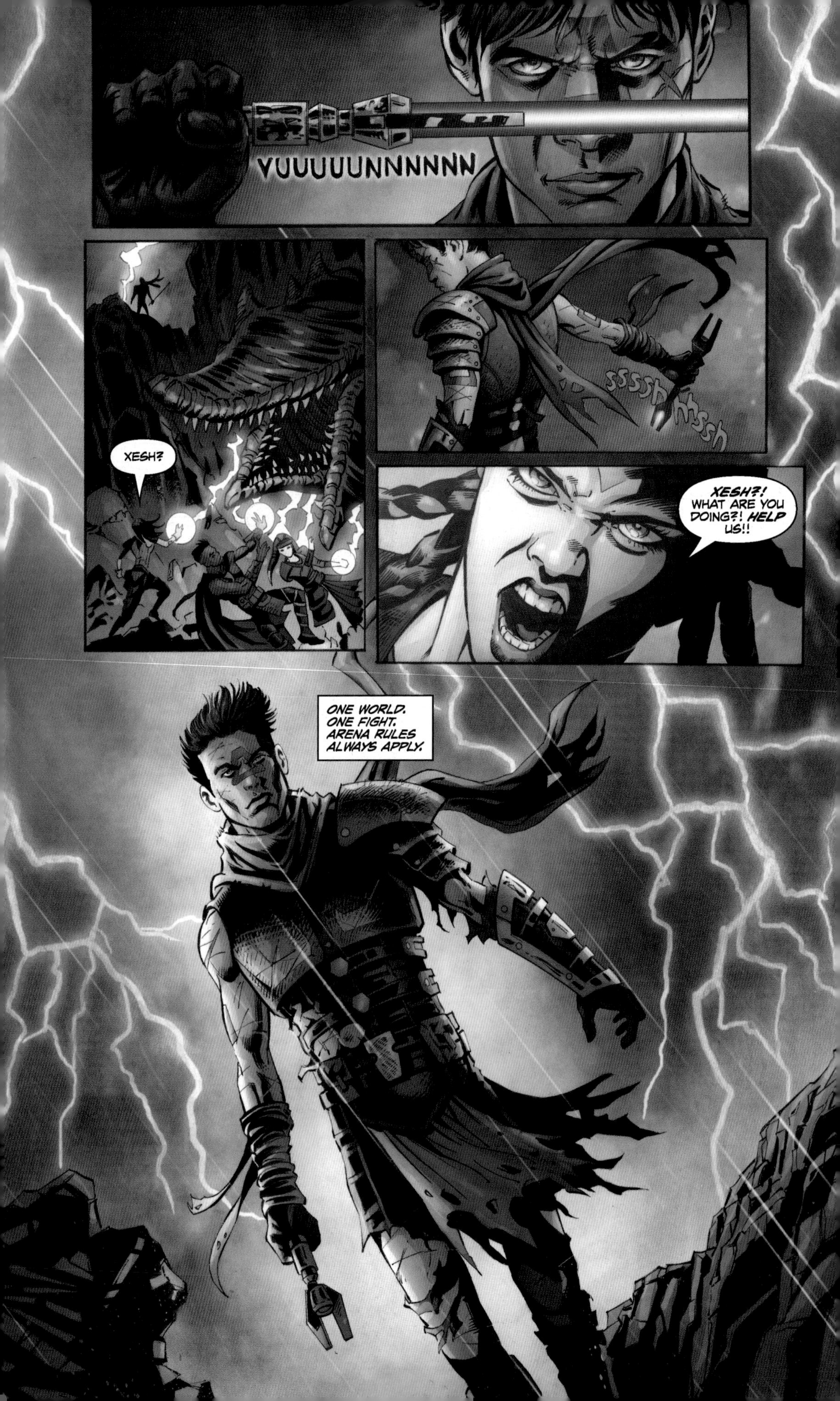
VUUUUUNNNNNN
XESH?
SSSSHHSSH
XESH?! WHAT ARE YOU DOING?! HELP US!!
ONE WORLD. ONE FIGHT. ARENA RULES ALWAYS APPLY.

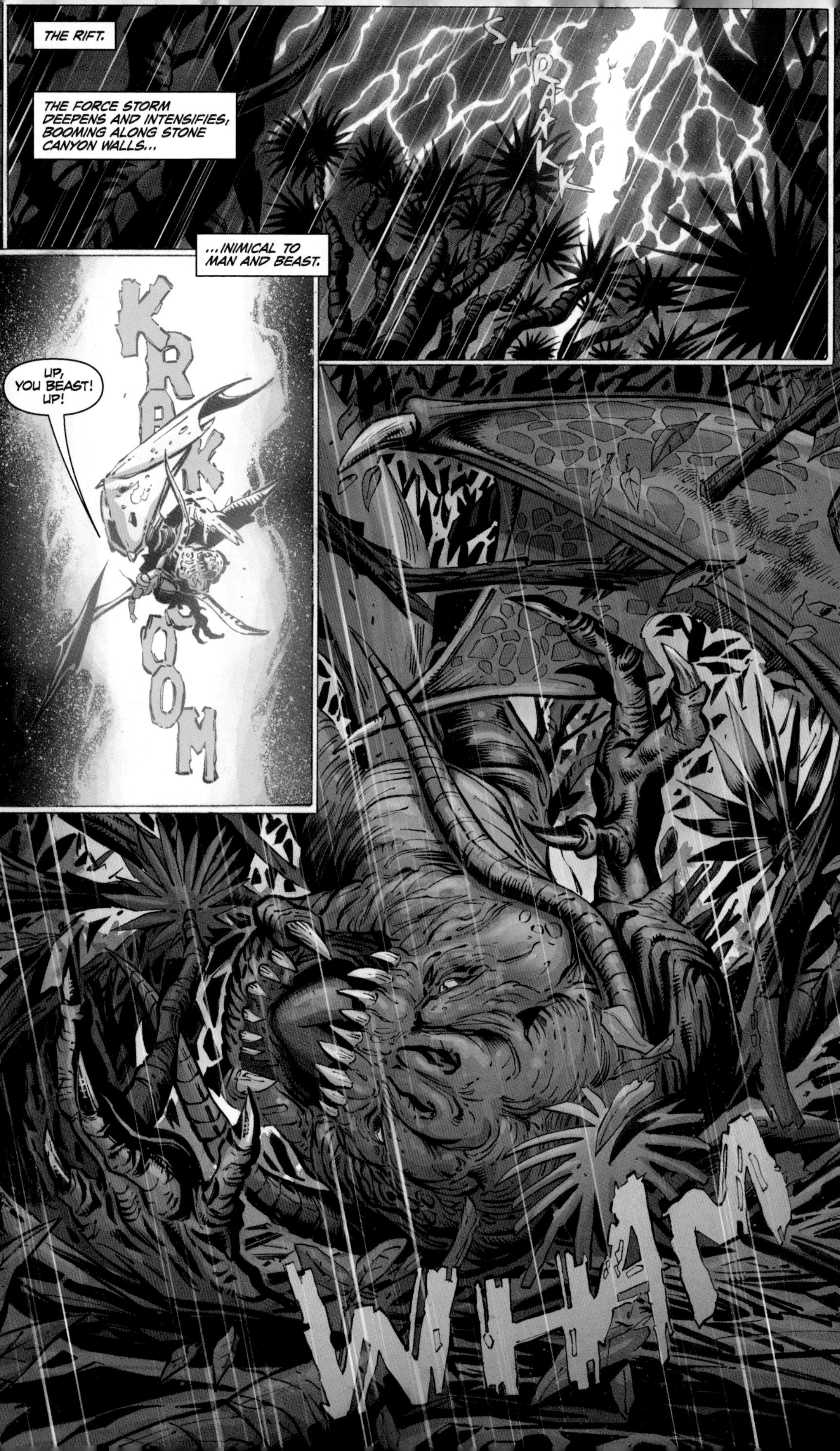
THE RIFT.
THE FORCE STORM DEEPENS AND INTENSIFIES, BOOMING ALONG STONE CANYON WALLS...
SHRAKKK
...INIMICAL TO MAN AND BEAST.
KRAKOOOM
UP, YOU BEAST! UP!
WHAM

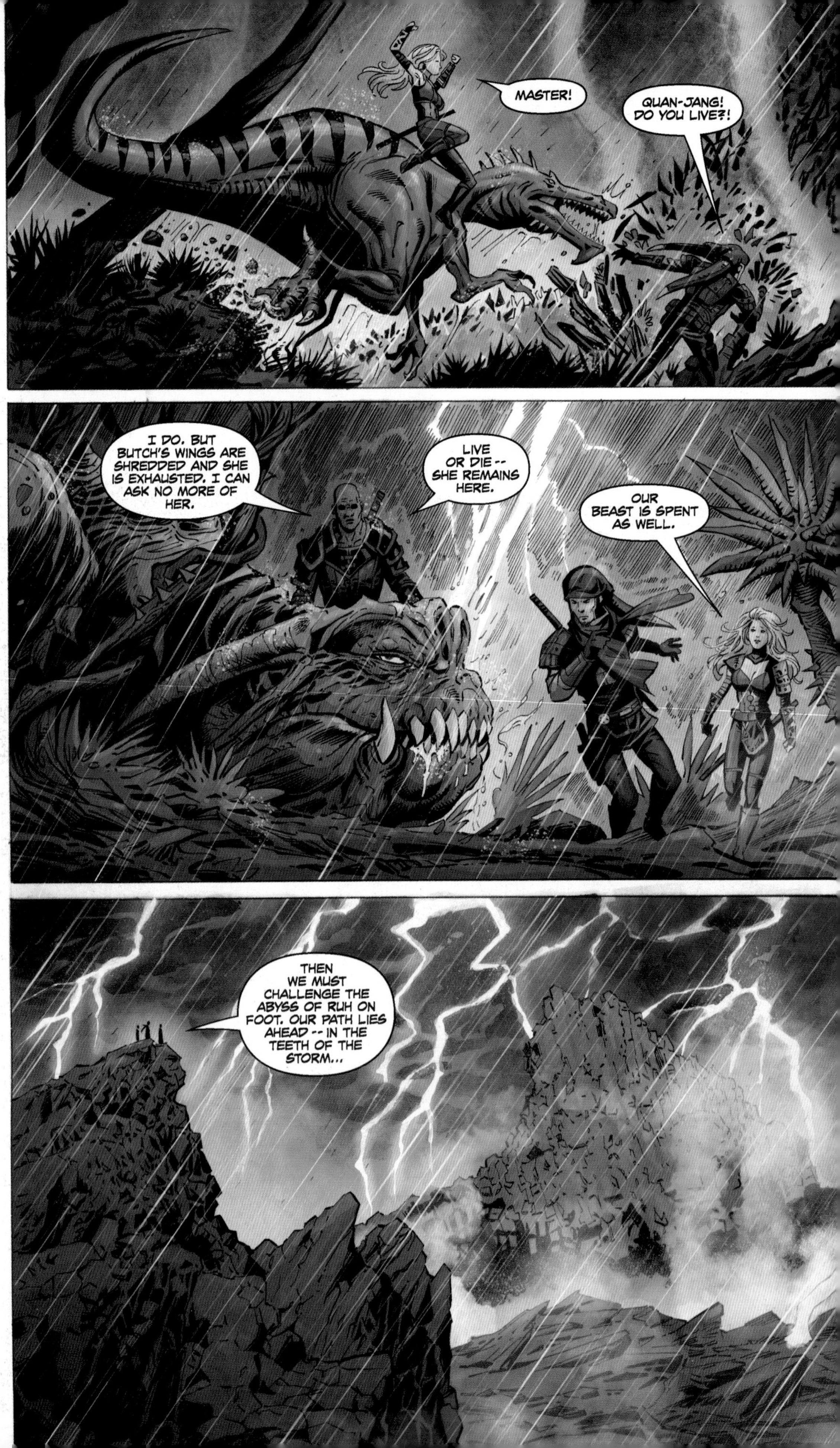

MASTER!
QUAN-JANG! DO YOU LIVE?!
I DO. BUT BUTCH'S WINGS ARE SHREDDED AND SHE IS EXHAUSTED. I CAN ASK NO MORE OF HER.
LIVE OR DIE -- SHE REMAINS HERE.
OUR BEAST IS SPENT AS WELL.
THEN WE MUST CHALLENGE THE ABYSS OF RUH ON FOOT. OUR PATH LIES AHEAD -- IN THE TEETH OF THE STORM...

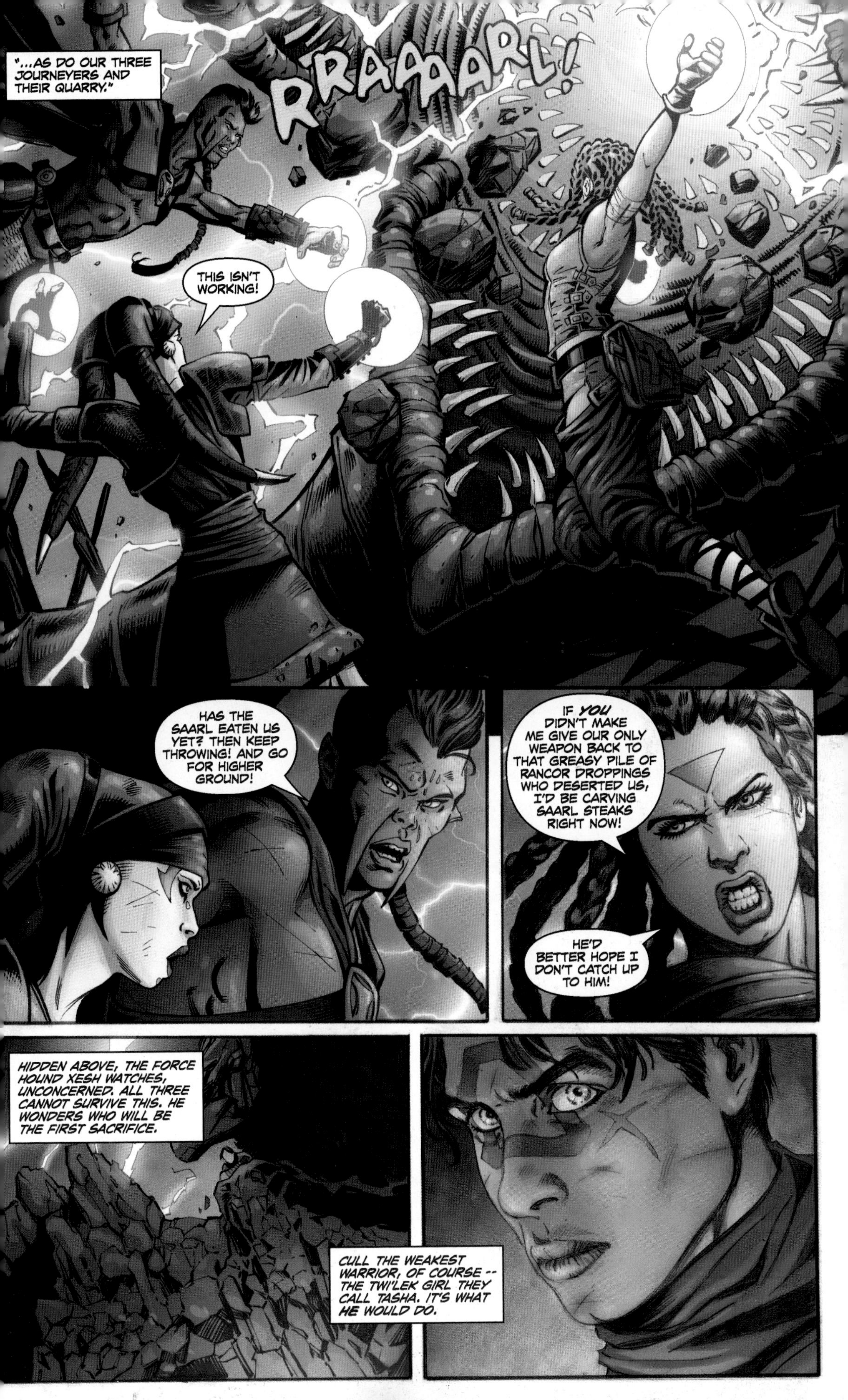
"...AS DO OUR THREE JOURNEYERS AND THEIR QUARRY."
RRAAAARL!
THIS ISN'T WORKING!
HAS THE SAARL EATEN US YET? THEN KEEP THROWING! AND GO FOR HIGHER GROUND!
IF YOU DIDN'T MAKE ME GIVE OUR ONLY WEAPON BACK TO THAT GREASY PILE OF RANCOR DROPPINGS WHO DESERTED US, I'D BE CARVING SAARL STEAKS RIGHT NOW!
HE'D BETTER HOPE I DON'T CATCH UP TO HIM!
HIDDEN ABOVE, THE FORCE HOUND XESH WATCHES, UNCONCERNED. ALL THREE CANNOT SURVIVE THIS. HE WONDERS WHO WILL BE THE FIRST SACRIFICE.
CULL THE WEAKEST WARRIOR, OF COURSE -- THE TWI'LEK GIRL THEY CALL TASHA. IT'S WHAT HE WOULD DO.

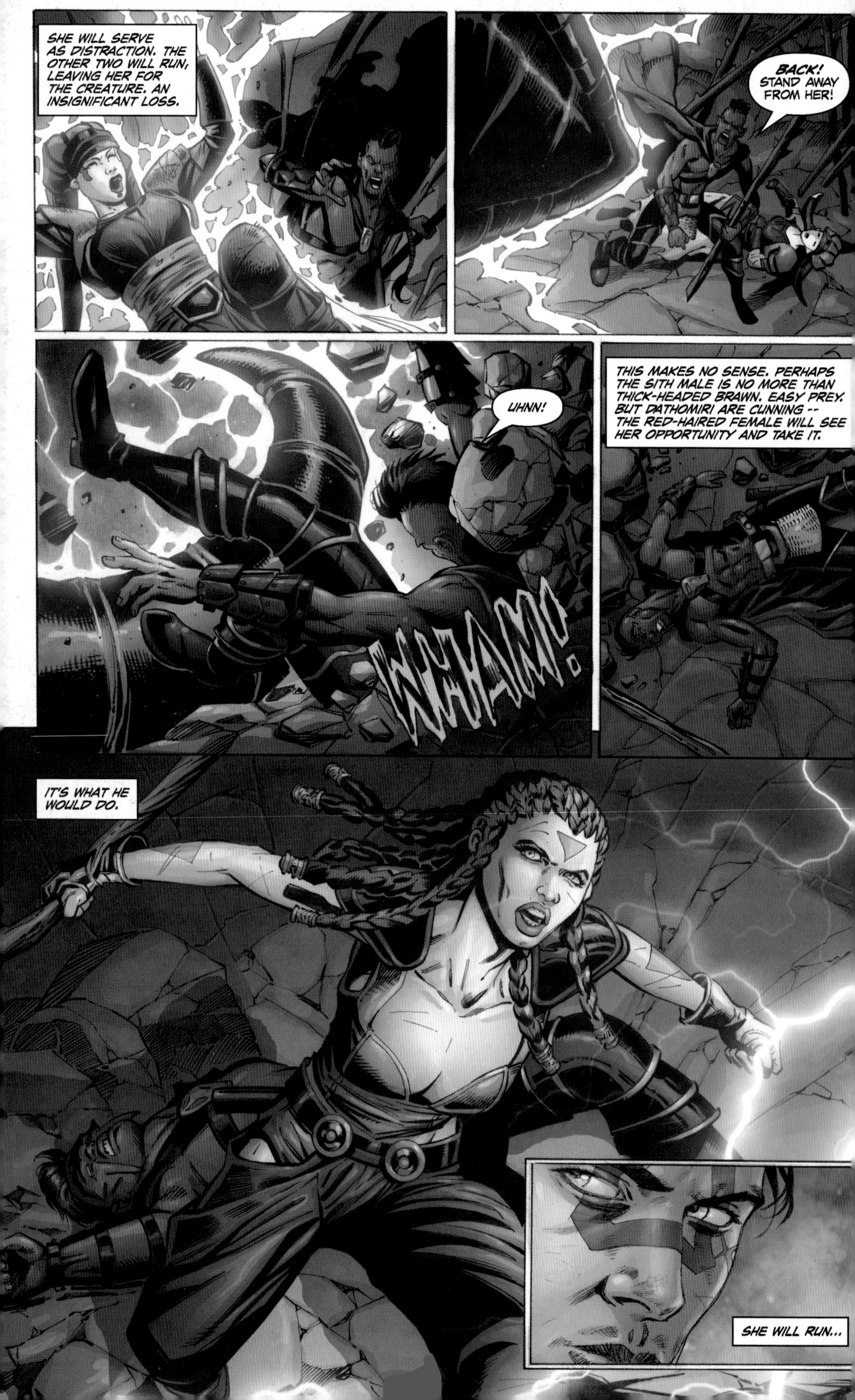
SHE WILL SERVE AS DISTRACTION. THE OTHER TWO WILL RUN, LEAVING HER FOR THE CREATURE. AN INSIGNIFICANT LOSS.
BACK! STAND AWAY FROM HER!
UHNN!
WHAM!
THIS MAKES NO SENSE. PERHAPS THE SITH MALE IS NO MORE THAN THICK-HEADED BRAWN. EASY PREY. BUT DATHOMIRI ARE CUNNING -- THE RED-HAIRED FEMALE WILL SEE HER OPPORTUNITY AND TAKE IT.
IT'S WHAT HE WOULD DO.
SHE WILL RUN...

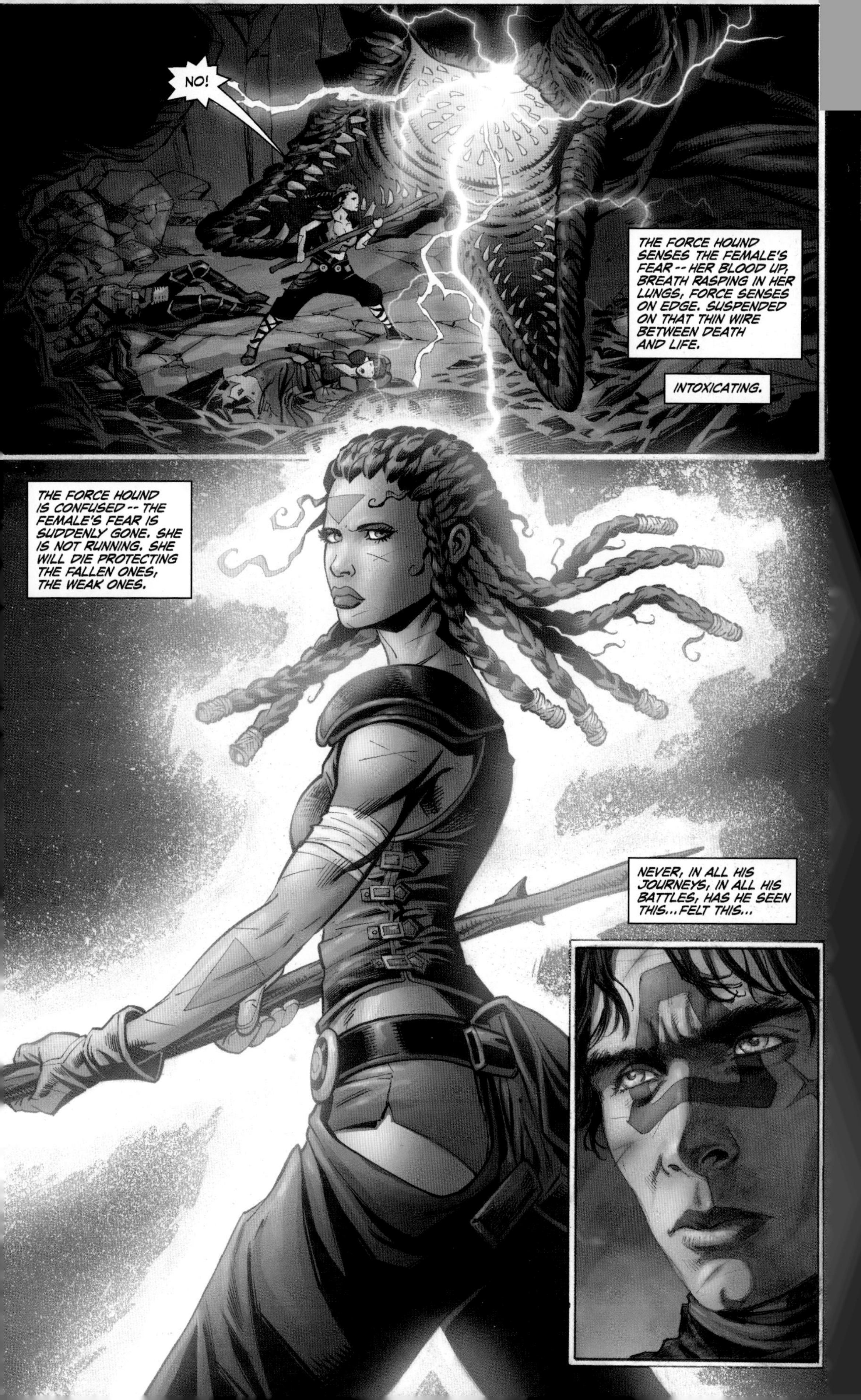
NO!
THE FORCE HOUND SENSES THE FEMALE'S FEAR -- HER BLOOD UP, BREATH RASPING IN HER LUNGS, FORCE SENSES ON EDGE. SUSPENDED ON THAT THIN WIRE BETWEEN DEATH AND LIFE.
INTOXICATING.
THE FORCE HOUND IS CONFUSED -- THE FEMALE'S FEAR IS SUDDENLY GONE. SHE IS NOT RUNNING. SHE WILL DIE PROTECTING THE FALLEN ONES, THE WEAK ONES.
NEVER, IN ALL HIS JOURNEYS, IN ALL HIS BATTLES, HAS HE SEEN THIS...FELT THIS...

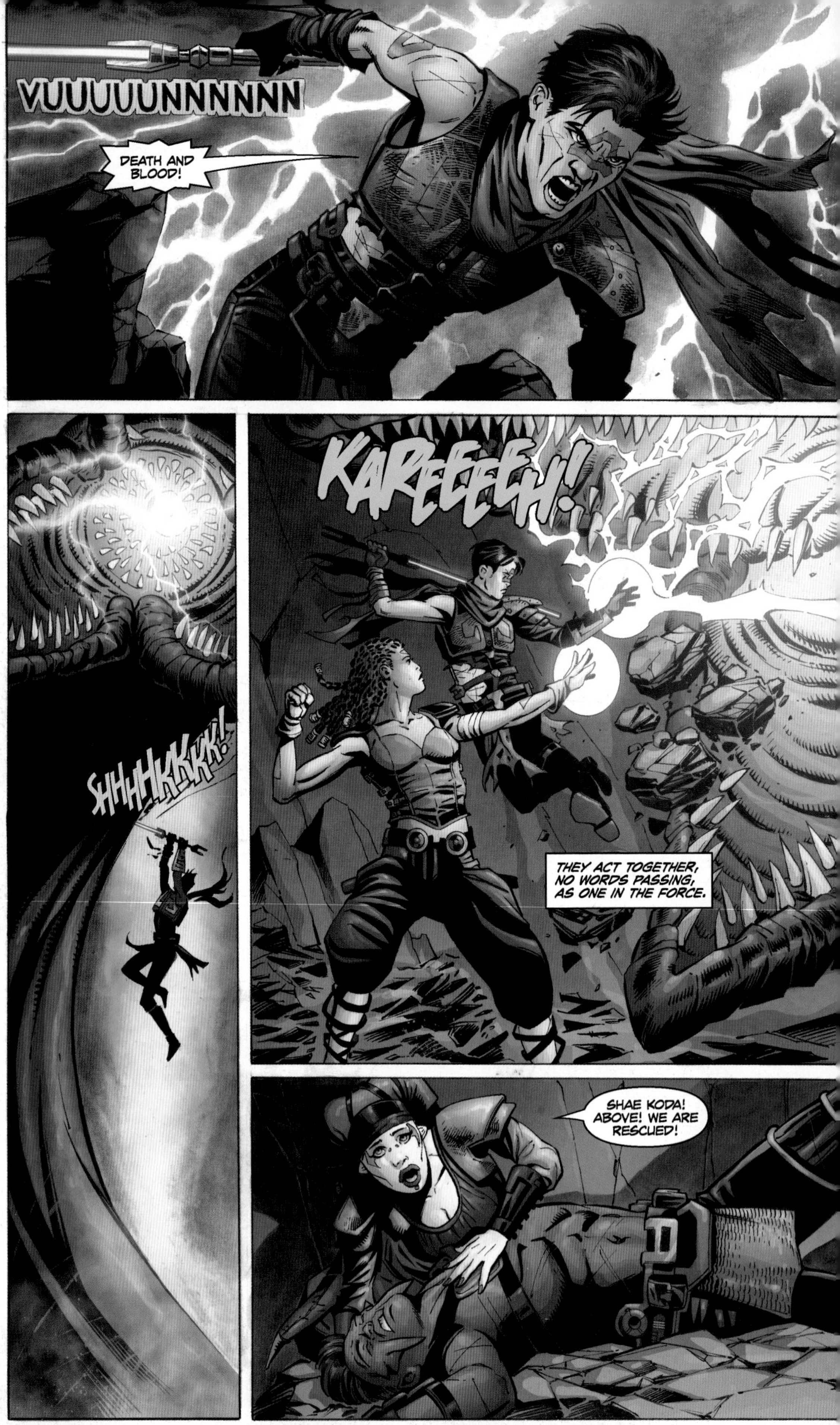
VUUUUUNNNNNN
DEATH AND BLOOD!
SHHHKKKKK!
KAREEEECH!
THEY ACT TOGETHER, NO WORDS PASSING, AS ONE IN THE FORCE.
SHAE KODA! ABOVE! WE ARE RESCUED!

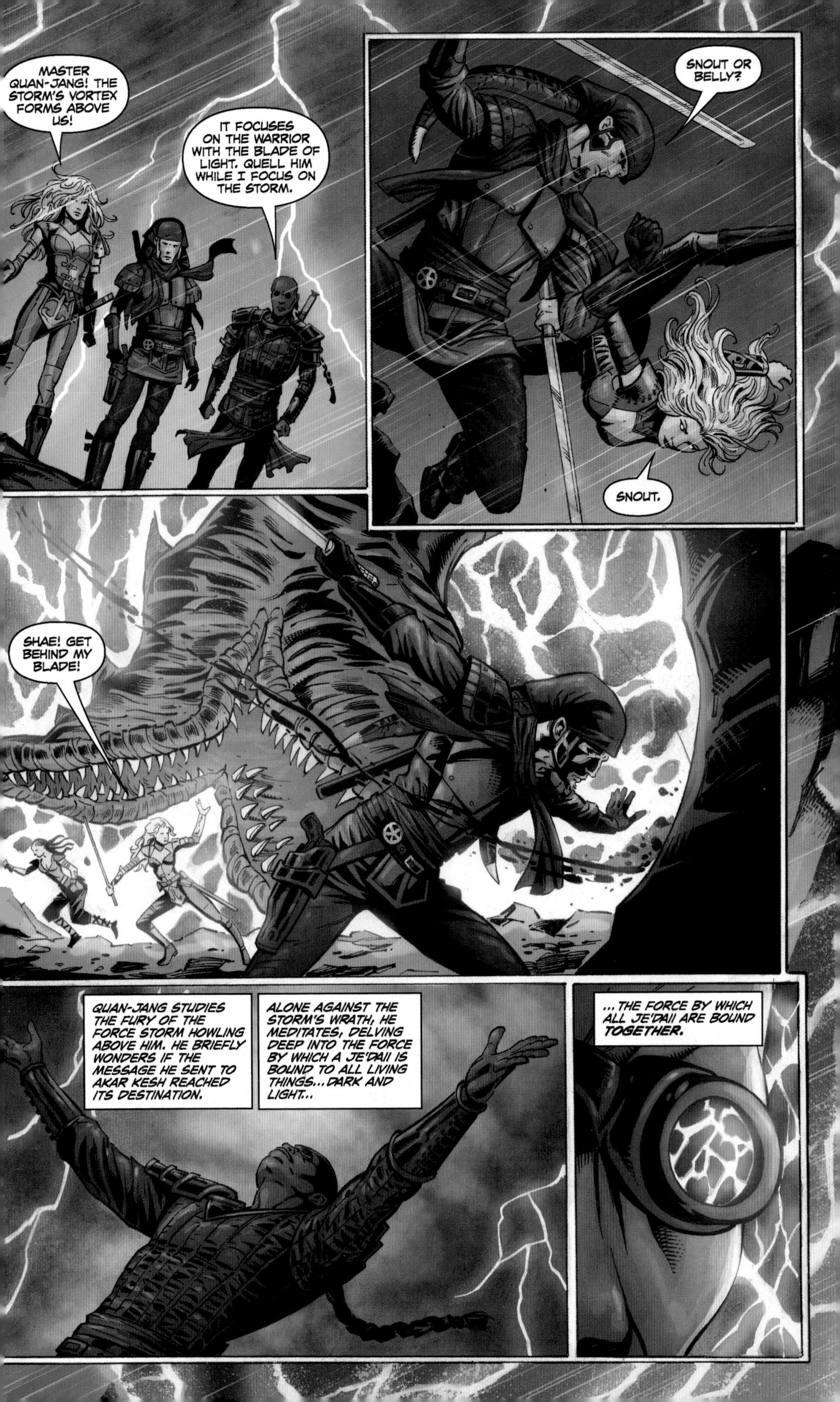
MASTER QUAN-JANG! THE STORM'S VORTEX FORMS ABOVE US!
IT FOCUSES ON THE WARRIOR WITH THE BLADE OF LIGHT. QUELL HIM WHILE I FOCUS ON THE STORM.
SNOUT OR BELLY?
SNOUT.
SHAE! GET BEHIND MY BLADE!
QUAN-JANG STUDIES THE FURY OF THE FORCE STORM HOWLING ABOVE HIM. HE BRIEFLY WONDERS IF THE MESSAGE HE SENT TO AKAR KESH REACHED ITS DESTINATION.
ALONE AGAINST THE STORM'S WRATH, HE MEDITATES, DELVING DEEP INTO THE FORCE BY WHICH A JE'DAII IS BOUND TO ALL LIVING THINGS...DARK AND LIGHT...
...THE FORCE BY WHICH ALL JE'DAII ARE BOUND TOGETHER.

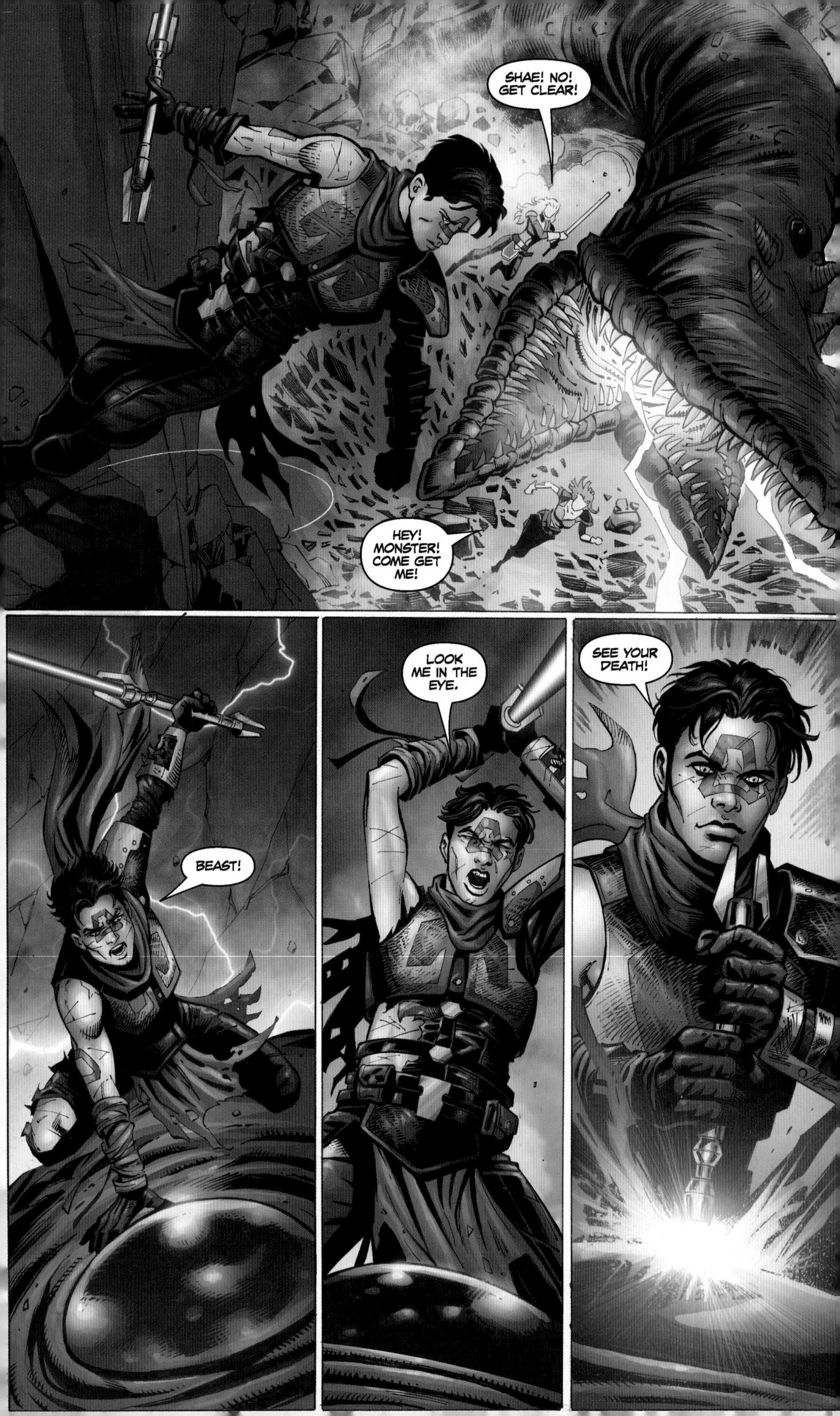
SHAE! NO! GET CLEAR!
HEY! MONSTER! COME GET ME!
BEAST!
LOOK ME IN THE EYE.
SEE YOUR DEATH!

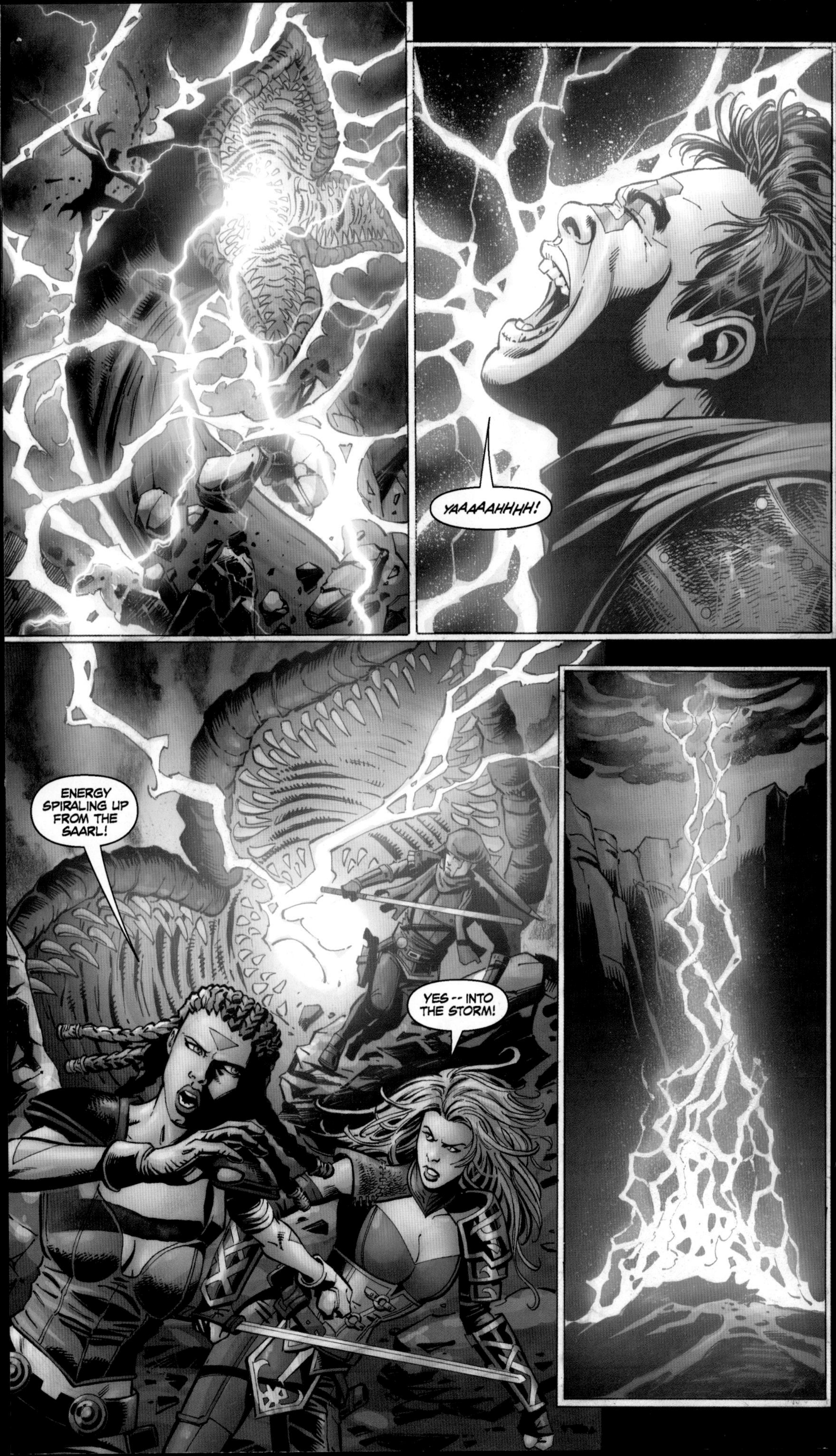
YAAAAAHHHH!
ENERGY SPIRALING UP FROM THE SAARL!
YES -- INTO THE STORM!

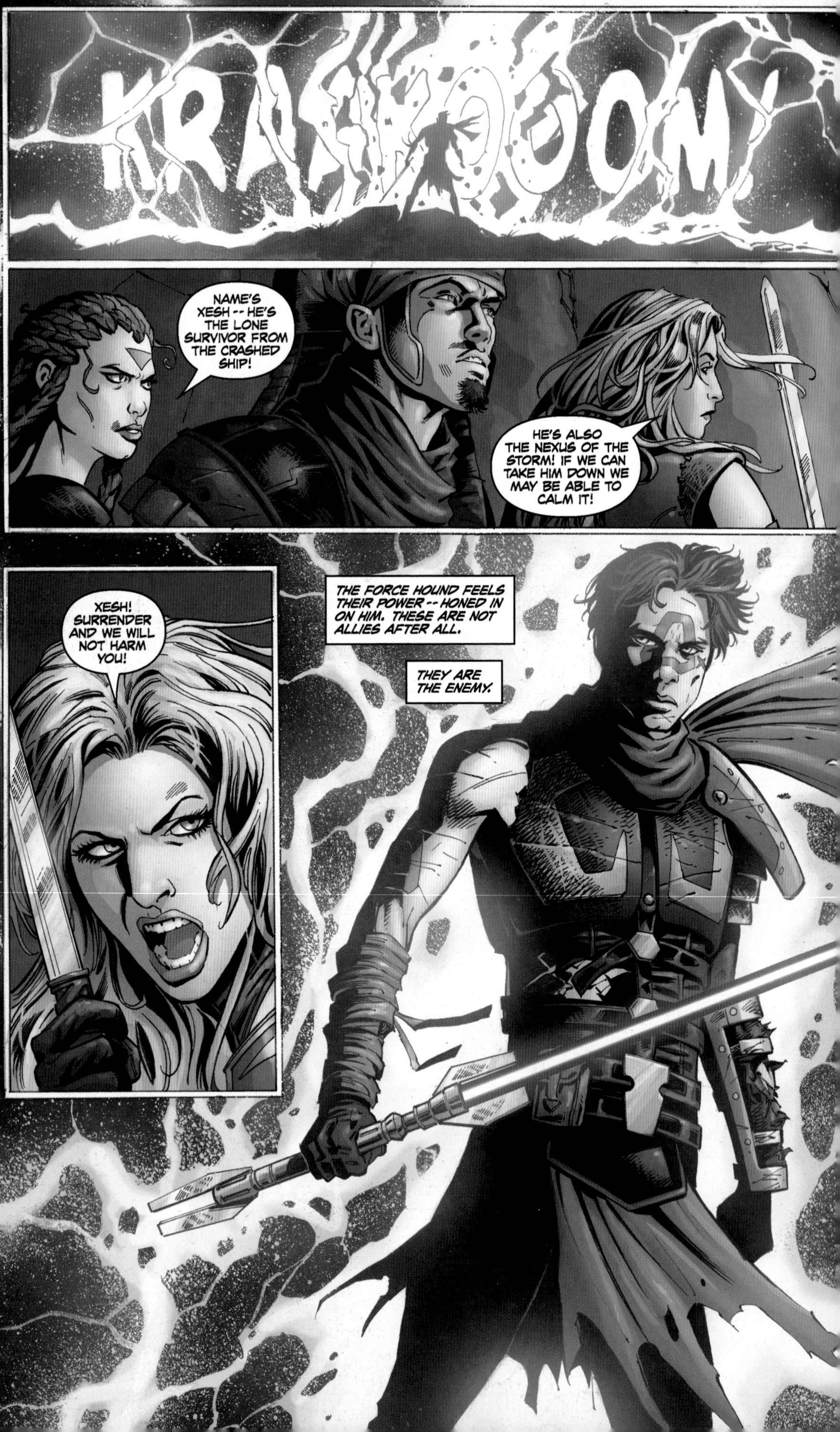
KRAKKOOOM!
NAME'S XESH -- HE'S THE LONE SURVIVOR FROM THE CRASHED SHIP!
HE'S ALSO THE NEXUS OF THE STORM! IF WE CAN TAKE HIM DOWN WE MAY BE ABLE TO CALM IT!
XESH! SURRENDER AND WE WILL NOT HARM YOU!
THE FORCE HOUND FEELS THEIR POWER -- HONED IN ON HIM. THESE ARE NOT ALLIES AFTER ALL.
THEY ARE THE ENEMY.

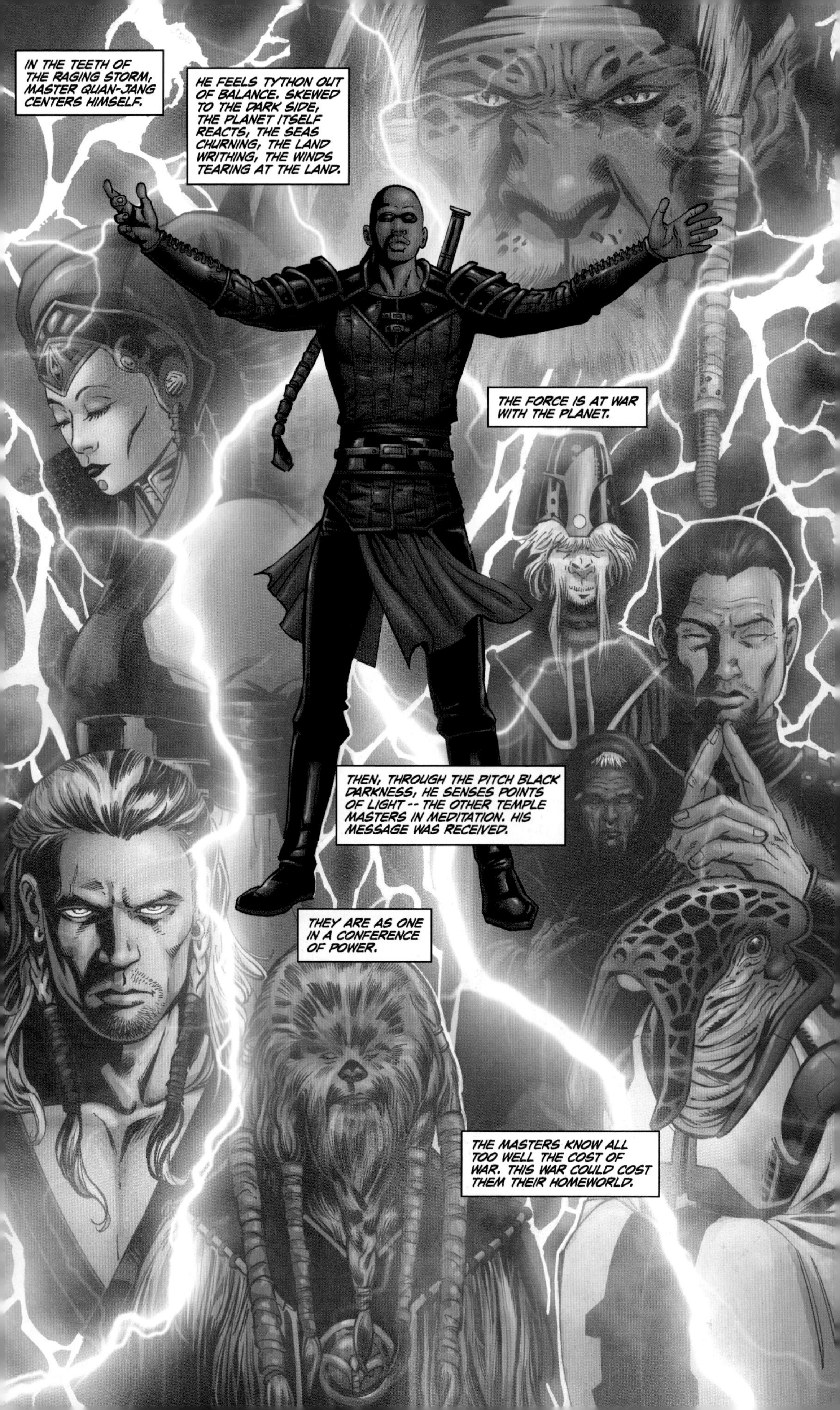
IN THE TEETH OF THE RAGING STORM, MASTER QUAN-JANG CENTERS HIMSELF.
HE FEELS TYTHON OUT OF BALANCE. SKEWED TO THE DARK SIDE, THE PLANET ITSELF REACTS, THE SEAS CHURNING, THE LAND WRITHING, THE WINDS TEARING AT THE LAND.
THE FORCE IS AT WAR WITH THE PLANET.
THEN, THROUGH THE PITCH BLACK DARKNESS, HE SENSES POINTS OF LIGHT -- THE OTHER TEMPLE MASTERS IN MEDITATION. HIS MESSAGE WAS RECEIVED.
THEY ARE AS ONE IN A CONFERENCE OF POWER.
THE MASTERS KNOW ALL TOO WELL THE COST OF WAR. THIS WAR COULD COST THEM THEIR HOMEWORLD.

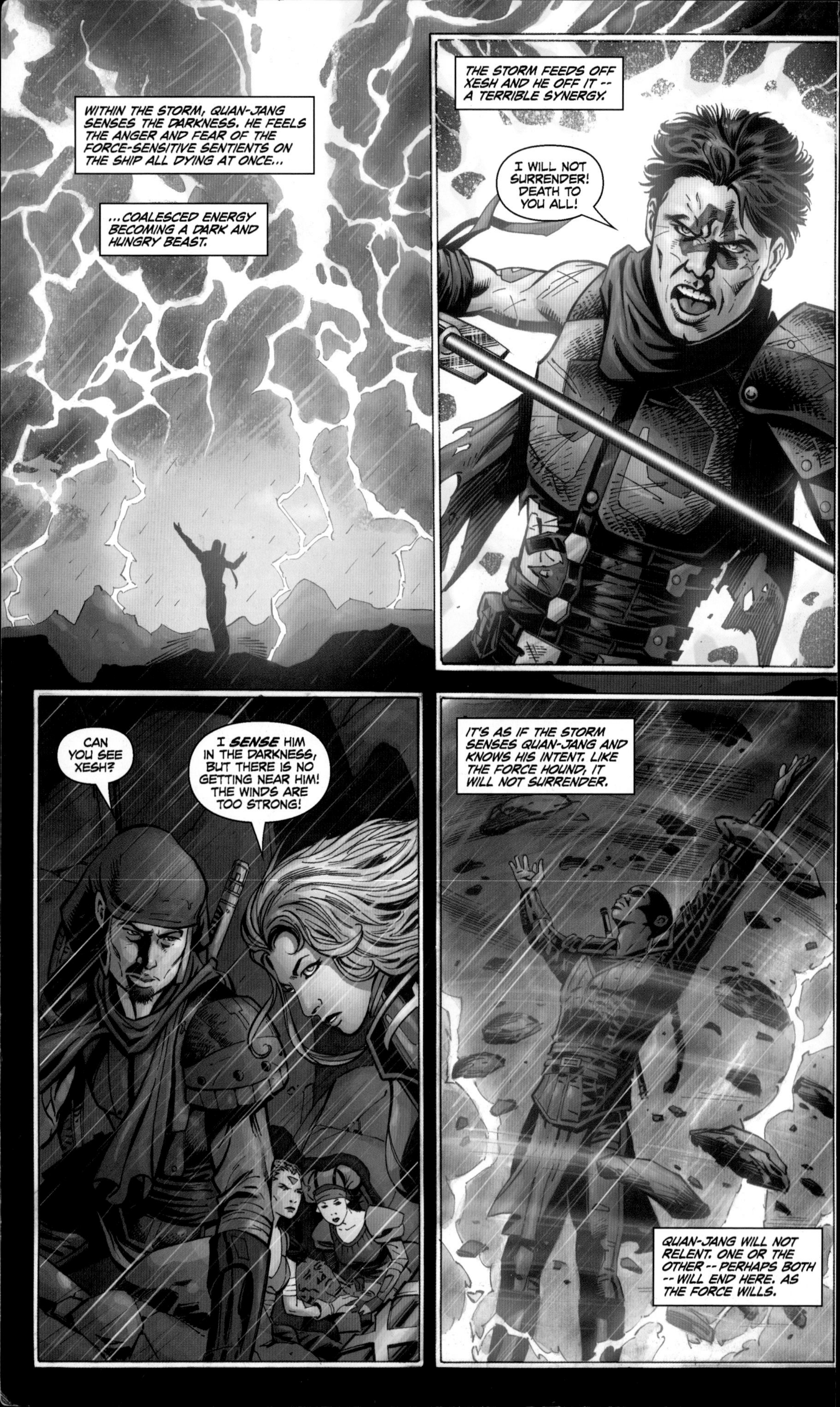
WITHIN THE STORM, QUAN-JANG SENSES THE DARKNESS. HE FEELS THE ANGER AND FEAR OF THE FORCE-SENSITIVE SENTIENTS ON THE SHIP ALL DYING AT ONCE...
...COALESCED ENERGY BECOMING A DARK AND HUNGRY BEAST.
THE STORM FEEDS OFF XESH AND HE OFF IT -- A TERRIBLE SYNERGY.
I WILL NOT SURRENDER! DEATH TO YOU ALL!
CAN YOU SEE XESH?
I SENSE HIM IN THE DARKNESS, BUT THERE IS NO GETTING NEAR HIM! THE WINDS ARE TOO STRONG!
IT'S AS IF THE STORM SENSES QUAN-JANG AND KNOWS HIS INTENT. LIKE THE FORCE HOUND, IT WILL NOT SURRENDER.
QUAN-JANG WILL NOT RELENT. ONE OR THE OTHER -- PERHAPS BOTH -- WILL END HERE. AS THE FORCE WILLS.

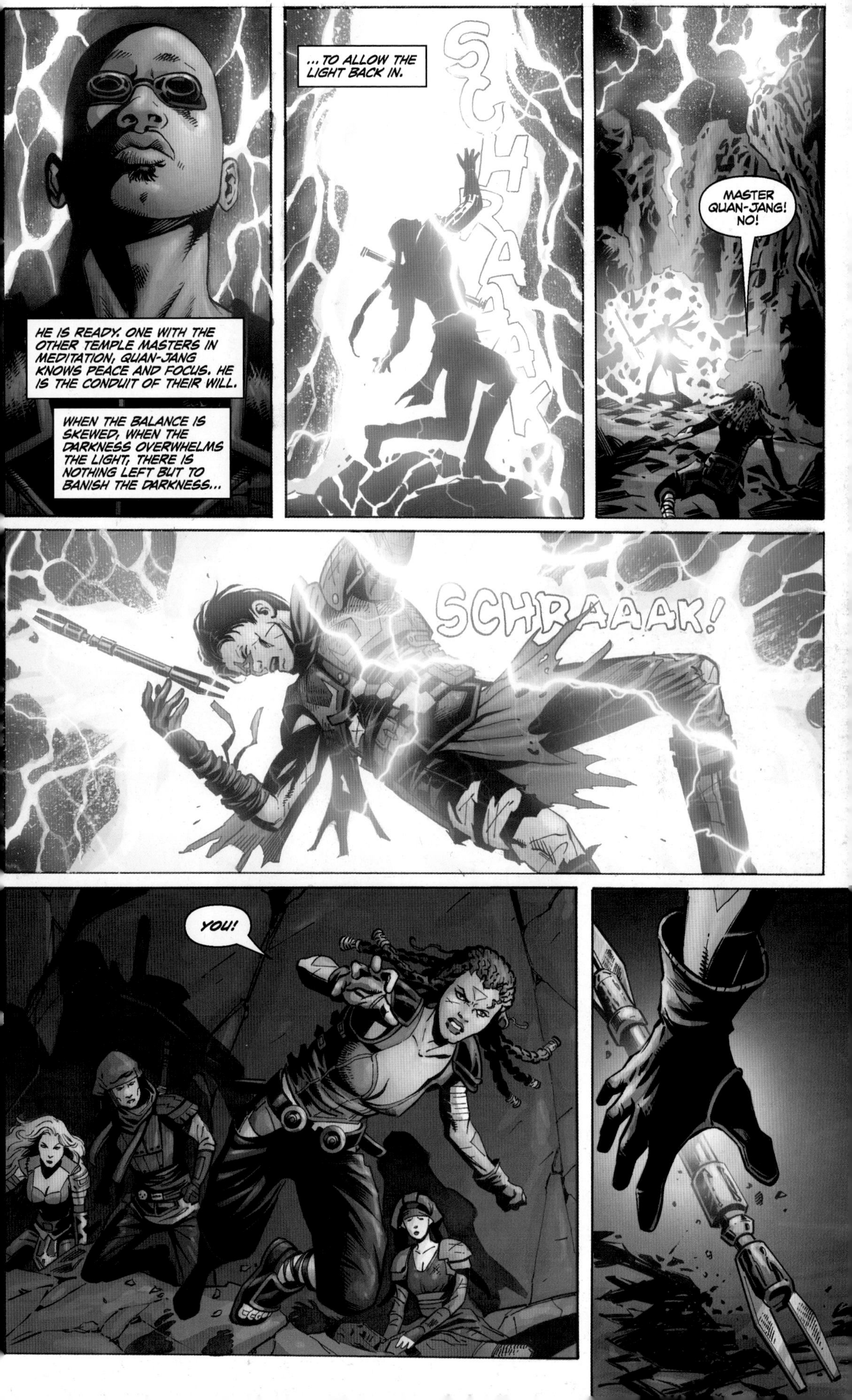

HE IS READY. ONE WITH THE OTHER TEMPLE MASTERS IN MEDITATION, QUAN-JANG KNOWS PEACE AND FOCUS. HE IS THE CONDUIT OF THEIR WILL.
WHEN THE BALANCE IS SKEWED, WHEN THE DARKNESS OVERWHELMS THE LIGHT, THERE IS NOTHING LEFT BUT TO BANISH THE DARKNESS...
...TO ALLOW THE LIGHT BACK IN.
SCHRAAAK
MASTER QUAN-JANG! NO!
SCHRAAAK!
YOU!

MY MASTER MAY BE DEAD BECAUSE OF YOU! YOU DESERVE *DEATH!*

I EXPECT IT. I SOUGHT A GOOD DEATH IN BATTLE, BUT THIS IS MY FATE. SO BE IT.

WHEN YOUR PEOPLE EAT MY BODY, YOU SHOULD HAVE THE HONOR PORTION -- MY HEART. YOU WERE VERY BRAVE.

STRANGER, THAT IS NOT OUR WAY.

YOU...ARE VERY ODD... BEINGS...

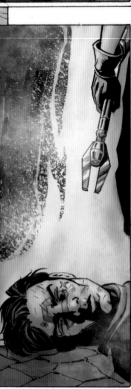

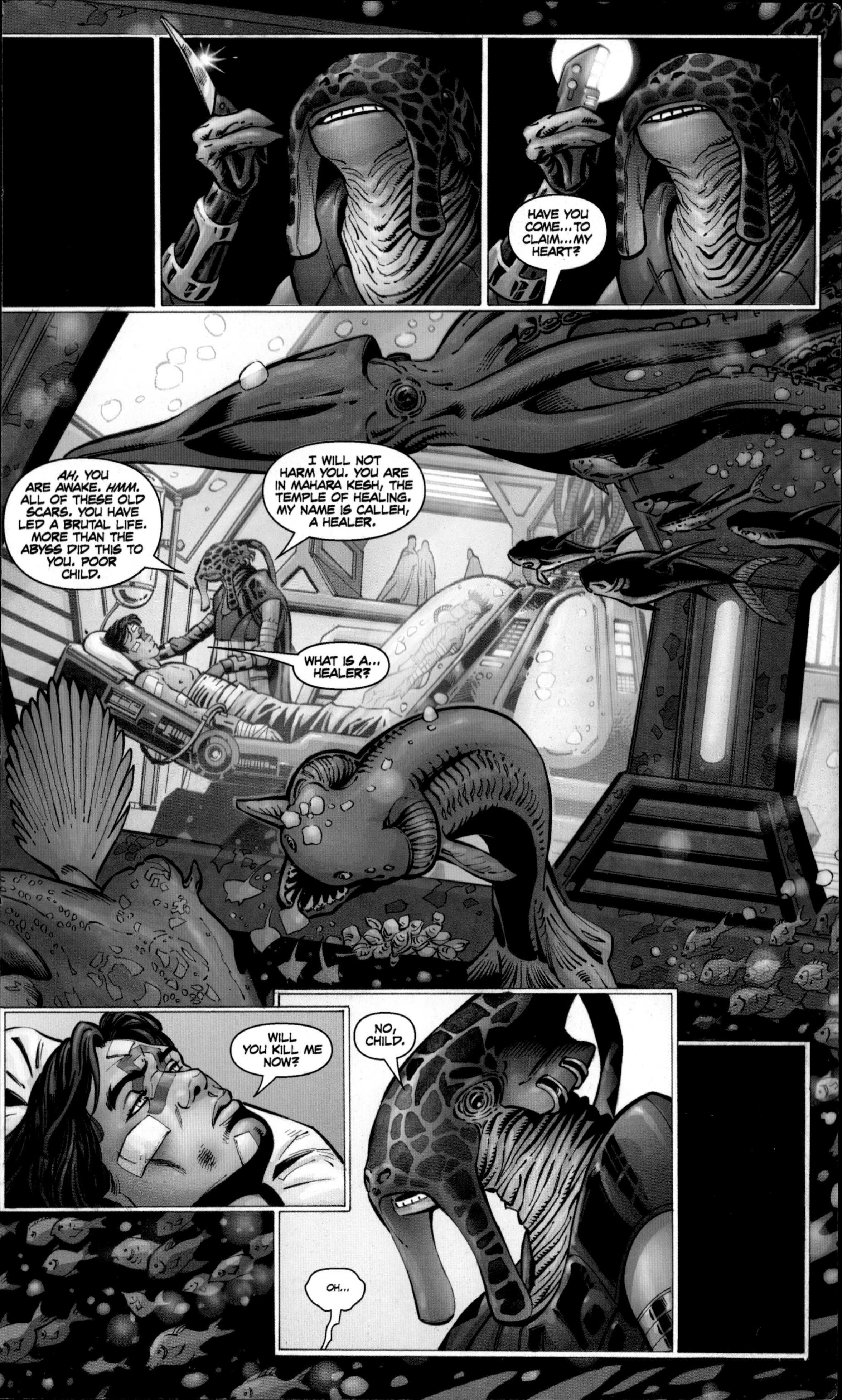
HAVE YOU COME... TO CLAIM... MY HEART?
AH, YOU ARE AWAKE. *HMM.* ALL OF THESE OLD SCARS. YOU HAVE LED A BRUTAL LIFE. MORE THAN THE ABYSS DID THIS TO YOU. POOR CHILD.
I WILL NOT HARM YOU. YOU ARE IN MAHARA KESH, THE TEMPLE OF HEALING. MY NAME IS CALLEH, A HEALER.
WHAT IS A... HEALER?
WILL YOU KILL ME NOW?
NO, CHILD.
OH...

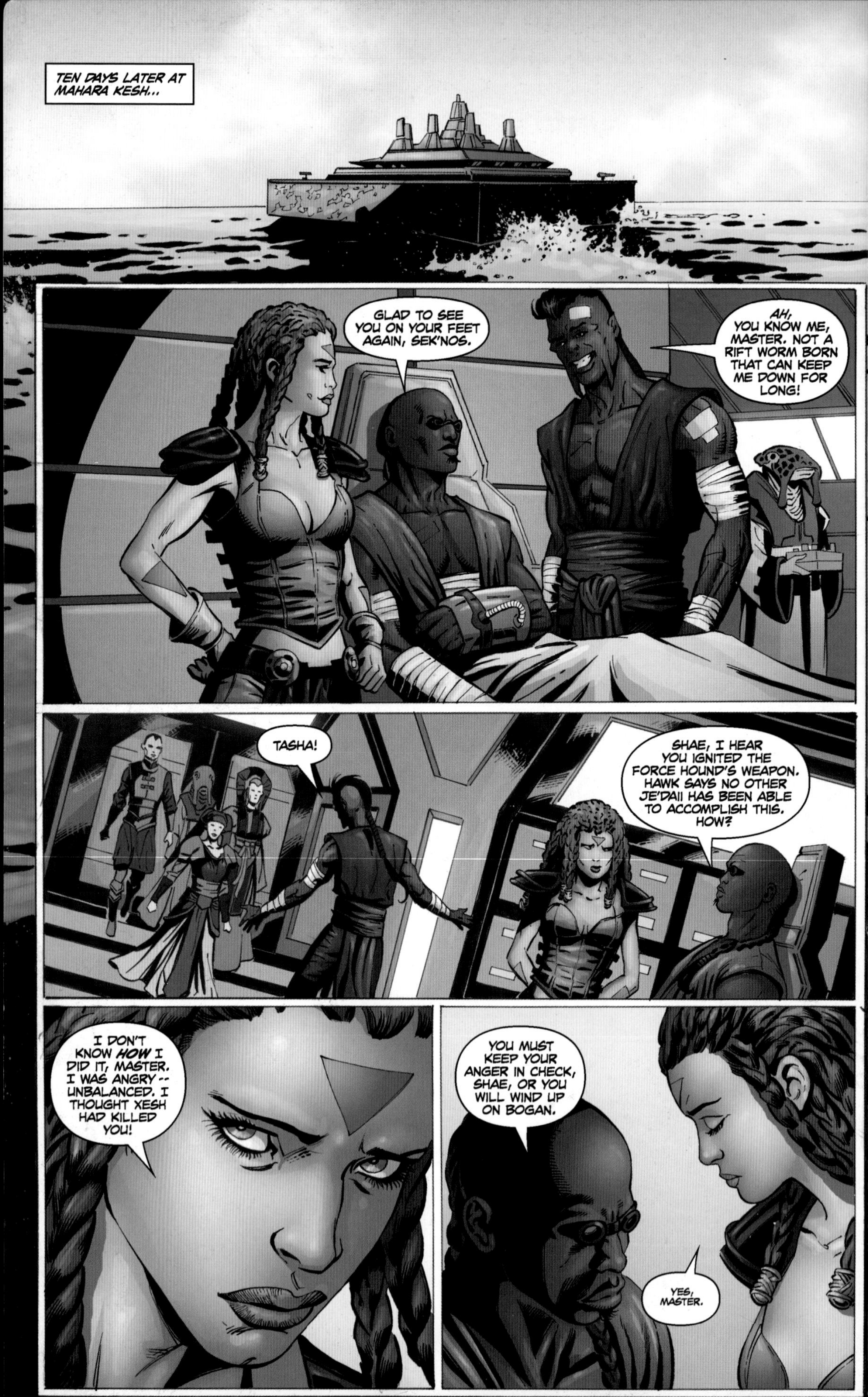
TEN DAYS LATER AT MAHARA KESH...
GLAD TO SEE YOU ON YOUR FEET AGAIN, SEK'NOS.
AH, YOU KNOW ME, MASTER. NOT A RIFT WORM BORN THAT CAN KEEP ME DOWN FOR LONG!
TASHA!
SHAE, I HEAR YOU IGNITED THE FORCE HOUND'S WEAPON. HAWK SAYS NO OTHER JE'DAII HAS BEEN ABLE TO ACCOMPLISH THIS. HOW?
I DON'T KNOW HOW I DID IT, MASTER. I WAS ANGRY -- UNBALANCED. I THOUGHT XESH HAD KILLED YOU!
YOU MUST KEEP YOUR ANGER IN CHECK, SHAE, OR YOU WILL WIND UP ON BOGAN.
YES, MASTER.

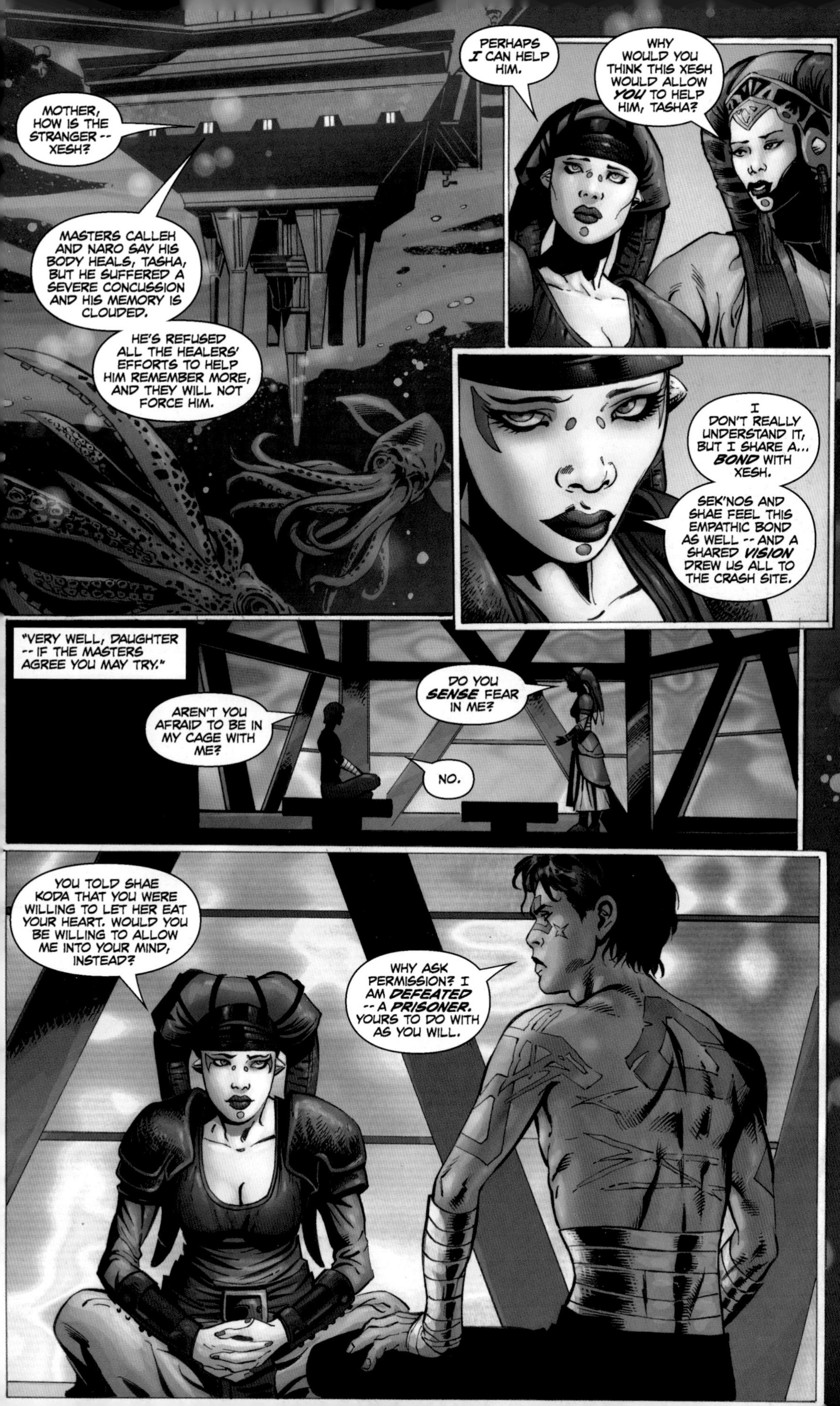

MOTHER, HOW IS THE STRANGER -- XESH?
MASTERS CALLEH AND NARO SAY HIS BODY HEALS, TASHA, BUT HE SUFFERED A SEVERE CONCUSSION AND HIS MEMORY IS CLOUDED.
HE'S REFUSED ALL THE HEALERS' EFFORTS TO HELP HIM REMEMBER MORE, AND THEY WILL NOT FORCE HIM.
PERHAPS *I* CAN HELP HIM.
WHY WOULD YOU THINK THIS XESH WOULD ALLOW *YOU* TO HELP HIM, TASHA?
I DON'T REALLY UNDERSTAND IT, BUT I SHARE A... *BOND* WITH XESH.
SEK'NOS AND SHAE FEEL THIS EMPATHIC BOND AS WELL -- AND A SHARED *VISION* DREW US ALL TO THE CRASH SITE.
"VERY WELL, DAUGHTER -- IF THE MASTERS AGREE YOU MAY TRY."
AREN'T YOU AFRAID TO BE IN MY CAGE WITH ME?
DO YOU *SENSE* FEAR IN ME?
NO.
YOU TOLD SHAE KODA THAT YOU WERE WILLING TO LET HER EAT YOUR HEART. WOULD YOU BE WILLING TO ALLOW ME INTO YOUR MIND, INSTEAD?
WHY ASK PERMISSION? I AM *DEFEATED* -- A *PRISONER*. YOURS TO DO WITH AS YOU WILL.

IT IS MY WILL THAT YOU SHOULD NOT COME TO HARM. DON'T YOU WANT TO REMEMBER WHO YOU ARE?

YES. I WANT THAT.

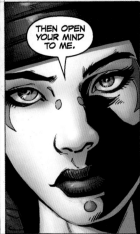

THEN OPEN YOUR MIND TO ME.

BY THE MOONS! I SEE...

"...A DARK WORLD, WITH HUGE SHIPS LIKE THE ONE THAT CRASHED HERE...

"...ALL IMBUED WITH DARKNESS. THEY HAVE CREATED ARMIES... TAKEN WORLDS... SLAUGHTERED AND ENSLAVED THEIR INHABITANTS!

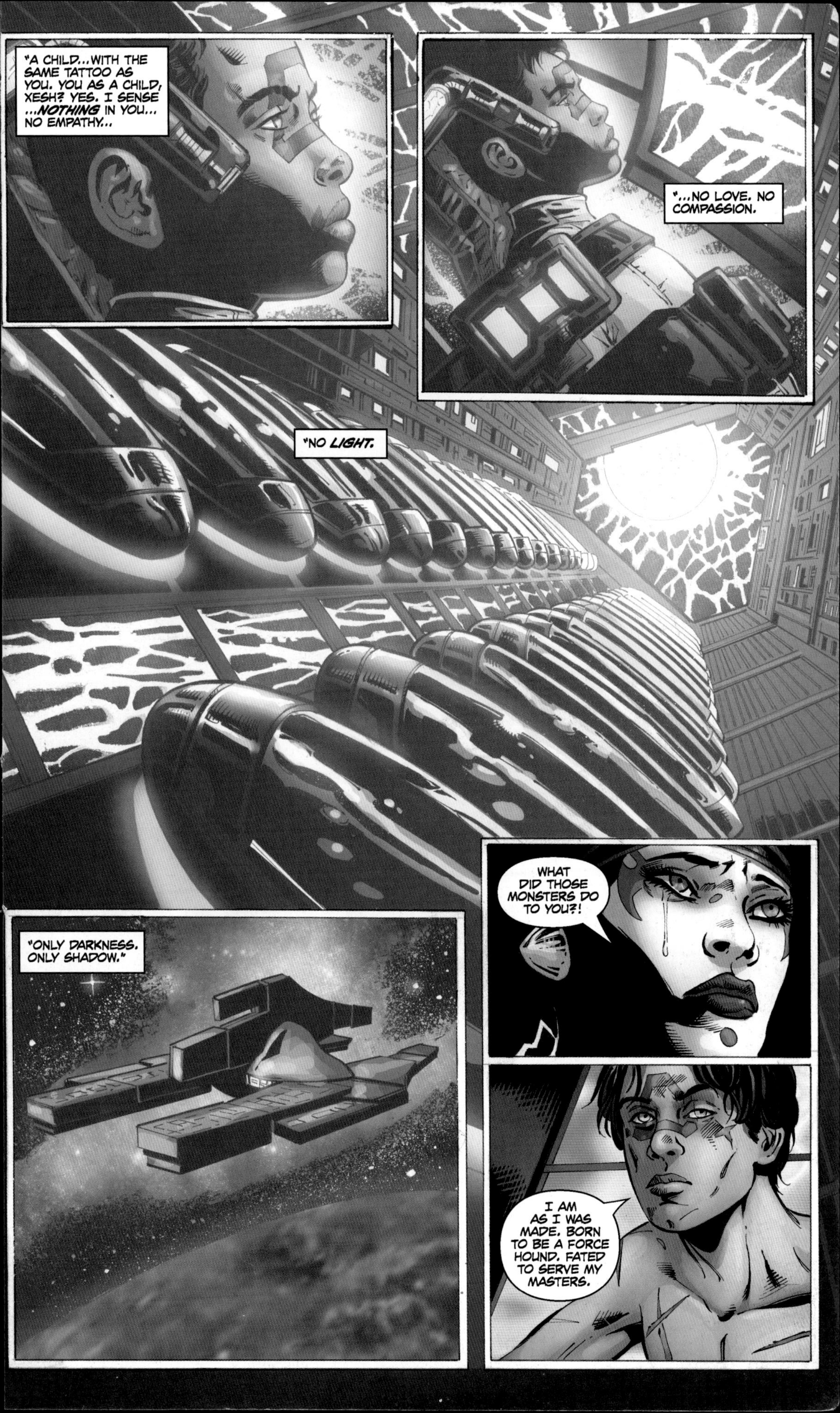
"A CHILD...WITH THE SAME TATTOO AS YOU. YOU AS A CHILD, XESH? YES. I SENSE ...*NOTHING* IN YOU... NO EMPATHY...
"...NO LOVE. NO COMPASSION.
"NO *LIGHT.*
"ONLY DARKNESS. ONLY SHADOW."
WHAT DID THOSE MONSTERS DO TO YOU?!
I AM AS I WAS MADE. BORN TO BE A FORCE HOUND. FATED TO SERVE MY MASTERS.

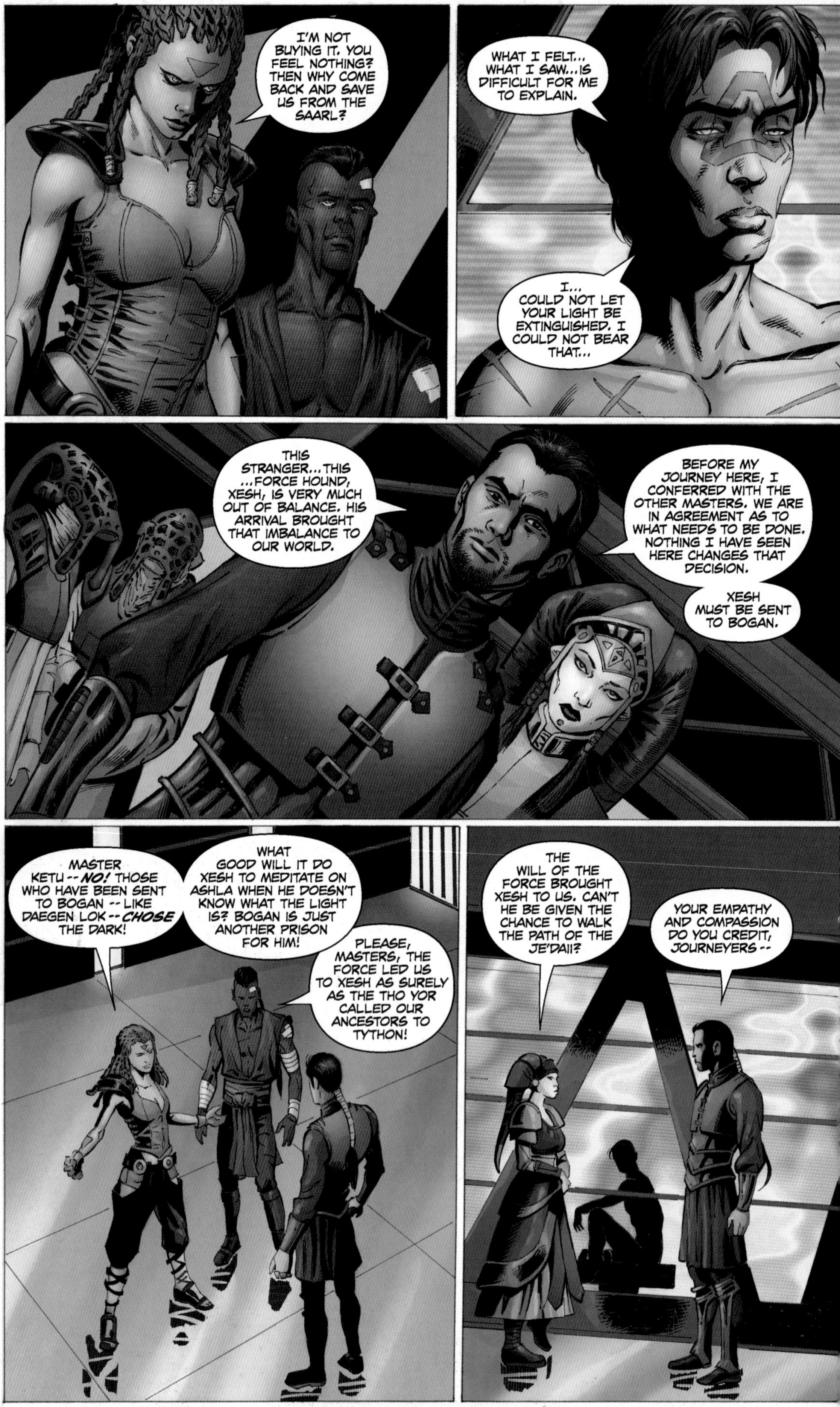

I'M NOT BUYING IT. YOU FEEL NOTHING? THEN WHY COME BACK AND SAVE US FROM THE SAARL?
WHAT I FELT... WHAT I SAW...IS DIFFICULT FOR ME TO EXPLAIN.
I... COULD NOT LET YOUR LIGHT BE EXTINGUISHED. I COULD NOT BEAR THAT...
THIS STRANGER...THIS ...FORCE HOUND, XESH, IS VERY MUCH OUT OF BALANCE. HIS ARRIVAL BROUGHT THAT IMBALANCE TO OUR WORLD.
BEFORE MY JOURNEY HERE, I CONFERRED WITH THE OTHER MASTERS. WE ARE IN AGREEMENT AS TO WHAT NEEDS TO BE DONE. NOTHING I HAVE SEEN HERE CHANGES THAT DECISION.
XESH MUST BE SENT TO BOGAN.
MASTER KETU -- ***NO!*** THOSE WHO HAVE BEEN SENT TO BOGAN -- LIKE DAEGEN LOK -- ***CHOSE*** THE DARK!
WHAT GOOD WILL IT DO XESH TO MEDITATE ON ASHLA WHEN HE DOESN'T KNOW WHAT THE LIGHT IS? BOGAN IS JUST ANOTHER PRISON FOR HIM!
PLEASE, MASTERS, THE FORCE LED US TO XESH AS SURELY AS THE THO YOR CALLED OUR ANCESTORS TO TYTHON!
THE WILL OF THE FORCE BROUGHT XESH TO US. CAN'T HE BE GIVEN THE CHANCE TO WALK THE PATH OF THE JE'DAII?
YOUR EMPATHY AND COMPASSION DO YOU CREDIT, JOURNEYERS --

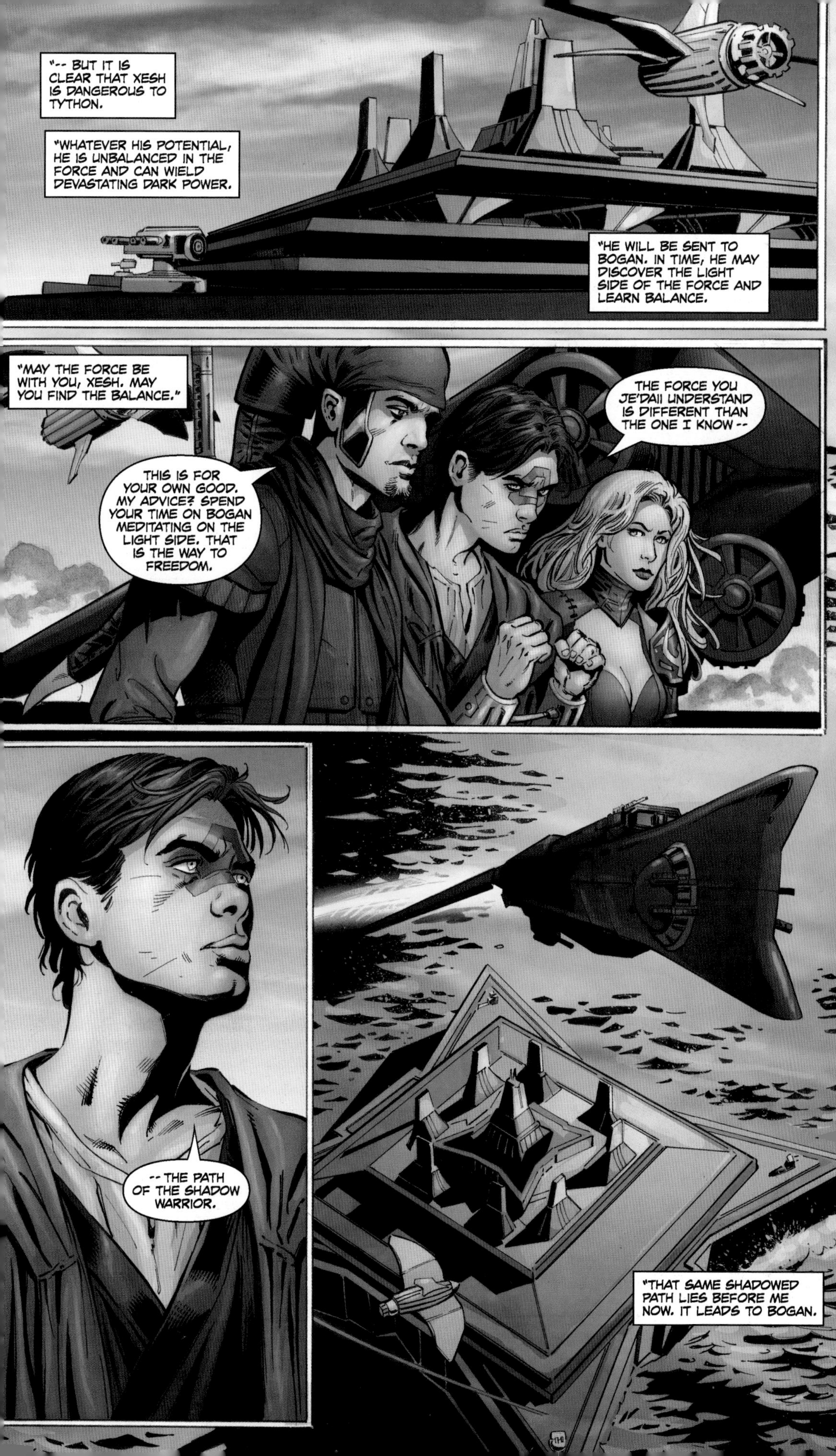
"-- BUT IT IS CLEAR THAT XESH IS DANGEROUS TO TYTHON.
"WHATEVER HIS POTENTIAL, HE IS UNBALANCED IN THE FORCE AND CAN WIELD DEVASTATING DARK POWER.
"HE WILL BE SENT TO BOGAN. IN TIME, HE MAY DISCOVER THE LIGHT SIDE OF THE FORCE AND LEARN BALANCE.
"MAY THE FORCE BE WITH YOU, XESH. MAY YOU FIND THE BALANCE."
THIS IS FOR YOUR OWN GOOD. MY ADVICE? SPEND YOUR TIME ON BOGAN MEDITATING ON THE LIGHT SIDE. THAT IS THE WAY TO FREEDOM.
THE FORCE YOU JE'DAII UNDERSTAND IS DIFFERENT THAN THE ONE I KNOW --
-- THE PATH OF THE SHADOW WARRIOR.
"THAT SAME SHADOWED PATH LIES BEFORE ME NOW. IT LEADS TO BOGAN.

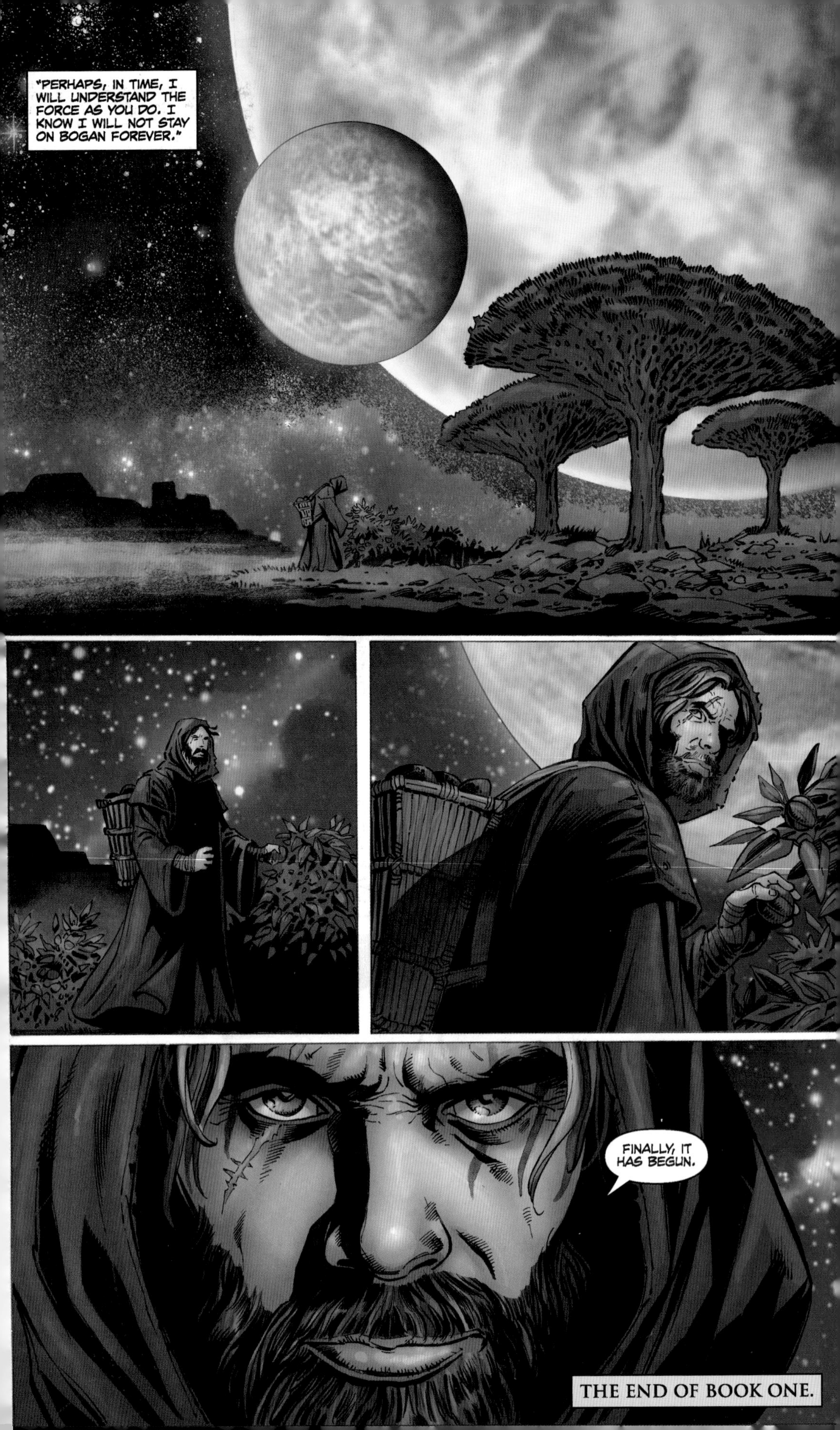
"PERHAPS, IN TIME, I WILL UNDERSTAND THE FORCE AS YOU DO. I KNOW I WILL NOT STAY ON BOGAN FOREVER."
FINALLY, IT HAS BEGUN.
THE END OF BOOK ONE.

STAR WARS GRAPHIC NOVEL TIMELINE (IN YEARS)

Omnibus: Tales of the Jedi—5,000–3,986 BSW4

Knights of the Old Republic—3,964–3,963 BSW4

The Old Republic—3653, 3678 BSW4

Knight Errant—1,032 BSW4

Jedi vs. Sith—1,000 BSW4

Omnibus: Rise of the Sith—33 BSW4

Episode I: The Phantom Menace—32 BSW4

Omnibus: Emissaries and Assassins—32 BSW4

Omnibus: Quinlan Vos—Jedi in Darkness—31–30 BSW4

Omnibus: Menace Revealed—31–22 BSW4

Honor and Duty—22 BSW4

Blood Ties—22 BSW4

Episode II: Attack of the Clones—22 BSW4

Clone Wars—22–19 BSW4

Clone Wars Adventures—22–19 BSW4

General Grievous—22–19 BSW4

Episode III: Revenge of the Sith—19 BSW4

Dark Times—19 BSW4

Omnibus: Droids—5.5 BSW4

Omnibus: Boba Fett—3 BSW4–10 ASW4

Omnibus: At War with the Empire—1 BSW4

Episode IV: A New Hope—SW4

Classic Star Wars—0–3 ASW4

Omnibus: A Long Time Ago . . . —0–4 ASW4

Empire—0 ASW4

Omnibus: The Other Sons of Tatooine—0 ASW4

Omnibus: Early Victories—0–3 ASW4

Jabba the Hutt: The Art of the Deal—1 ASW4

Episode V: The Empire Strikes Back—3 ASW4

Omnibus: Shadows of the Empire—3.5–4.5 ASW4

Episode VI: Return of the Jedi—4 ASW4

Omnibus: X-Wing Rogue Squadron—4–5 ASW4

Heir to the Empire—9 ASW4

Dark Force Rising—9 ASW4

The Last Command—9 ASW4

Dark Empire—10 ASW4

Crimson Empire—11 ASW4

Jedi Academy: Leviathan—12 ASW4

Union—19 ASW4

Chewbacca—25 ASW4

Invasion—25 ASW4

Legacy—130–137 ASW4

Old Republic Era
25,000 – 1000 years before
Star Wars: A New Hope

Rise of the Empire Era
1000 – 0 years before
Star Wars: A New Hope

Rebellion Era
0 – 5 years after
Star Wars: A New Hope

New Republic Era
5 – 25 years after
Star Wars: A New Hope

New Jedi Order Era
25+ years after
Star Wars: A New Hope

Legacy Era
130+ years after
Star Wars: A New Hope

Vector
Crosses four eras in the timeline

Volume 1 contains:
Knights of the Old Republic Volume 5
Dark Times Volume 3
Volume 2 contains:
Rebellion Volume 4
Legacy Volume 6

BSW4 = before *Episode IV: A New Hope*. ASW4 = after *Episode IV: A New Hope*.

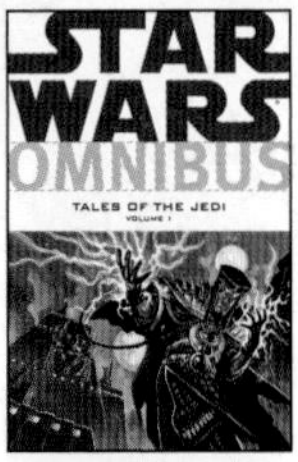
STAR WARS
OMNIBUS
TALES OF THE JEDI
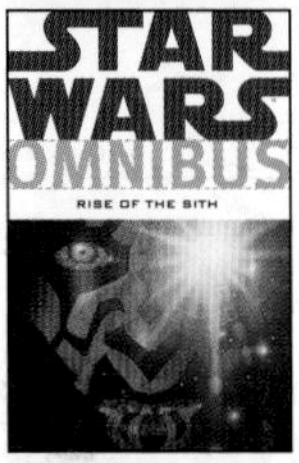
STAR WARS
OMNIBUS
RISE OF THE SITH
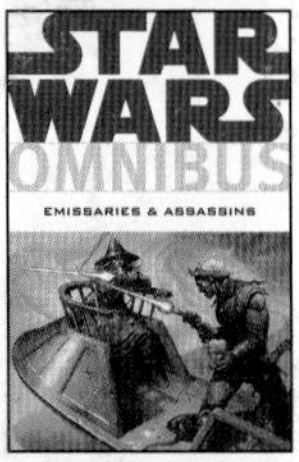
STAR WARS
OMNIBUS
EMISSARIES & ASSASSINS
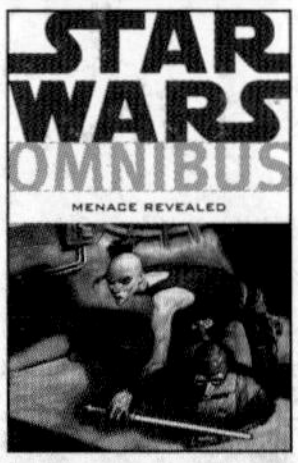
STAR WARS
OMNIBUS
MENACE REVEALED
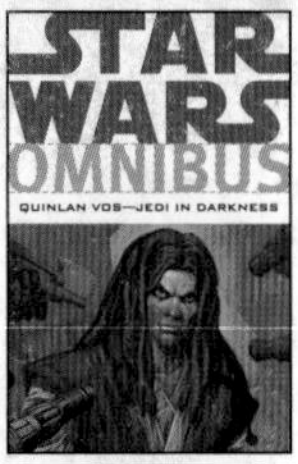
STAR WARS
OMNIBUS
QUINLAN VOS—JEDI IN DARKNESS
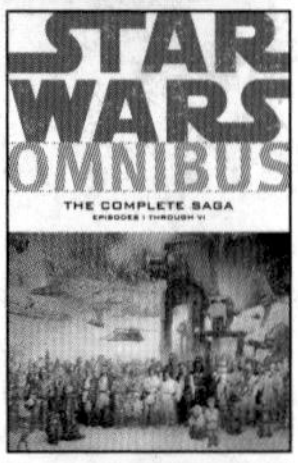
STAR WARS
OMNIBUS
THE COMPLETE SAGA
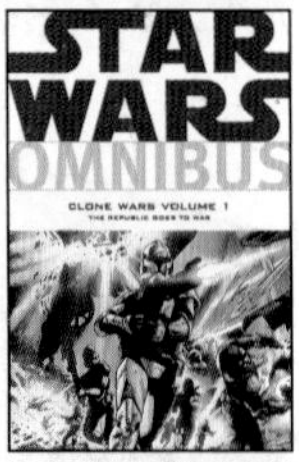
STAR WARS
OMNIBUS
CLONE WARS VOLUME 1
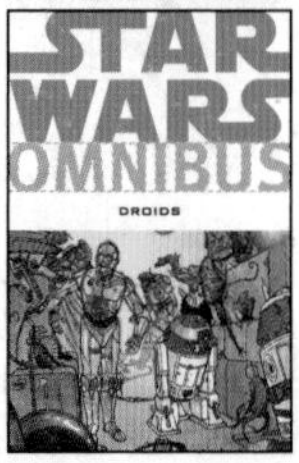
STAR WARS
OMNIBUS
DROIDS

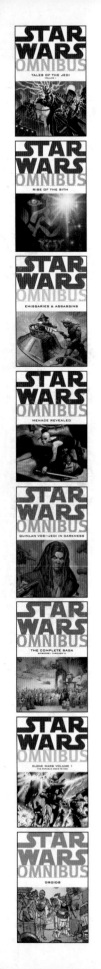

STAR WARS OMNIBUS COLLECTIONS

STAR WARS: TALES OF THE JEDI

Including the *Tales of the Jedi* stories "The Golden Age of the Sith," "The Freedon Nadd Uprising," and "Knights of the Old Republic," these huge omnibus editions are the ultimate introduction to the ancient history of the *Star Wars* universe!

Volume 1: ISBN 978-1-59307-830-0 | $24.99 **Volume 2: ISBN 978-1-59307-911-6 | $24.99**

STAR WARS: RISE OF THE SITH

These thrilling tales illustrate the events leading up to *Episode I: The Phantom Menace*, when the Jedi Knights preserved peace and justice . . . as well as prevented the return of the Sith.

ISBN 978-1-59582-228-4 | $24.99

STAR WARS: EMISSARIES AND ASSASSINS

Discover more stories featuring Anakin Skywalker, Amidala, Obi-Wan, and Qui-Gon set during the time of *Episode I: The Phantom Menace*!

ISBN 978-1-59582-229-1 | $24.99

STAR WARS: MENACE REVEALED

Included here are one-shot adventures, short story arcs, specialty issues, and early *Dark Horse Extra* comic strips! All of these tales take place after *Episode I: The Phantom Menace*, and lead up to *Episode II: Attack of the Clones*.

ISBN 978-1-59582-273-4 | $24.99

STAR WARS: QUINLAN VOS—JEDI IN DARKNESS

From his first appearance as a mind-wiped amnesiac to his triumphant passage to the rank of Jedi Master, few Jedi had more brushes with the powers of the dark side and the evil of the underworld than Quinlan Vos.

ISBN 978-1-59582-555-1 | $24.99

STAR WARS: THE COMPLETE SAGA—EPISODES I THROUGH VI

The comics adaptations of the complete *Star Wars* film saga—in one volume! From the first fateful encounter with Darth Maul to Luke Skywalker's victory over the Sith and Darth Vader's redemption, it's all here.

ISBN 978-1-59582-832-3 | $24.99

STAR WARS: CLONE WARS

The Jedi Knights who were once protectors of the peace must become generals, leading the clone armies of the Republic to war! These stories follow *Attack of the Clones* and feature Jedi heroes Obi-Wan Kenobi, Anakin Skywalker, Mace Windu, and Quinlan Vos.

Volume 1: The Republic Goes to War ISBN 978-1-59582-927-6 | $24.99
Volume 2: The Enemy on All Sides ISBN 978-1-59582-958-0 | $24.99
Volume 3: The Republic Falls ISBN 978-1-59582-980-1 | $24.99

STAR WARS: DROIDS

Before the fateful day Luke Skywalker met Artoo and Threepio, those troublesome droids had some amazing adventures all their own—and they stick together in a dangerous galaxy where anything can happen!

ISBN 978-1-59307-955-0 | $24.99

STAR WARS: DROIDS AND EWOKS

Based on the children's television cartoon series of the same names, *Droids and Ewoks* explores further adventures in the lives of the Ewoks on Endor and the droids R2-D2 and C-3PO.

ISBN 978-1-59582-953-5 | $24.99

DARK HORSE BOOKS

AVAILABLE AT YOUR LOCAL COMICS SHOP OR BOOKSTORE!

To find a comics shop in your area, call 1-888-266-4226

For more information or to order direct: • On the web: DarkHorse.com • E-mail: mailorder@darkhorse.com • Phone: 1-800-862-0052 Mon.–Fri. 9 AM to 5 PM Pacific Time